# THE EAST IS STILL RED

## Chinese Socialism in the 21st Century

Carlos Martinez

PRAXIS PRESS 2023

## Advance comments on ***The East Is Still Red***

Cheng Enfu (Chief Professor of the University of the Chinese Academy of Social Sciences, President of the World Association for Political Economy):
*The inspiring idea that "the left must resolutely oppose the new Cold War against China led by the United States" proposed by this book, should become the international strategic principle of the left around the world.*

Margaret Kimberley (Executive Editor, Black Agenda Report):
*As the new cold war accelerates, it is vital to have thorough analysis regarding China. Carlos Martinez is an important thought leader at this critical juncture.*

Professor Roland Boer (Renmin University of China):
*The book will soon become an indispensable resource for anyone who wants to know the facts concerning China.*

Danny Haiphong (Host of The Left Lens)
*This book is essential reading for understanding China today and why it's so important to oppose the US-led New Cold War against it.*

Ben Norton (Founder and editor-in-chief of Geopolitical Economy Report):
*Carlos Martinez has done an invaluable service in helping us understand the new phase in China's project to build socialism.*

Qiao Collective (A diaspora Chinese media collective challenging US aggression on China):
*Carlos Martinez's body of work on the history and continued reinvention of Chinese socialism had a formative influence on many of us in the diaspora who came together as Qiao Collective in 2020. Carlos has always treated this veritable revolutionary epic with the respect and attention to detail it deserves.*

Professor Ken Hammond (New Mexico State University):
*This is a most welcome contribution to the discourse about China on the Left, and for a broader audience of the politically engaged.*

Elias Jabbour (Associate professor of theory and policy of economic planning at Rio de Janeiro State University's School of Economics):
*In this book, the reader will have access to a wide source of information and living theory necessary to understand China and its unique socialism.*

Daniel Kovalik (Educator and author):
*This book represents a message of hope – that socialism has a future, and China is leading in its own, unique way.*

# THE EAST IS STILL RED

## Chinese Socialism in the 21st Century

**Carlos Martinez**

**ISBN-13:** 978-1-899155-16-3
**EAN:** 9781899155163

Published by Praxis Press 2023
Email: praxispress@me.com
Website: www.redletterspp.com

Praxis Press
c/o 26 Alder Road
Glasgow, G43 2UU
Scotland, Great Britain

Cover image: Ben Stahnke
Interior images: Carlos Martinez

Beijing Daxing International Airport

# CONTENTS


Acknowledgments vii

Introduction ix

1 No Great Wall 1

2 Neither Washington nor Beijing? 31

3 Will China suffer the same fate as the Soviet Union? 65

4 China's long war on poverty 89

5 Manufacturing consent for the containment and encirclement of China 109

6 China is building an ecological civilisation 135

7 Oppose the New Cold War on China 167

Appendix

The universalisation of 'liberal democracy' 187

Recommended reading 203

Index 205

About the author 210

Xian: Terracotta Warriors

# Acknowledgments

First and foremost, I must express my enduring gratitude to my friend and comrade Keith Bennett, whose contribution to this book would be difficult to measure. The fundamental concepts I set forward are to a significant degree grounded in his extensive knowledge and deep understanding of Marxism and of modern China, developed over the course of half a century. On a practical level, he has provided invaluable feedback on each chapter, and the end result is far better for it.

I am immensely grateful to the numerous activists, scholars and friends who have generously shared their time, knowledge, and perspectives with me. In particular, I would like to extend my heartfelt thanks to Danny Haiphong, Radhika Desai, Alan Freeman, Jenny Clegg, Ken Hammond, Lee Siu-Hin, Dirk Nimmegeers, Ben Norton, Sara Flounders, Chen Weihua, Cheng Enfu, Francisco Domínguez, Vijay Prashad, Roland Boer, John Riddell, Hugh Goodacre, Ben Chacko, Elias Jabbour, Tings Chak, Andrew Murray, Chen Shuoying, Mick Dunford, Margaret Kimberley, Carlos Garrido, Qiao Collective, Dan Kovalik, Brian Becker, Victor Figueroa, John Catalinotto, John Ross, and the dearly-missed Jude Woodward.

Thanks are due to Praxis Press and the indefatigable Kenny Coyle for their unwavering belief in this project. Special mentions must go to Ben Stahnke for his encouragement and his wonderful artwork, and to Tineke Jager for an amazingly thorough job of proof-reading the draft.

While they would disagree quite strongly with some of the formulations I propose here, my parents – Harpal Brar and Ella Rule – were the first people to spark my interest in Chinese socialism and in Marxist theory. I'm very grateful to have had my first political experiences in a context where support for the socialist world and for anti-imperialist struggle was encouraged.

Lastly, I must thank Beth, Amar and Nikhil; their patience, understanding and encouragement have been indispensable.

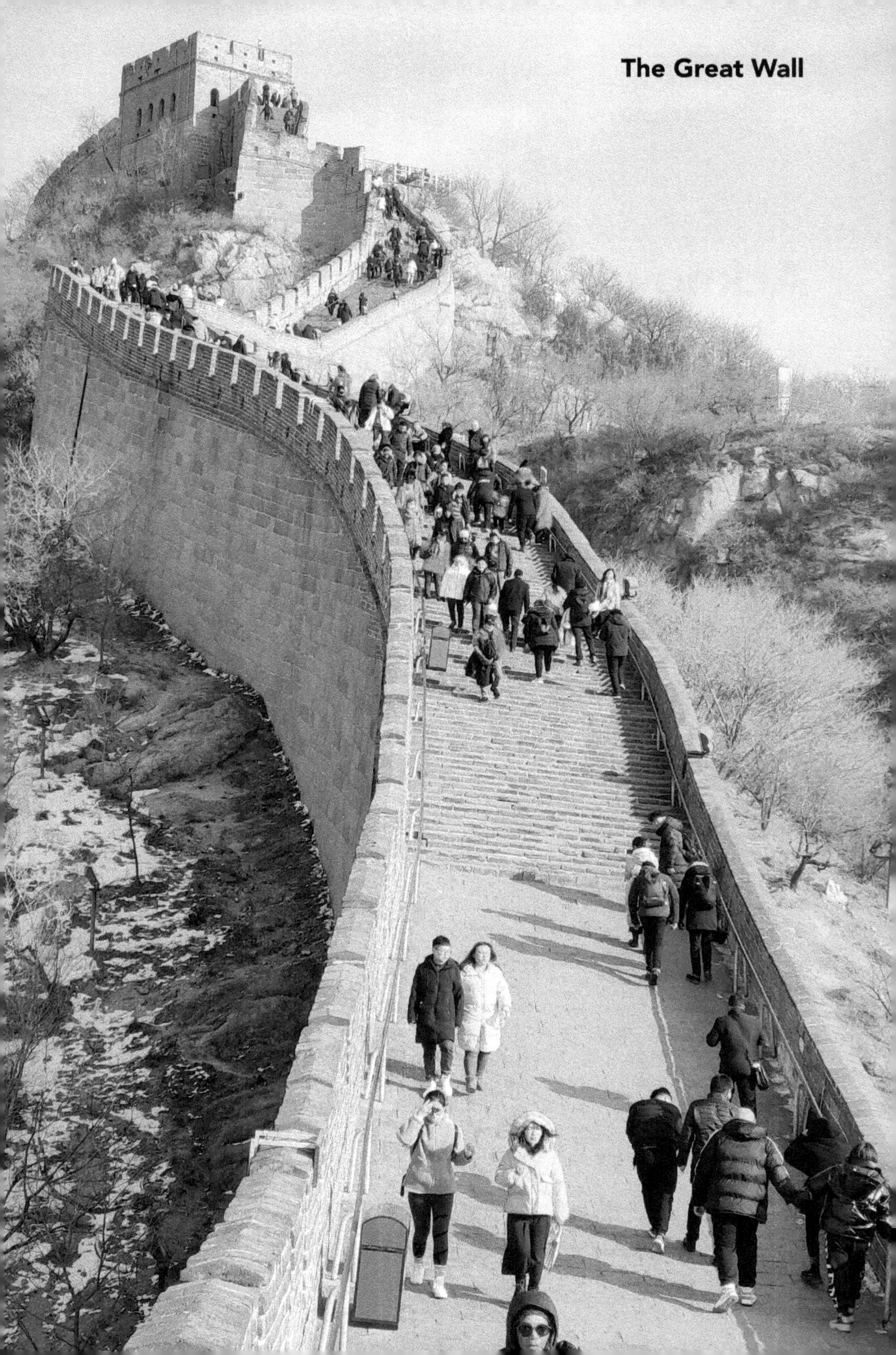
The Great Wall

# Introduction

# The East is still red

Modern China is the subject of a great deal of ignorance and misunderstanding in the imperialist countries. People in Britain, the US, Australia, Canada and Western Europe are subjected to an extraordinary quantity of anti-China propaganda, particularly in the years since the US launched its New Cold War, of which China is a primary target.

Even among socialists and communists, there are misconceptions and important gaps in understanding. Sometimes these are the ideological residue of the dark days of the Sino-Soviet Split – the nearly three decades from 1960 when the two largest socialist countries were locked in bitter ideological conflict. But more often, people simply find it difficult to get their heads round the idea that today's China, with its stock markets and billionaires and multinational corporations, is still socialist.

Travel to Beijing, Shanghai or Guangzhou and you will find McDonalds, KFC and Starbucks. There's abundant private capital; there are big businesses, wealthy individuals and significant inequality. There are rich people and poor people; there's exploitation of labour; there's integration into global value chains. Many on the Western left in particular look at such a situation and feel that it's somehow not what our movement has been fighting for.

On the other hand, the People's Republic of China has some interesting characteristics that make it rather different from the average capitalist country. Although inequality has dramatically increased since the launch of *Reform and Opening Up* in 1978, the standard of living for ordinary workers and farmers has risen precipitously along with it. Wealth under capitalism generally has its counterpart in poverty and exploitation (at home and/or abroad), but in China practically everyone enjoys a far better standard of life than they did.

No other country has achieved what China has achieved in terms of poverty alleviation – ensuring that people in their hundreds of millions have reliable access to food, shelter, clothing, clean water, modern energy, education and healthcare. Pre-liberation China was one of the poorest countries in the world. Millions would die every year due to malnutrition, even in non-famine years. The vast majority of the population was illiterate. In the absence of medical services in the countryside – where around nine-tenths of the population resided – to contract a serious illness was, more often than not, to receive a death sentence.

Life expectancy has more than doubled since the founding of the People's Republic of China in 1949. China has achieved near-universal literacy. Everybody has access to education and healthcare. The social and economic position of women has improved beyond recognition. The UN Development Programme describes China as having achieved "the most rapid decline in absolute poverty ever witnessed".[1] This is surely a phenomenon we should explore and understand: why has an enormous developing country like China had greater successes tackling poverty than any other country, including the advanced capitalist states of the West?

On tackling climate change and promoting biodiversity, China has emerged as a global leader. In relation to the Covid-19 pandemic, China established the gold standard in terms of going all out to protect human life – China's Covid suppression measures saved literally millions of lives.

The fact that China is able to prioritise the immediate and long-term needs of the masses of the people – eradicating poverty, transitioning to green energy systems, suppressing Covid-19, improving people's living standards – doesn't reflect some mystical, etherial quality of Chinese culture; it reflects the fact that the Communist Party of China (CPC) came to power via a revolution that was led by, supported by and sustained by the working class and peasantry. It was a revolution that created a workers' state – or more fully a "people's democratic dictatorship led by the working class and based on the worker-peasant alliance."[2] Thus China's extraordinary achievements are built on specifically socialist foundations.

## Not any other 'ism'

> Socialism with Chinese Characteristics is socialism. It is not any other sort of 'ism.' The foundational, scientific principles of socialism cannot be abandoned; only if they are abandoned would our system no longer be socialist. From first to the last our Party has emphasised that Socialism with Chinese Characteristics adheres to the basic principles of scientific socialism and is imbued with characteristically Chinese

> features bestowed by the conditions of the times. (Xi Jinping)[3]

The Chinese leadership has always been clear that its political and economic system is socialism, albeit what the post-Mao leadership defined as the *primary stage* of socialism, during which the emphasis is on the development of the productive forces in order to create the material conditions for a more advanced stage. Deng Xiaoping described this theory in conversation with Robert Mugabe in 1985:

> A Communist society is one in which there is no exploitation of man by man, there is great material abundance and the principle of from each according to his ability, to each according to his needs is applied. It is impossible to apply that principle without overwhelming material wealth. In order to realise communism, we have to accomplish the tasks set in the socialist stage. They are legion, but the fundamental one is to develop the productive forces so as to demonstrate the superiority of socialism over capitalism and provide the material basis for communism.[4]

The Australian Marxist academic Roland Boer talks of "the dialectical relation between ownership and the liberation of the productive forces." In the Western context, one typically finds a "one-sided definition of socialism as the [common] ownership of the means of production", reflecting the reality that the productive forces in the major capitalist countries are already advanced. However, "proletarian revolutions have been successful overwhelmingly in places that had undeveloped productive forces, so one finds that there is greater attention to liberating productive forces."[5] This helps to explain why China puts such an enormous emphasis on prosaic matters like productive forces – things that are easy to take for granted when you live in an advanced capitalist country that has accumulated wealth over hundreds of years – assisted to a considerable degree by colonisation, slavery and plunder.

While there is a great deal of private capital in China, the economy is still very much dominated and directed by the state. Xi Jinping insists:

> We must be extremely clear that our nation's basic economic system is an important pillar of the Chinese socialist system and the basis of the socialist market economy, and therefore the dominant role of public ownership and the leading role of the state sector must not change.[6]

The Chinese state maintains tight control over the 'commanding heights' of the economy: heavy industry, energy, transport, communications, and foreign trade. China's financial system is dominated by the big four majority state-owned banks, which are primarily accountable to the government rather than to private shareholders. This level of intervention and regulation – a far cry from the free market fundamentalism and 'small government' neoliberalism that prevails in the West – means that capital isn't able to seize control of the overall economic course, and that the economy is directed in order to benefit the people as a whole.

In John Pilger's important documentary *The Coming War on China,* Shanghai-based political analyst Eric X Li provides a concise explanation of this relationship between the market and the state, contrasting it with the situation in the United States:

"In China you have a vibrant market economy but capital doesn't rise above political authority. Capital does not have enshrined rights. In America the interests of capital and capital itself have risen above the American nation. Political authority cannot check the power of capital – and that's why America is a capitalist country but China's not."[7]

The Marxist sociologist Albert Szymanski made a similar point in his detailed 1979 investigation of Soviet socialism, *Is the Red Flag Flying?*: that an economic system is defined in terms of its *dominant* relations of production. These are not necessarily "the relations of production in which the largest number of producers are involved, nor the set of productive relations that produce the greatest amount of surplus value," but rather "those relations whose basic logic structures the form and movement of the whole social formation."[8]

He observes that in 1860 there were more slaves, agricultural freeholders and artisans than there were industrial workers, and yet the US was nonetheless a capitalist society. "It is likewise possible to have a socialist society in which the majority of the producing classes are not working in collectively owned and controlled enterprises, provided that the logic of such enterprises structures the rest of the economy."

Szymanski's analysis is pertinent to contemporary China. Although the number of employees of private enterprises has overtaken the number of employees of state- and collectively-owned companies, the basic economic agenda is set by the state. Private production is encouraged by the state because it contributes to modernisation, technological development and employment.

Discussing Vietnam's socialist market economy – which has largely taken a similar form to China's – US Marxist Vince Sherman writes that the socialist state allows capital to flourish "only to the degree that it helps in the economic development of the whole country and serves the greater class interests of the working class and peasantry."[9] China and Vietnam have proven that it is possible to leverage market mechanisms to more rapidly develop the productive forces and to improve the living standards of the people.

There has been comparatively little in the way of actual privatisation in China, in terms of transferring ownership of state enterprises into the hands of private capital; indeed, the state sector is several times bigger than it was in 1978, when the reforms were launched. Rather, private enterprise was allowed to develop alongside the state sector, and has grown at an even faster rate than the state sector (bear in mind that it started from a very low base). Martin Jacques explains:

> Rather than root-and-branch privatisation, the Chinese government has sought to make the numerous state-owned enterprises that remain as efficient and competitive as possible. As a result, the top 150 state-owned firms, far from being lame ducks, have instead become enormously profitable, their aggregate profits reaching $150 billion in 2007… Unlike in Japan or Korea, where privately owned firms overwhelmingly predominate, most of China's best-performing companies are to be found in the state sector.[10]

Of the world's five largest companies, three are Chinese state-owned enterprises (SOEs).[11] SOEs are compelled to align their operations with overall government strategy. For example, China's national plans include extending railway, road and energy infrastructure throughout the country, including relatively sparsely populated rural areas in the western and central regions. Private firms that allocate resources exclusively on the basis of generating a profit would run a mile from these projects, but state companies are organised on different principles. This helps to explain the fact that China is able to carry out enormous people-centred projects – for example developing renewable energy plants and building temporary hospitals to treat Covid patients – at record-breaking speed.

China's land was never privatised; it remains owned and managed at the village level. Peter Nolan observes: "Public ownership of land was a powerful countervailing force to the social inequality which inevitably accompanied elements of the market reform."

De-collectivisation "was not followed by the establishment of private property rights. Because the Chinese Communist Party wished to prevent the emergence of a landlord class, it did not permit the purchase and sale of farmland… The village community remained the owner, controlling the terms on which land was contracted out and operated by peasant households. It endeavoured to ensure that farm households had equal access to farmland… The massively dominant form was distribution of land contracts on a locally equal per capita basis."[12]

The complexities of the socialist market economy are discussed in more detail in Chapter 1, *No Great Wall – on the continuities of the Chinese Revolution*. Suffice it to say that the organisation of production in China differs fundamentally to the organisation of production in a capitalist society.

## Opening up has stimulated scientific and technological advance

China's opening up to foreign investment and its integration into global markets is often presented as prima facie evidence of its having become a capitalist country. British academic Jenny Clegg points out that China's joining of the World Trade Organisation in 2001 was seen by many as "the outcome of a gradual process of capitalist restoration – a final step in sweeping away the last obstacle in the way of China's transition from socialism."[13]

Clegg goes on to explain that WTO membership had nothing to do with capitalist restoration and everything to do with developing China's productive forces, strengthening its defences against imperialist aggression and destabilisation. China joined the WTO in order to be able to "insert itself into the global production chains linking East Asia to the US and other markets, thus making itself indispensable as a production base for the world economy. This would make it far more difficult for the United States to impose a new Cold War isolation."[14] Clegg's words were written in 2009, a few years before the US started pursuing its New Cold War on China (which is discussed at length in the final chapter, *The left must resolutely oppose the US-led New Cold War on China*). The difficulties the US is facing in attempting to 'decouple' from China provide a strong vindication of the Chinese leadership's strategic vision.

Economically, China's integration in the global value chains has allowed it to be a part of "the unprecedented global technological revolution, offering a short cut for the country to accelerate its industrial transformation and upgrade its economic structure."[15]

The opportunity to rapidly learn from the advanced capitalist countries' developments in science and technology was the principal reason for opening up. Blockaded by the western countries after the revolution, and then cut off from Soviet support with the emergence of the Sino-Soviet split, China by the late 1970s was still relatively backward from a technological point of view, in spite of having made some great advances and having developed a standard of living for its people that was far ahead of other countries at a similar level of development.

Deals with foreign investors were drawn up such that foreign companies trying to expand their capital in China were compelled to share skills and technology, and operate under Chinese regulation. A report by the Center for Economic and Policy Research (CEPR) on China's development from 1960 to 2016 observes:

> Foreign investment was regulated to make it compatible with state development planning. Technology transfer and other

> performance requirements — conditions attached to foreign investment to make sure that the host country gets some benefit from foreign investment, such as the use of locally produced inputs, or the hiring of local managers — were common and are still an issue of contention with the United States today.[16]

This is another example of the complex dynamic between planning and markets in China. The existence of a strong, people-oriented state has allowed China to attract foreign capital in such a way as to bolster, rather than supplant, a comprehensive national development programme. Martin Jacques writes, for example:

> In order to gain access to the vast and rapidly growing China market, Boeing was required to assist the main Chinese aircraft manufacturer in Xi'an to successively establish a capacity to produce spare parts and then manufacture whole sections of aircraft, and finally to assist in the development of a capacity to produce complete aircraft within China. In order to gain the right to invest in car production in China, Ford Motor Company was required to first invest for several years in upgrading the technical capacity of the Chinese automobile spare parts industry through a sequence of joint ventures.[17]

China is now one of the world's leading innovators in science and technology; it's a global leader in numerous key areas including renewable energy, space exploration, digital networking, quantum computing, nanotechnology and advanced manufacturing. It has displaced the US as the world leader in both scientific research publication[18] and patent grants.[19]

## A workers' state

The class nature of the state is one of the core themes of Marxism. Marx and Engels were the first to conclusively demonstrate that the state is not an impartial body sitting above society and operating for the common good; rather, its responsibility is to represent the interests of a given social class and the system of production relations associated with it. In the case of capitalism, "the executive of the modern state is nothing but a committee for managing the common affairs of the whole bourgeoisie".[20]

In a socialist society, the state must serve the interests of the working class and its allies; it must protect working class power, defend it from the inevitable attacks from capital, and build a better life for the people. Albert Szymanski wrote of the Soviet Union that, "in a socialist society surrounded by a capitalist world, the necessity to develop industrially, to feed the people, to protect itself and catch up with the leading capitalist countries, imposes a fairly limited set of options on a socialist power elite."[21] This applies equally to contemporary China. As Xi Jinping describes it:

> The working class is China's leading class; it represents China's advanced productive forces and relations of production; it is our Party's most steadfast and reliable class foundation; and it is the main force for realising a moderately prosperous society in all respects, and upholding and building socialism with Chinese characteristics... To uphold and build Chinese socialism in the future, we must rely wholeheartedly on the working class, enhance its position as China's leading class, and give full play to its role as our main force. Relying fully on the working class is not just a slogan or label.[22]

Chinese Marxists posit that the fundamental defining characteristic of socialist society is not the relative proportions of public and private ownership, but the consolidation of political power in the working class and its allies. A socialist state can clearly incorporate market mechanisms, as long as these operate under the guidance of the state and introduce some benefit for working people; so long as capital is not allowed to become politically dominant. As Deng insisted: "If markets serve socialism they are socialist; if they serve capitalism they are capitalist."[23] Or as Sitaram Yechury, General Secretary of the Communist Party of India (Marxist), puts it:

> In the final analysis, it boils down to the question of who controls the state or whose class rule it is. Under bourgeois class rule, it is the profit indicators that are the driving force. Under working-class rule, it is the society's responsibilities that are the priorities.[24]

A government's priorities can provide a useful indicator as to its ideology and the social forces it represents. The top priorities of the Chinese government in the present era are very much consistent with the demands of the Chinese people, in particular: protecting China's unity and territorial integrity; improving living standards; clamping down on corruption; protecting the environment; eradicating poverty; maintaining peace and stability; protecting people's health and wellbeing; and re-establishing China's national prestige, all but wiped out in the 'century of humiliation' preceding the establishment of the PRC in 1949. The average citizen of the US or Britain would surely be pleased if their government embraced a set of priorities focussed on the interests of the masses; unfortunately the close correlation between wealth and power in capitalist society means that the interests of the masses are never the top priority. Hence Deng Xiaoping's 1987 comment that "only the socialist system can eradicate poverty."[25]

The question of environmental protection is instructive. A capitalist state has limited freedom of action on this issue, due to the always-urgent need to expand capital, to generate profits. As a result, the major capitalist countries have made disastrously slow progress on ecological issues. A comprehensive strategy of environmental protection requires a huge investment: a production of use values that may not have corresponding exchange values; that is, production for people, not profit. In China, the government has a clear mandate to lead just such a strategy – even though there is a complex tension between development and conservation, both of which are essential for the Chinese people.

As I detail in Chapter 6, *China is building an ecological civilisation*, China has emerged as a global leader in the fight against climate breakdown. The reason that China can consolidate such enormous resources towards renewable energy production and distribution, biodiversity protection, low-carbon transport, forestation and pollution reduction is that its economic development proceeds according to state plans, not market anarchy. Fossil fuel companies do not have the sway over policy in China that they do in the West. As the veteran US communist activist and writer Deirdre Griswold has observed:

> China's economic planners have the power to make decisions that cost a lot of money, but will benefit the people — and the world — over the long run. They're not driven by profits and each quarter's bottom line. In countries where the super-rich run and control everything, you get a well-financed campaign of lies by the polluting corporations to turn public opinion against science and the environmental movement. But not in China.[26]

Another useful indicator of the class nature of the Chinese state is the government's vigilance in tackling corruption. Breaking laws and exerting political pressure in the name of expansion of capital is par for the course in capitalist countries, and precious little is done to combat it – including in Britain, where what Seumas Milne terms the "revolving-door colonisation of public life" has become pervasive.[27] Meanwhile in China, resolute action has been taken over the last decade in particular to wipe out the corruption that proliferated as a byproduct of market reforms. Soon after his election as CPC General Secretary in 2012, Xi Jinping asserted:

> In the new circumstances our Party faces many severe challenges as well as many pressing issues within the Party that need to be addressed, particularly corruption, being divorced from the people, and being satisfied merely with going through formalities and bureaucracy on the part of some Party officials.[28]

In his work report to the 20th National Congress of the CPC in 2022, Xi was able to truthfully report that "we have waged a battle against corruption on a scale unprecedented in our history", successfully dealing with literally hundreds of thousands of cases at all levels of society. The government chose to "offend a few thousand rather than fail 1.4 billion", and as a result significantly deepened the people's confidence in and support for the government.[29]

China's progress in these areas has been possible precisely because of the location of political power in the Chinese working people.

## Commitment to Marxism

> Only socialism can save China, and only Chinese socialism can lead our country to development – a fact that has been fully proved through the long-term practice of the Party and the state. (Xi Jinping)[30]

Through more than four decades of reform and opening up, the CPC has retained its commitment to Marxism. Deng Xiaoping was clear from the very beginning of the reform process that China must keep to the socialist road.

> Some people are now openly saying that socialism is inferior to capitalism. We must demolish this contention… Deviate from socialism and China will inevitably revert to semi-feudalism and semi-colonialism. The overwhelming majority of the Chinese people will never allow such a reverse… Although it is a fact that socialist China lags behind the developed capitalist countries in its economy, technology and culture, this is not due to the socialist system but basically to China's historical development before liberation; it is the result of imperialism and feudalism. The socialist revolution has greatly narrowed the gap in economic development between China and the advanced capitalist countries.[31]

In no country in the world is Marxism studied as widely as it is in China. Xi Jinping has a doctorate in Marxist theory. Marxism is part of the core curriculum at every level of the education system. The close to a hundred million members of the party are required to engage in Marxist study. Marx is considered the "teacher of revolution for the proletariat and working people all over the world" and "the greatest thinker of modern times".[32] Peter Nolan observes that "Marx's ideas remain centrally important for the Chinese Communist Party."[33]

A 2015 article in the *Washington Times* complains:

> Marxism is highly relevant to everyday life in the world's most populous country, a mandatory curricular course taught at every level of the education system from kindergarten to graduate school. Tens of millions of devoted 'political teachers' in the schools, unknown millions of 'ideological workers' at every level of the society, and the ubiquitous 'political commissars' in the People's Liberation Army — they all collectively serve as the official clergy of Marxism.[34]

Some consider that the CPC merely pays lip-service to Marxism in order to disguise its capitulation to capitalism, but it's quite a stretch of the imagination to believe that such a conspiracy "has been going for over 40 years and includes the CPC leadership, tens of thousands of scholars, tens of millions of CPC members, and hundreds of millions of Chinese citizens."[35] Furthermore it's difficult to understand *why* the Chinese leadership would go to such lengths to pretend to be Marxists.

All available evidence indicates that not only is the Communist Party of China committed to Marxism, but it is a leading force for the development and enhancement of Marxism in the 21st century. This is obviously of the most profound significance to progressive humanity, and a source of tremendous hope. In 1989, Deng Xiaoping commented to Julius Nyerere that, "so long as socialism does not collapse in China, it will always hold its ground in the world."[36] Those words continue to resonate. China has become – as Xi Jinping recently commented – the standard-bearer of the global socialist movement.[37]

Reflecting on the collapse of the Soviet Union and the European people's democracies, Deng urged people not to lose confidence in socialism:

> Feudal society replaced slave society, capitalism supplanted feudalism, and, after a long time, socialism will necessarily supersede capitalism. This is an irreversible general trend of historical development, but the road has many twists and turns. Over the several centuries that it took for capitalism to replace feudalism, how many times were monarchies restored! So, in a sense, temporary restorations are usual and can hardly be avoided. Some countries have suffered major setbacks, and socialism appears to have been weakened. But the people have been tempered by the setbacks and have drawn lessons from them, and that will make socialism develop in a healthier direction. So don't panic, don't think that Marxism has disappeared, that it's not useful any more and that it has been defeated. Nothing of the sort![38]

Indeed, Marxism has not disappeared and has not been defeated, and the socialist countries are at the cutting edge of preventing its disappearance and defeat. As such, it's essential to understand and support all the socialist countries, and all those states – such as Venezuela – that are exploring new paths towards socialism. China has a particular significance, since "its size and level of development give it an objectively critical role in the global transition to socialism."[39]

Having achieved its goal of eliminating extreme poverty by the centenary of the founding of the CPC in 2021, China is pursuing its second centenary goal: building a "great modern socialist country that is prosperous, strong, democratic, culturally advanced, harmonious and beautiful" by the centenary of the PRC's founding, in 2049.[40] The CPC is pursuing a socialist modernisation that is environmentally sustainable, that features common prosperity rather than polarisation, and that is achieved through the efforts of the Chinese people rather than via the domination of other countries' land, labour, resources and markets. Surely such a project is of interest to people that consider themselves socialists.

Rather than denouncing Chinese socialism for its perceived impurities and flaws, those on the Western left should accept that "only the wearer of the shoes knows if they fit or not."[41] As Vince Sherman commented in relation to Vietnam: "Actually existing socialism will always fall short of the socialist ideal because it is precisely that ideal implemented within the confines of reality."[42]

Our movement has a responsibility to learn about China; to build solidarity and friendship with China. If the first century of human experience of building socialism teaches us anything, it is that the road from capitalism to socialism is a long and complicated one, and that 'actually existing socialism' varies enormously according to time, place and circumstances. China is building a form of socialism that suits its conditions, using the means it has at its disposal, in the extraordinarily challenging circumstances of global imperialist hegemony. No socialist experiment thus far – be it the Paris Commune, the Soviet Union, China, Cuba, Mozambique, Venezuela or anywhere else – can claim to have discovered a magic wand that can be waved such that peace, prosperity, equality and comprehensive human development are achieved overnight. China is forging its own path, and this is worthy of study and support.

Is China socialist? Perhaps it is fitting to give Fidel Castro – someone with a certain amount of expertise on the subject – the last word:

> If you want to talk about socialism, you must not forget what socialism has done in China. Once it was a country of hunger, poverty, disasters — today there is none of that. Today China feeds, clothes, cares for, and educates 1.2 billion people... I think China is a socialist country, and Vietnam is a socialist country as well. And they insist that they've introduced all the

> necessary reforms, precisely to stimulate development and to continue advancing towards the objectives of socialism... In Cuba, for example, we have many forms of private property. We have tens of thousands of landowners who own, in some cases, up to 45 hectares; in Europe they would be considered latifundistas. Practically all Cubans own their own homes and, what's more, we are more than open to foreign investment. But none of this detracts from Cuba's socialist character. (Fidel Castro, 1993)[43]

That socialists and communists should support and defend Chinese socialism is in my view axiomatic. China provides a powerful living example of what can be achieved under a socialist system; by a Marxist-led government firmly grounded in the masses of the people. My central objective in writing this book is to present some of these achievements; to explain the escalating hostility by the imperialist powers towards China; and to contribute to clearing up various popular misconceptions. I hope it will have something useful to offer to those who seek to deepen their knowledge and understanding of Chinese socialism.

## NOTES


1 Cited in Neil Hirst. *The Energy Conundrum: Climate Change, Global Prosperity, and the Tough Decisions We Have to Make*. New Jersey: World Scientific, 2018, p68

2 Mao Zedong 1949, *On the People's Democratic Dictatorship*, Marxist Internet Archive, accessed 1 February 2023, <https: / / www.marxists.org / reference / archive / mao / selected-works / volume-4 / mswv4_65.htm>.

3 Xi Jinping 2013, *Uphold and Develop Socialism with Chinese Characteristics*, Palladium, accessed 2 February 2023, <https: / / www.palladiummag.com / 2019 / 05 / 31 / xi-jinping-in-translation-chinas-guiding-ideology / >.

4 Deng Xiaoping 1985, *Reform Is the Only Way For China to Develope Its Productive Forces*, Marxist Internet Archive, accessed 2 February 2023, <https: / / www.marxists.org / reference / archive / deng-xiaoping / 1985 / 112.htm>.

5 Roland Boer. *Socialism with Chinese Characteristics: A Guide for Foreigners*. Singapore: Springer, 2021, p310

6 Xi Jinping 2015, *Opening Up New Frontiers for Marxist Political Economy in Contemporary China*, Qiushi, accessed 2 February 2023, <http: / / en.qstheory.cn / 2020-11 / 08 / c_560906.htm>.

7 John Pilger. *The Coming War on China*, accessed 4 February 2023, <https: / / johnpilger.com / videos / the-coming-war-on-china>.

8 Albert Szymanski. *Is the Red Flag Flying? The Political Economy of the Soviet Union*. Imperialism Series, no. 5. London: Zed Press, 1979, p14

9 Vince Sherman 2013, *Actually Existing Socialism in Vietnam*, Return to the Source, accessed 4 February 2023, <https: / / return2source.wordpress.com / 2013 / 01 / 08 / actually-existing-socialism-in-vietnam / >.

10 Martin Jacques. *When China Rules the World: The End of the Western World and the Birth of a New Global Order*. 2. ed. New York, NY: Penguin Books, 2012, p228

11 Wang Tianyu 2021, *Explainer: Why does China have so many state-owned enterprises?*, CGTN, accessed 4 February 2023, <https: / / news.cgtn.com / news / 2021-06-14 / Explainer-Why-China-has-so-many-state-owned-enterprises-115vt8ntcZ2 / index.html>.

12 Peter Nolan. *China's Rise, Russia's Fall: Politics, Economics and Planning in the Transition from Stalinism*. New York: St. Martin's Press, 1995, p191

13 Jenny Clegg. *China's Global Strategy: Towards a Multipolar World*. London ; New York: Pluto Press , 2009, p124

14 *ibid*, p128

15 *ibid*, p129

16 Mark Weisbrot et al 2017, *The Scorecard on Development, 1960–2016: China and the Global Economic Rebound*, Center for Economic and Policy Research, accessed 5 February 2023, <https: / / cepr.net / report / the-

scorecard-on-development-1960-2016-china-and-the-global-economic-rebound / >.

17 Nolan, *China's Rise, Russia's Fall*, p188

18 Niall McCarthy 2020, *The countries leading the world in scientific research*, World Economic Forum, accessed 5 February 2023, <https: / / www.weforum.org / agenda / 2020 / 01 / top-ten-countries-leading-scientific-publications-in-the-world / >.

19 *Ranking of the 20 national patent offices with the most patent grants in 2021*, Statista, accessed 5 February 2023, <https: / / www.statista.com / statistics / 257152 / ranking-of-the-20-countries-with-the-most-patent-grants / >.

20 Karl Marx and Friedrich Engels. *The Communist Manifesto*. London: Penguin Classics, 2015, p4

21 Szymanski, *op cit*, p28

22 Xi Jinping 2013, *Hard Work Makes Dreams Come True*, The National People's Congress of the People's Republic of China, accessed 8 February 2023, <https: / / www.npc.gov.cn / englishnpc / c23934 / 202006 / 34c5df6240994461a8d3bf47cfe8e8fa.shtml>.

23 Deng Xiaoping 1987, *Planning and the Market Are Both Means of Developing the Productive Forces*, Marxist Internet Archive, accessed 8 February 2023, <https: / / www.marxists.org / reference / archive / deng-xiaoping / 1987 / 83.htm>.

24 Siteram Yechury: *Economy: Reforms for Restoration of Capitalism* (1991), in Jodi Dean and Vijay Prashad. *Red October: The Russian Revolution and the Communist Horizon*. New Delhi, India: LeftWord, 2017.

25 Deng Xiaoping 1987, *China can only take the socialist road*, China Daily, accessed 10 February 2023, <https: / / www.chinadaily.com.cn / china / 19thcpcnationalcongress / 2010-10 / 25 / content_29714437.htm>.

26 Dierdre Griswold 2017, *China takes another big step away from CO2*, Workers World, accessed 10 February 2023, <https: / / www.workers.org / 2017 / 01 / 29359 / >.

27 Seumas Milne 2013, *Corporate power has turned Britain into a corrupt state*, The Guardian, accessed 10 February 2023, <https: / / www.theguardian.com / commentisfree / 2013 / jun / 04 / corporate-britain-corrupt-lobbying-revolving-door>.

28 Xi Jinping 2012, *The People's Wish for a Good Life Is Our Goal*, The National People's Congress of the People's Republic of China, accessed 10 February 2023, <https: / / www.npc.gov.cn / englishnpc / c23934 / 202005 / c800ae87a9744e399486456f8cbe417c.shtml>.

29 Xi Jinping 2022, *Full text of the report to the 20th National Congress of the Communist Party of China*, Xinhua, accessed 10 February 2023, <https: / / english.news.cn / 20221025 / 8eb6f5239f984f01a2bc45b5b5db0c51 / c.html>.

30 Xi Jinping. *The Governance of China (Volume 1)*. First edition. Beijing:

Foreign Languages Press, 2014, p7

31 Deng Xiaoping 1979, *Uphold the Four Cardinal Principles*, Marxist Internet Archive, accessed 10 February 2023, <https: / / www.marxists.org / reference / archive / deng-xiaoping / 1979 / 115.htm>.

32 *Marx's theory still shines with truth: Xi*, Xinhua, accessed 10 February 2023, <http: / / www.xinhuanet.com / english / 2018-05 / 04 / c_137155329.htm>.

33 Peter Nolan. *Understanding China: The Silk Road and the Communist Manifesto*. Routledge Studies on the Chinese Economy 60. London ; New York: Routledge, Taylor & Francis Group, 2016, p57

34 Miles Yu 2015, *Inside China: Marxism: The opium of the Chinese masses*, Washington Times, accessed 10 February 2023, <https: / / www.washingtontimes.com / news / 2015 / oct / 15 / inside-china-marxism-the-opium-of-the-chinese-mass / >.

35 Boer, *op cit*, p12

36 Deng Xiaoping 1989, *We Must Adhere To Socialism and Prevent Peaceful Evolution Towards Capitalism*, Marxist Internet Archive, accessed 12 February 2023, <https: / / www.marxists.org / reference / archive / deng-xiaoping / 1989 / 173.htm>.

37 William Zheng 2022, *Xi Jinping article gives insight into China's direction ahead of Communist Party congress*, South China Morning Post, accessed 10 February 2023, <https: / / www.scmp.com / news / china / politics / article / 3192677 / xi-article-gives-insight-chinas-direction-ahead-party-congress>.

38 Deng Xiaoping 1992, *Excerpts From Talks Given In Wuchang, Shenzhen, Zhuhai and Shanghai*, Marxist Internet Archive, accessed 12 February 2023, <https: / / www.marxists.org / reference / archive / deng-xiaoping / 1992 / 179.htm>.

39 *About Friends of Socialist China*, Friends of Socialist China, accessed 12 February 2023, <https: / / socialistchina.org / about / >.

40 Yang Sheng and Zhang Changyue 2022, *CPC charts course for modern socialist China in all respects*, Global Times, accessed 12 February 2023, <https: / / www.globaltimes.cn / page / 202210 / 1277280.shtml>.

41 Xi Jinping 2013, *Only the Wearer of the Shoes Knows If They Fit or Not -- Maintaining full confidence in the path, theory, and system of Chinese socialism*, China Story, accessed 12 February 2023, <https: / / www.chinastory.cn / ywdbk / english / v1 / detail / 20190719 / 1012700000042741563521134436657063_1.html>.

42 Vince Sherman 2013, *Actually Existing Socialism in Vietnam*, Return to the Source, accessed 12 February 2023, <https: / / return2source.wordpress.com / 2013 / 01 / 08 / actually-existing-socialism-in-vietnam / >.

43 Fidel Castro 1993, *Fidel Castro interviewed by Jas Gawronski (1993)*, Red Sails, accessed 31 January 2023, <https: / / redsails.org / fidel-and-gawronski / >.

# 1

# No Great Wall – the continuities of the Chinese Revolution

The Communist Party of China (CPC) was formed in July 1921. From that time up to the present day, it has led the Chinese Revolution – a revolution to eliminate feudalism, to regain China's national sovereignty, to end foreign domination of China, to build socialism, to create a better life for the Chinese people, and to contribute to a peaceful and prosperous future for humanity.

Some of these goals have already been achieved; others are ongoing. Thus the Chinese Revolution is a continuing process, and its basic political orientation remains the same.

Feudalism was dismantled in CPC-controlled territories from the early 1930s onwards, and throughout the country in the period immediately following the establishment of the People's Republic in 1949. Similarly, warlord rule was ended and a unified China essentially established in 1949; Hong Kong was returned to Chinese rule in 1997 and Macao in 1999. Only Taiwan continues to be governed separately and to serve foreign interests. And yet in a world system still principally defined by US hegemony, the imperialist threat remains – and is intensifying with the development of a US-led hybrid war against China. Therefore the project of protecting China's sovereignty and resisting imperialism continues. Similarly, the path to socialism is constantly evolving.

In the course of trying to build socialism in a vast semi-colonial, semi-feudal country, mistakes have certainly been made. The collected works of Marx and Lenin bubble over with profound ideas, but they contain no templates or formulae. Chinese Marxists have had to continuously engage in "concrete analysis of concrete conditions",[1] applying and developing socialist theory, creatively adapting it to an ever-changing material reality. In their foreword to Agnes Smedley's biography of Zhu De, *The Great Road*, Leo Huberman and Paul Sweezy wrote that the Chinese communists, "in the midst of their struggle for survival … have proceeded to evolve a more flexible and sophisticated theory which enriched Marxism by reflecting and absorbing the stubborn realities of the Chinese scene."[2]

As Liu Shaoqi, a prominent CPC leader until his denunciation during the Cultural Revolution, explained:

> Because of the distinctive peculiarities in China's social and historical development and her backwardness in science, it is a unique and difficult task to apply Marxism systematically to China and to transform it from its European form into a Chinese form… Many of these problems have never been solved or raised by the world's Marxists, for here in China the main section of the masses are not workers but peasants, and the fight is directed against foreign imperialist oppression and medieval survivals, and not against domestic capitalism.[3]

This chapter argues that, while the Chinese Revolution has taken numerous twists and turns, and while the CPC leadership has adopted different strategies at different times, there is a common thread running through modern Chinese history: of the CPC dedicating itself to navigating a path to socialism, development and independence, improving the lot of the Chinese people, and contributing to a peaceful and prosperous future for humanity.

## Historical background

The CPC was formed in response to a clear need for revolutionary leadership. The 1911 bourgeois revolution that had finally overthrown the Qing dynasty and established the Republic of China had come to a dead end, owing to the manoeuvring of the imperialist powers and their comprador agents. Most of the country was run by warlords. The feudal economy remained in place and the bulk of the population remained permanently on the brink of starvation, indebted to landlords. The various imperialist powers maintained their footholds, with Britain, the US, Japan and Germany competing for control of China's land and resources.

Young people in particular were searching for a path forward. "Youth organisations and study circles sprang up in great profusion", writes Israel Epstein,[4] including the New People's Study Society in Hunan, led by a certain Mao Zedong. A turning point came on 4 May 1919, when the students of Beijing marched on the government buildings in protest at the Treaty of Versailles, which legalised the Japanese seizure of Shandong province and rejected China's demands for the abolition of foreign spheres of influence and the withdrawal of foreign troops. The demonstrations caught the imagination of students, workers and radical intellectuals throughout the country. "The May 4 Movement was a climactic point of the Chinese revolution. It took place after, and was one of the results of, the October Revolution in Russia."[5] Han Suyin described the May 4 Movement as "a leap of consciousness, a radicalisation, which would determine the course of history."[6]

The CPC, formed two years later, was the first organisation to put forward the slogan 'Down with imperialism', recognising that China's weakness and backwardness were inherently bound up with foreign domination. Some relatively forward-thinking elements of the emerging capitalist class had hoped that the US or Japan might help China to establish itself as a modern capitalist power, but the communists recognised that this reflected a fundamental misunderstanding of the nature of imperialism. The major capitalist powers were compelled by the nature of their economic system to compete for control of China – a country offering an abundance of land, people, natural resources, and geostrategic advantage. Japan, the US, Britain, Germany and others wouldn't hesitate to support feudal warlords where it suited their interests; nor would they hesitate to suppress the Chinese people's desire for independence and progress. The CPC's anti-imperialist position quickly won it the support of a significant section of the population.

Soon after its formation, at its Third Congress in 1923, the CPC pushed for a united front with the Guomindang (GMD)[7], a revolutionary nationalist party set up by Sun Yat-sen in 1912 (the veteran politician and doctor Sun was elected as provisional president of the Republic of China following the overthrow of the Qing dynasty). The idea of the united front was to construct an anti-imperialist alliance incorporating workers, peasants, intellectuals and the patriotic elements of the capitalist class, with a view to decisively ending feudalism, uniting the country under a single central government, and driving out the imperialist powers. Denied recognition or support by the West, the GMD was in the process of orienting towards the Soviet Union, which had already demonstrated itself to be a supporter of Chinese sovereignty (the Bolsheviks had indicated their support for Sun Yat-sen as early as 1912[8] and, once in power, renounced all privileges in China granted to the tsarist regime). Recognising that the CPC would be more effective in mobilising the masses of the working class and peasantry, the GMD agreed to the CPC's proposal, and the CPC leadership took joint membership of both organisations.

This first united front started to fracture after the death in 1925 of Sun Yat-sen. The GMD's right wing gained the ascendancy under the leadership of Chiang Kai-shek (who would later go on to become the highly authoritarian leader of Taiwan from 1949 until his death in 1975). Chiang "believed that communism was inhuman and that, unless defeated, it would mean oppression for the Chinese people and the destruction of their traditional culture."[9] Fearing that the communists were gaining too much popular support, Chiang orchestrated a coup against them, in collaboration with the various foreign powers that had recognised in Chiang a potential partner in the pursuit of an 'acceptable' political conjuncture in China.

When, in April 1927, Shanghai was liberated from warlord control as the result of an insurrection of the local working class (led primarily by CPC forces), Chiang's forces won control of the city by means of a massacre of its liberators, killing an estimated 5,000 people. This marked the start of a several-year campaign of mass killings by Chiang's forces against communists and progressive workers. With CPC members formally ejected from the GMD and the united front dismantled, Chiang Kai-shek set up a new regime in Nanjing, under which "communism became a crime punishable by death."[10] The government focused its efforts not on resisting imperialism or uniting the country but on suppressing communists. Facing something close to physical annihilation, the membership of the CPC fell from 58,000 at the start of 1927 to 10,000 by the end of the year.

These disastrous events led the communists to a strategic reorientation. It was clear that a united front policy focused on the major urban centres was no longer a viable option. Meanwhile, "as every schoolboy knows, 80 per cent of China's population are peasants,"[11] and, as William Hinton writes in the preface to his classic account *Fanshen*, "without understanding the land question one cannot understand the Revolution in China."[12] The CPC was moving towards the development of a rural-based revolutionary movement.

Following a failed uprising in his native Hunan, Mao Zedong fled with his forces into the Jinggang mountains, in the border region of Jiangxi and Hunan provinces. This became the birthplace of the Chinese Red Army and the site of the first liberated territory. The Jiangxi Soviet expanded over the course of several years to incorporate parts of seven counties and a population of more than half a million.

Han Suyin notes that Mao Zedong "was the first in the party who abandoned the city orientation and devised a major strategy born from China's reality." The working class were a growing force, but constituted less than one percent of the population. "Mao saw that setting up rural bases, dedicated to the liberation of the peasantry from the oppression of landlordism, was the only way in which revolution would succeed."[13] Not only was the mass of the peasantry against feudal exploitation, but it could also understand the connection between foreign domination and domestic poverty. The period of foreign aggression from 1840 had led to wars and instability, much of the burden of which fell on the peasantry, which was expected to provide soldiers and sustenance. Any agricultural surplus from good harvest years was redirected to the state (or local warlord), leaving grain reserves empty and thus contributing to vast famines.

The CPC and Red Army grew in strength and experience during this time. Chiang Kai-shek's obsessive focus on eliminating communism led Mao and his comrades to develop a theory of guerrilla warfare that would prove decisive in the CPC's rise to power. However, China was rendered vulnerable to attack by Chiang's pacification programme. Even when the Japanese occupied Northeast China in September 1931, siphoning 'Manchukuo' off as an 'independent' puppet state a year later, Chiang's clearly stated policy was: "Internal pacification first, before external resistance".

Between 1929 and 1934, Chiang's forces led a series of brutal encirclement campaigns in an attempt to bury the Jiangxi Soviet. After suffering a series of defeats at the hands of a highly motivated and skilled Red Army, the Guomindang mobilised warlord armies from around the country, organising a force of more than a million troops. The communists had no choice but to abandon the liberated territory and break the siege. This process became the Long March: the extraordinary year-long retreat to the North-West, covering over 9,000 kilometres and ending with the establishment of a revolutionary base area at Yan'an, Shaanxi. This area would serve as the centre of the CPC's operations until shortly before the formation of the People's Republic of China in 1949.

In the liberated territories, the communists led the creation of a new rural political economy that – along with their determined struggle against Japanese militarism – would earn them the support of the broad masses of the peasantry. In his classic account *Red Star Over China*, Edgar Snow paints a vivid picture of life in the red base areas:

> Land was redistributed and taxes were lightened. Collective enterprise was established on a wide scale… Unemployment, opium, prostitution, child slavery, and compulsory marriage were reported to be eliminated, and the living conditions of the workers and poor peasants in the peaceful areas greatly improved. Mass education made much progress in the stabilised soviets. In some counties the Reds attained a higher degree of literacy among the populace in three or four years than had been achieved anywhere else in rural China after centuries.[14]

Opium production was ended and replaced by food agriculture. Antiquated feudal practices such as foot-binding, infanticide and the keeping of slave girls were prohibited. Peng Dehuai, one of the top Red Army leaders and later the Defence Minister of the PRC, commented on the decisive importance of the CPC's progressive and popular policies in the liberated areas:

> Only by implanting itself deeply in the hearts of the people, only by fulfilling the demands of the masses, only by consolidating a base in the peasant soviets, and only by sheltering in the shadow of the masses, can partisan warfare bring revolutionary

> victory… Tactics are important, but we could not exist if the majority of the people did not support us.[15]

By the mid 1930s, the Japanese armed forces were consolidating and expanding their occupation of Northeast China, aided and abetted by the Western powers, who were motivated by the idea of cooperating with Japan to attack the Soviet Union. Chiang Kai-shek's position was becoming untenable. He granted concession after concession to the Japanese, but he could no longer justify his refusal to defend China's national sovereignty. In July 1937, Japanese forces marched out of their puppet state of Manchukuo, going on to occupy Beijing and Shanghai.

In this context, more progressive elements within the GMD took the initiative, detaining Chiang in the northwestern city of Xi'an and forcing him to agree to cooperate with the CPC against Japanese occupation. Thus was formed the Second United Front. The red base at Yan'an (Shaanxi province) was recognised as a provincial government and the CPC was legalised; the Red Army was re-designated as the Eighth Route Army and New Fourth Army.

## New Democracy

In the period of the Second United Front, the CPC won enormous prestige for its leadership of the national defence efforts and for its commitment to improving the lives of the population in the territories under its control. Yan'an became a pole of attraction for revolutionary and progressive youth throughout the country. British academic Graham Hutchings writes:

> Yan'an seemed to stand for a new type of society. Visitors, foreign and Chinese, found it brimming with purpose, equality and hope. Many students and intellectuals chose to leave areas under the control of a central government they felt lacked a sense of justice, as well as the will to confront the national enemy, for life in the border regions and the communist or 'progressive' camp.[16]

Indeed Yan'an remains a crucial component of the PRC's origin story – following the conclusion of the 20th National Congress of the CPC in October 2022, Xi Jinping led the members of the politburo on a delegation to Yan'an, emphasising the need to "carry forward the great founding spirit of the Party, the Yan'an Spirit, and our fighting spirit."[17]

It was increasingly clear that the communists were the most cohesive, committed and competent political force in China; the only political party with the potential to restore China's sovereignty, unity and dignity. Mao and the CPC leadership took the time to theorise the type of society they were trying to build; what the substance of their revolution was. The results of these debates and discussions are synthesised in Mao's 1940 pamphlet *On New Democracy*, which describes the Chinese Revolution as necessarily having two stages: "first of New Democracy and then of socialism."[18]

New Democracy was not to be a socialist society, but a "democratic republic under the joint dictatorship of all anti-imperialist and anti-feudal people led by the proletariat." Extending a friendly hand to patriotic non-communist forces, Mao invoked the spirit of Sun Yat-sen, calling for "a republic of the genuinely revolutionary new Three People's Principles with their Three Great Policies." (The *Three People's Principles* were – approximately – nationalism, people's government, and social welfare; the *Three Great Policies* were alliance with the Soviet Union, alliance with the CPC, and support for the workers and peasants).

The key elements of this stage of the revolution were to defeat imperialism and to establish independence, as an essential step on the road to the longer-term goal of building socialism. How long would this stage last? It would "need quite a long time and cannot be accomplished overnight. We are not utopians and cannot divorce ourselves from the actual conditions confronting us."[19]

Such a society would not be a dictatorship of the proletariat; that is, the working class would not exercise exclusive political control. Rather, political power would be shared by all the anti-imperialist classes: the working class, the peasantry, the petty bourgeoisie and the national bourgeoisie (ie those elements of the capitalist class that stood against foreign domination).

In economic terms, New Democracy would include elements of both socialism and capitalism.

> The state enterprises will be of a socialist character and will constitute the leading force in the whole national economy, but the republic will neither confiscate capitalist private property in general nor forbid the development of such capitalist production as does not 'dominate the livelihood of the people', for China's economy is still very backward.

Land reform would be carried out, and the activities of private capital would be subjected to heavy regulation.

In conversation with Edgar Snow, Mao envisaged China taking its place within an ever-more globalised world – perhaps anticipating the 'opening up' of four decades later:

> When China really wins her independence, then legitimate foreign trading interests will enjoy more opportunities than ever before. The power of production and consumption of 450 million people is not a matter that can remain the exclusive interest of the Chinese, but one that must engage the many

> nations. Our millions of people, once really emancipated, with their great latent productive possibilities freed for creative activity in every field, can help improve the economy as well as raise the cultural level of the whole world.[20]

Following Japan's defeat in 1945, the CPC and GMD attempted to negotiate a post-war government alliance. However, the agreement forged in Chongqing in October 1945 fell apart as Chiang's forces continued their military attacks on the CPC-controlled areas. A bitter four-year civil war ensued, resulting in the communists' victory, Chiang Kai-shek's flight to Taiwan, and the establishment of the People's Republic of China on 1 October 1949. The newly-installed government, led by the CPC, attempted to build the type of society described in *On New Democracy*. Its governance was based on the Common Programme – an interim constitution drawn up by the Chinese People's Political Consultative Conference (a united front body created by the CPC), with 662 delegates representing 45 different organisations. The Common Programme did not call for the immediate establishment of a socialist society, and it promised to encourage private business. As Mao had written earlier in the year, "our present policy is to regulate capitalism and not to destroy it."[21] Patriotic capitalists were invited to participate in government.

The most important immediate economic change was the comprehensive dismantling of feudalism: the abolition of the rural class system and the distribution of land to the peasantry (a process already well underway in the areas under CPC control). Land reform resulted in a large agricultural surplus which, along with Soviet support, created the conditions for a rapid state-led industrialisation. Hutchings notes that "dramatic improvements in life expectancy and literacy rates and increases in living standards accompanied the appearance of factories, roads, railways and bridges across the country."[22] Along with this came an unprecedented shift in the status of women, who had suffered every oppression and indignity under feudalism. Via a system of "barefoot doctors", basic medical care was made available to the peasantry. "As a consequence, fertility rose, infant mortality declined, life expectancy began to climb, and the population stabilised and then grew for the first time since the Japanese invasion of 1937."[23]

The New Democracy period only lasted a few years. By 1954, the government was promoting collectivisation in the countryside and shifting private production into state hands. By the time of the Great Leap Forward in 1958, there was no more talk of a slow and cautious road to socialism; the plan now was to "surpass Britain and catch up to America" within 15 years.

The reasons for moving on from New Democracy are complex and contested, and reflect a shifting global political environment. The CPC had envisaged – or at least hoped for – mutually beneficial relations with the West, as is hinted at in the quote above that "legitimate foreign trading interests will enjoy more opportunities than ever before". However, by the time of the founding of the PRC, the Cold War was already in full swing. After the defeat of Japan in 1945, and with the outbreak of civil war between the communists and the nationalists, the US came down on the side of the latter, on the basis that Chiang understood the civil war to be "an integral part of the worldwide conflict between communism and capitalism"[24] and was resolutely on the side of capitalism.

The US made its hostility to the People's Republic manifestly clear from early on. The US involvement in the Korean War, starting in June 1950, was to no small degree connected to "the West's determination ... to 'contain' revolutionary China."[25] The genocidal force directed against the Korean people – including the repeated threat of nuclear warfare – was also a warning to China's communists (although the warning was returned with interest, when hundreds of thousands of Chinese volunteers joined hands with their Korean brothers and sisters, rapidly pushing the US-led troops back to the 38th parallel and forcing an effective stalemate).

Soon after the arrival of US troops in Korea, US President Truman announced that his government would act to prevent Taiwan's incorporation into the PRC, since this would constitute "a threat to the security of the Pacific area and to United States forces performing their lawful and necessary functions in that area."[26] Truman ordered the Seventh Fleet of the US Navy into the Taiwan Strait in order to prevent China from occupying it (such, incidentally, are the imperialist origins of the notion of Taiwanese independence). Along with these acts of physical aggression, the US imposed a total embargo on China, depriving the country of various important materials required for reconstruction.

The dangerously hostile external environment made New Democracy less viable. There are parallels here with the Soviet abandonment of the New Economic Policy (NEP) in 1929. Much like New Democracy, the NEP had consisted of a mixed economy, with private business encouraged in order to increase production and enhance productivity. Introduced in 1921, the NEP proved highly successful, allowing the Soviet Union to recover economically from war whilst minimising internal class conflict. By the end of the decade, however, new external dangers were emerging and it became clear to the Soviet leadership that the imperialist powers were starting to mobilise for war. From 1929 the Soviet economy shifted to something like a wartime basis, with near-total centralisation, total state ownership of industry, collectivisation of agriculture, and a major focus on heavy industry and military production.

Similarly in China in the mid-1950s, the shifting regional situation contributed to an economic and political shift. Beyond that, there was undoubtedly a subjective factor of the CPC leadership wanting to accelerate the journey to socialism – to "accomplish socialist industrialisation and socialist transformation in fifteen years or a little longer", as Mao put it in

1953.[27] With the death of Stalin in March 1953 and the gradual deterioration of relations between the CPC and the new Soviet leadership under Nikita Khrushchev, the Chinese came to feel that the Soviets were abandoning the path of revolutionary struggle and that responsibility for blazing a trail in the construction of socialism had fallen to China. To move from a position of economic and scientific backwardness to becoming an advanced socialist power would require nothing less than a great leap.

## Mao as monster?

To this day, the most popular method for casually denigrating the People's Republic of China and the record of the CPC is to cite the alleged crimes of Mao Zedong who, from the early 1930s until his death in 1976, was generally recognised as the top leader of the Chinese Revolution. If the CPC was so dedicated to improving the lot of the Chinese people, why did it engage in such disastrous campaigns as the Great Leap Forward and the Cultural Revolution?

The Great Leap Forward (GLF), launched in 1958, was an ambitious programme designed to achieve rapid industrialisation and collectivisation; to fast-track the construction of socialism and allow China to make a final break with centuries-old underdevelopment and poverty; in Mao's words, to "close the gap between China and the US within five years, and to ultimately surpass the US within seven years".[28] In its economic strategy, it represented "a rejection of plodding Soviet-style urban industrialisation,"[29] reflecting the early stages of the Sino-Soviet split. The Chinese were worried that the Khrushchev leadership in Moscow was narrowly focused on the avoidance of conflict with the imperialist powers, and that its support to China and the other socialist countries would be sacrificed at the altar of 'peaceful coexistence'. Hence China would have to rely on its own resources.

For all its shortcomings, the core of the GLF was pithily described by Indian Marxist Vijay Prashad as an "attempt to bring small-scale industry to rural areas."[30] Mao considered the countryside would once again become the "true source for revolutionary social transformation" and "the main arena where the struggle to achieve socialism and communism will be determined."[31] Agricultural collectivisation was fast-tracked, and there was a broad appeal to the revolutionary spirit of the masses. Ji Chaozhu (at the time an interpreter for the Ministry of Foreign Affairs and later China's ambassador to the UK (1987-91) notes in his memoirs:

> The peasants were left with small plots of their own, for subsistence farming only. All other activity was for the communal good, to be shared equally. Cadres were to join the peasants in the fields, factories, and construction sites. Even Mao made an appearance at a dam-building project to have his picture taken with a shovel in hand.[32]

The GLF was not overall a success. Liu Mingfu writes that "the Great Leap Forward did not realise the goal of surpassing the UK and US. It actually brought China's economy to a standstill and then recession. It caused a large number of unnatural deaths and pushed China's global share of GDP from 5.46 percent in 1957 to 4.01 percent in 1962, lower than its share of 4.59 percent in 1950."[33]

The disruption to the basic economic structure of society combined with the sudden withdrawal of Soviet experts in 1960 and a series of terrible droughts and floods to produce poor harvests. Meanwhile, with millions of peasants drafted into the cities to work in factories, "no one was available to reap and to thresh."[34] The historian Alexander Pantsov opines that the "battle for steel had diverted the Chinese leadership's attention from the grain problem, and the task of harvesting rice and other grain had fallen on the shoulders of women, old men, and children... A shortage of grain developed, and Mao gave the command to decrease the pace of the Great Leap."[35] Ji Chaozhu observes that "malnutrition leading to edema was common in many areas, and deaths among the rural population increased."[36]

Certain of the GLF's goals were achieved – most notably the irrigation of arable land. However, it didn't achieve its overall objective, and the disruption it caused contributed to a deepening of poverty and malnutrition. It was called off in 1962. It remains a highly controversial topic in Chinese history. For anticommunists, the GLF provides incontrovertible proof of the monstrous, murderous nature of the CPC – and Mao Zedong in particular. Western bourgeois historians seem to have settled on a figure of 30 million for the estimated number of lives lost in famine resulting from the Great Leap. On the basis of a rigorous statistical analysis, Indian economist Utsa Patnaik concludes that China's death rate rose from 12 per thousand in 1958 (a historically low figure resulting from land reform and the extension of basic medical services throughout the country) to a peak of 25.4 per thousand in 1960.

> If we take the remarkably low death rate of 12 per thousand that China had achieved by 1958 as the benchmark, and calculate the deaths in excess of this over the period 1959 to 1961, it totals 11.5 million. This is the maximal estimate of possible 'famine deaths.'[37]

Patnaik observes that even the peak death rate in 1960 "was little different from India's 24.8 death rate in the same year, which was considered quite normal and attracted no criticism." This is an important point. Malnutrition was at that time a scourge throughout the developing world (sadly it remains so in some parts of the planet). China's history is rife with terrible famines, including in 1907, 1928 and 1942. It is only in the modern era, under the leadership of precisely that 'monstrous' CPC, that malnutrition has become a thing of the past in China.

In other words, the failure of the GLF has been cynically manipulated by bourgeois academics to denigrate the entire history of the Chinese Revolution. The GLF was not some outrageous crime against humanity; it was a legitimate attempt to accelerate the building of a prosperous and advanced socialist society. It turned out not to be successful and was therefore dropped.

In the aftermath of the GLF, Mao's more radical wing of the CPC leadership became somewhat marginalised, and the initiative fell to those wanting to prioritise social stability and economic growth over ongoing class struggle. Principal among these were Liu Shaoqi (head of state of the PRC from 1959, and widely considered to be Mao's successor) and Vice Premier Deng Xiaoping. Liu, Deng, Chen Yun and Zhou Enlai put forward the concept of the *Four Modernisations* (in agriculture, industry, defence, and science and technology) which would come to constitute a cornerstone of post-Mao economic policy.

In the years that followed, Mao and a group of his close comrades began to worry that the deprioritisation of class struggle reflected an anti-revolutionary 'revisionist' trend that could ultimately lead to capitalist restoration. As Mao saw it, revisionist elements were able to rely on the support of the intelligentsia – particularly teachers and academics – who, themselves coming largely from non-working class backgrounds, were promoting capitalist and feudal values among young people. It was necessary to "exterminate the roots of revisionism" and "struggle against those in power in the party who were taking the capitalist road."[38]

The Cultural Revolution started in 1966 as a mass movement of university and school students, incited and encouraged by Mao and others on the left of the leadership. Student groups formed in Beijing calling themselves Red Guards and taking up Mao's call to "thoroughly criticise and repudiate the reactionary bourgeois ideas in the sphere of academic work, education, journalism, literature and art".[39] The students produced 'big-character posters' (*dazibao*) setting out their analysis against, and making their demands of, anti-revolutionary bourgeois elements in authority. Mao was enthusiastic, writing the students in support of their initiative: "I will give enthusiastic support to all who take an attitude similar to yours in the Cultural Revolution movement."[40] He produced his own *dazibao* calling on the revolutionary masses to "Bombard the Headquarters" – that is, to rise up against the reformers and "bourgeois elements" in the party.

These developments were synthesised by the CPC Central Committee, which in August 1966 adopted its *Decision Concerning the Great Proletarian Cultural Revolution:*

> Although the bourgeoisie has been overthrown, it is still trying to use the old ideas, culture, customs and habits of the ex-

> ploiting classes to corrupt the masses, capture their minds and endeavour to stage a comeback. The proletariat must do the exact opposite: it must meet head-on every challenge of the bourgeoisie in the ideological field and use the new ideas, culture, customs and habits of the proletariat to change the mental outlook of the whole of society. At present, our objective is to struggle against and overthrow those persons in authority who are taking the capitalist road, to criticise and repudiate the reactionary bourgeois academic 'authorities' and the ideology of the bourgeoisie and all other exploiting classes and to transform education, literature and art and all other parts of the superstructure not in correspondence with the socialist economic base, so as to facilitate the consolidation and development of the socialist system.[41]

Thus the aims of the Cultural Revolution were to stimulate a mass struggle against the supposedly revisionist and capitalist restorationist elements in the party; to put a stop to the hegemony of bourgeois ideas in the realms of education and culture; and to entrench a new culture – socialist, collectivist, modern. The Cultural Revolution also marked a further escalation of the Sino-Soviet split, as the revisionist illness was considered to have a Soviet etiology (Liu Shaoqi, previously considered as Mao's successor and now the principal target of the radicals, was labelled *China's Khrushchev*). Singaporean scholar Li Mingjiang notes that, "throughout the Cultural Revolution, the Soviet Union was systematically demonised. Sino-Soviet hostilities reached an unprecedented level, as exemplified by Mao's designation of Moscow as China's primary enemy."[42]

Han Suyin describes the chaotic atmosphere of the early days of the Cultural Revolution:

> Extensive democracy. Great criticism. Wall posters everywhere. Absolute freedom to travel. Freedom to form revolutionary exchanges. These were the rights and freedoms given to the Red Guards, and no wonder it went to their heads and very soon became total licence... [In August 1966] the simmering Cultural Revolution exploded in a maelstrom of violence… Mao had not reckoned that he would lose control of the havoc he had launched.[43]

There was widespread disruption. Universities were closed.

> Red Guards occupied and ransacked the Foreign Ministry, while most ambassadors were recalled to Beijing for political education. The British embassy was attacked, and the Soviet

> embassy was laid under siege by youthful Maoists for several months.[44]

Many of those accused by the Cultural Revolution Group (CRG, a body of the CPC initially reporting to the Politburo Standing Committee but becoming the de facto centre of power) suffered horrible fates. Posters appeared with the slogan "Down with Liu Shaoqi! Down with Deng Xiaoping! Hold high the great red banner of Mao Zedong Thought." Liu's books were burned in Tiananmen Square – "they were declared to be poisonous weeds, yet they had been a mainstay of the theoretical construct which in Yan'an in 1945-47 had brought Mao to power."[45] He was expelled from all positions and arrested.

> Liu had been repeatedly tortured and interrogated, confined to an unheated cell, and denied medical care. He died in November 1969, his remains surreptitiously cremated under a false name. His death was kept from his wife for three years, and from the public for a decade.[46]

Peng Dehuai, former Defence Minister and the leader of the Chinese People's Volunteer Army's operations in the Korean War, had been forced into retirement in 1959 after criticising the Great Leap Forward. Jiang Qing – Mao's wife, and a leading figure in the CRG – sent Red Guards to Sichuan, where Peng was living.

> A band of thugs burst into his house, seized him, and brought him to the capital, where he was thrown into prison. Peng was tortured and beaten more than a hundred times, his ribs were broken, his face maimed, and his lungs damaged. He was repeatedly dragged to criticism and struggle meetings.[47]

He died in a prison hospital in 1974.

Even Premier Zhou Enlai, unfailingly loyal in spite of his quiet horror at the CRG's extremism, didn't escape unscathed: in November 1966, according to Han Suyin, he had a heart attack after 22 hours of being surrounded and shouted at by Red Guards.

Although Mao had intended it to last for just a few months, the Cultural Revolution continued for a decade, albeit with varying intensity: realising that the situation was getting out of control, in 1967 Mao called on the army to help establish order and re-organise production. However, it flared up again with the ascendancy of the 'Gang of Four' from 1972.

Historians in the capitalist countries tend to present the Cultural Revolution in the most facile and vacuous terms. To them, it was simply the quintessential example of Mao's obsessive love of violence and power;

just another episode in the long story of communist authoritarianism. But psychopathology is rarely the principal driving force of history. In reality, the Cultural Revolution was a radical mass movement; millions of young people were inspired by the idea of moving faster towards socialism, of putting an end to feudal traditions, of creating a more egalitarian society, of fighting bureaucracy, of preventing the emergence of a capitalist class, of empowering workers and peasants, of making their contribution to a global socialist revolution, of building a proud socialist culture unfettered by thousands of years of Confucian tradition. They wanted a fast track to a socialist future. They were inspired by Mao and his allies, who were in turn inspired by them.

Such a movement can get out of control easily enough, and it did. Mao can't be considered culpable for every excess, every act of violence, every absurd statement (indeed he intervened at several points to rein them in), but he was broadly supportive of the movement and ultimately did the most to further its aims. Mao had enormous personal influence – not solely powers granted by the party or state constitutions, but an authority that came from being the chief architect of a revolutionary process that had transformed hundreds of millions of people's lives for the better. He was as Lenin was to the Soviet people, as Fidel Castro remains to the Cuban people. Even when he made mistakes, these mistakes were liable to be embraced by millions of people. Han Suyin comments that "Mao was prone to making contradictory remarks, but each remark had the force of an edict."[48]

The Cultural Revolution is now widely understood in China to have been largely misguided. It was "the most severe setback … suffered by the Party, the state and the people since the founding of the People's Republic."[49] The political assumptions of the movement – that the party was becoming dominated by counter-revolutionaries and capitalist-roaders; that the capitalist-roaders in the party would have to be overthrown by the masses; that continuous revolution would be required in order to stay on the road to socialism – were explicitly rejected by the post-Mao leadership of the CPC, which pointed out that "the 'capitalist-roaders' overthrown … were leading cadres of Party and government organisations at all levels, who formed the core force of the socialist cause."[50]

Historian Rebecca Karl posits that this post-Mao leadership in fact benefitted from the Cultural Revolution, in the sense that it came to be seen as "the saviour of China from chaos."[51]

Perhaps the Cultural Revolution had a more directly useful outcome. Its principal aim was, after all, to prevent the ideological decay that was taking place in the Soviet Union at the time – an ideological decay that made a major contribution towards the Soviet people's loss of confidence in the socialist project and, ultimately, the end of Soviet socialism.[52] Indeed it can be argued that the Cultural Revolution set the parameters of how far *Reform and Opening Up* could go; it laid the ground for Deng Xiaoping's

*Four Cardinal Principles,* which the CPC continues to observe today: 1) We must keep to the socialist road; 2) We must uphold the people's democratic dictatorship; 3) We must uphold the leadership of the Communist Party; 4) We must uphold Marxism-Leninism and Mao Zedong Thought.[53]

Australian academic Roland Boer poses the question of why the CPC leadership felt it important to identify and emphasise the Four Cardinal Principles at that point, at the start of the economic reform programme: "Deng identifies the 'rightist' deviation as their target. The Reform and Opening Up may be seen by some as a path to capitalism and bourgeois liberalisation, and thus an abandonment of Marxism-Leninism."[54] As such, the Four Cardinal Principles and the Cultural Revolution share some common ground in terms of their basic motivation.

German political economist Isabella M Weber also makes an interesting point that "the disruption of social order during the Cultural Revolution" was a crucial factor in the development of a new generation of young intellectuals with a close understanding of the needs of peasantry and the situation in the countryside.

> A cohort of young intellectuals (born 1940–1960) who were 'sent up to the mountains and to the countryside' during the Cultural Revolution emerged as influential reform economists in the course of agricultural reform. Like the veteran revolutionaries before them, their intellectual and political formation was intimately connected to the agrarian question, to China's peasant majority, and to their struggle for material well-being. These young and old intellectuals with close ties to the countryside formed an unusual alliance that proved critical for China's reform… As a historical irony, these Cultural Revolution campaigns also established new links between the urban and rural spheres that became instrumental for the breakthrough in the early years of reform.[55]

Nonetheless, the turmoil of the Cultural Revolution impeded the country's development and brought awful tragedy to a significant number of people. What so many historians operating in a capitalist framework fail to understand is why, in spite of the chaos and violence of the Cultural Revolution, Mao is still revered in China. For the Chinese people, the bottom line is that his errors were "the errors of a great proletarian revolutionary."[56]

It was the CPC, led by Mao and on the basis of a political strategy principally devised by him, liberated China from foreign rule; that unified the country; that led the dismantling of feudalism; that distributed land to the peasants; that led the industrialisation of the country; that forged a path to women's liberation. British economist John Ross points out:

> In the 27 years between the establishment of the People's Republic of China in 1949 and the death of Mao Zedong in 1976, life expectancy in China increased by 31 years – or over a year per chronological year... China's rate of increase of life expectancy in the three decades after 1949 was the fastest ever recorded in a major country in human history.[57]

The excesses and errors associated with the last years of Mao's life have to be contextualised within this overall picture of unprecedented, transformative progress for the Chinese people. The pre-revolution literacy rate in China was less than 20 percent. By the time Mao died, it was around 93 percent. China's population had remained stagnant between 400 and 500 million for a hundred years or so up to 1949. By the time Mao died, it had reached 900 million. A thriving culture of literature, music, theatre and art grew up that was accessible to the masses of the people. Land was irrigated. Famine became a thing of the past. Universal healthcare was established. China – after a century of foreign domination – maintained its sovereignty and developed the means to defend itself from imperialist attack.

Hence the *Mao as monster* narrative has little resonance in China. As Deng Xiaoping himself put it, "without Mao's outstanding leadership, the Chinese revolution would still not have triumphed even today. In that case, the people of all our nationalities would still be suffering under the reactionary rule of imperialism, feudalism and bureaucrat-capitalism."[58] Furthermore, even the mistakes were not the product of the deranged imagination of a tyrant but, rather, creative attempts to respond to an incredibly complex and evolving set of circumstances. They were errors carried out in the cause of exploring a path to socialism – a historically novel process inevitably involving risk and experimentation.

## Reform and opening up: the great betrayal?

From 1978, the post-Mao Chinese leadership embarked on a process of 'reform and opening up' – gradually introducing market mechanisms to the economy, allowing elements of private property, and encouraging investment from the capitalist world. This programme of *socialism with Chinese characteristics* posited that, while China had established a socialist society, it would remain for some time in the primary stage of socialism, during which period it was necessary to develop a socialist market economy – combining planning, the development of a mixed economy and the profit motive – with a view to maximising the development of the productive forces.

Deng Xiaoping, who had been one of the most prominent targets of the Cultural Revolution and who had risen to become de facto leader of the CPC from 1978, theorised reform and opening up in the following terms:

> Marxism attaches utmost importance to developing the productive forces... [The advance towards communism] calls for highly developed productive forces and an overwhelming abundance of material wealth. Therefore, the fundamental task for the socialist stage is to develop the productive forces. The superiority of the socialist system is demonstrated, in the final analysis, by faster and greater development of those forces than under the capitalist system. As they develop, the people's material and cultural life will constantly improve... Socialism means eliminating poverty. Pauperism is not socialism, still less communism.[59]

The reform strategy aimed at "shaking off China's poverty and backwardness, gradually improving the people's living standards, restoring a position for China in international affairs commensurate with its current status, and enabling China to contribute more to mankind."[60]

Was this the moment the CPC gave up on its commitment to Marxism? Such is the belief of many. For supporters of capitalism, the idea that China 'ascended' to capitalism from 1978 onwards is a validation of their own ideology; China was socialist and poor, and then became capitalist and rich. This view is near-universal among mainstream economists. Even the well-known Keynesian Jeffrey Sachs, who is both politically progressive and friendly towards China, considers that the key turning point in Chinese history was not 1949 but 1978:

> After nearly 140 years of economic and social strife, marked by foreign incursions, domestic rebellions, civil wars, and internal policy blunders of historic dimensions, China settled down after 1978 to stable, open, market-based production and trade.[61]

On the other hand, for many on the left (particularly in the West), 1978 marked a turning point in the wrong direction – away from socialism, away from the cause of the working class and peasantry. The introduction of private profit, the decollectivisation of agriculture, the appearance of multinational companies and the rise of Western influence: these added up to a historic betrayal and an end to the Chinese Revolution.

The consensus view within the CPC is that socialism with Chinese characteristics is a strategy aimed at strengthening socialism, improving the lives of the Chinese people, and consolidating China's sovereignty. Although China had taken incredible steps forward since 1949, China in 1978 remained backward in many ways. The bulk of the population lived a very precarious existence, many lacking access to modern energy and safe water. China's per capita income was $210. Food production, and consequently average food consumption, was insufficient. "An estimated

30 percent of rural residents, about 250 million, lived below the poverty line, relying on small loans for production and state grants for food."[62] The low per capita income figure is deceptive in the sense that the poor in China had secure access to land and housing – by which measure they were doing much better than most of their counterparts in the developing world; nonetheless the vast majority were genuinely poor.

Meanwhile the capitalist world was making major advances in science and technology, and the gap in living standards between China and its neighbours was growing sufficiently wide as to threaten the legitimacy of the CPC government. Chinese economist Justin Yifu Lin notes that, at the time of the founding of the PRC, there was only a relatively small per capita income gap between China and its East Asian neighbours.

> But by 1978 Japan had basically caught up with the United States, and South Korea and Taiwan Province had narrowed the income gap with developed countries. China, although boasting a complete industrial system, an atomic bomb, and a man-made satellite, had a standard of living a far cry from that of the developed world.[63]

In Guangdong, the southern province bordering Hong Kong, many were fleeing because, in the words of Hua Guofeng (Mao's chosen successor as head of the CPC), "Hong Kong and Macao were wealthy and the PRC was poor." The leadership simply decided to "change the situation and make the PRC wealthy."[64]

Opening up to foreign capital, learning from foreign technology, and integrating into the global market would allow for a faster development of the productive forces. Export manufacturing would allow China to build up sufficient hard currency to acquire technology from rich countries and improve productivity. Foreign capital would be attracted by China's virtually limitless pool of literate and diligent workers.

All this was highly unorthodox compared to the experience of the socialist world up to that point (with some partial exceptions, such as Yugoslavia and Hungary). Deng Xiaoping's strong belief was that, unless the government delivered on a significant improvement in people's standard of living, the entire socialist project would lose its legitimacy and therefore be in peril. Assessing that China was around 20 years behind the advanced countries in science and technology, he stated:

> When a backward country is trying to build socialism, it is natural that during the long initial period its productive forces will not be up to the level of those in developed capitalist countries and that it will not be able to eliminate poverty completely. Accordingly, in building socialism we must do

> all we can to develop the productive forces and gradually eliminate poverty, constantly raising the people's living standards... If we don't do everything possible to increase production, how can we expand the economy? How can we demonstrate the superiority of socialism and communism? We have been making revolution for several decades and have been building socialism for more than three. Nevertheless, by 1978 the average monthly salary for our workers was still only 45 yuan, and most of our rural areas were still mired in poverty. Can this be called the superiority of socialism?[65]

Interestingly, this sentiment contains echoes of Mao in 1949:

> If we are ignorant in production, cannot grasp production work quickly ... so as to improve the livelihood of workers first and then that of other ordinary people, we shall certainly not be able to maintain our political power: we shall lose our position and we shall fail.[66]

Marx wrote in volume 3 of *Capital* that "the development of the productive forces of social labour is capital's historic mission and justification. For that very reason, it unwittingly creates the material conditions for a higher form of production."[67] The vision of the CPC leadership was to replace "unwittingly" with "purposefully": using capital, within strict limits and under heavy regulation, to bring China into the modern world.

Rather than selling out to capitalism, *reform and opening up* is better understood as a return to the policies of the New Democracy period. The CPC has always been adamant that what China is building is socialism, not capitalism – "it is for the realisation of communism that we have struggled for so many years... It was for the realisation of this ideal that countless people laid down their lives."[68] The basic guiding ideology of the CPC has not changed in its century of existence, as was summed up succinctly by Xi Jinping:

> Both history and reality have shown us that only socialism can save China and only socialism with Chinese characteristics can bring development to China.[69]

In borrowing certain techniques and mechanisms from capitalism, China is following a logic devised by the Bolsheviks during the New Economic Policy, using markets and investment to stimulate economic activity, whilst maintaining Communist Party rule and refusing to allow the capitalist class to dominate political power. As Lenin put it in 1921:

> We must not be afraid of the growth of the petty bourgeoisie and small capital. What we must fear is protracted starvation, want and food shortage, which create the danger that the working class will be utterly exhausted and will give way to petty-bourgeois vacillation and despair. This is a much more terrible prospect.[70]

Modern China has gone much further than the NEP, in the sense that private property is not limited to "the petty bourgeoisie and small capital"; there are some extremely wealthy individuals and companies controlling vast sums of capital. And yet their political status is essentially the same as it was in the early days of the PRC; their existence as a class is predicated on their acceptance of the overall socialist programme and trajectory of the country. As long as they are helping China to develop, they are tolerated, even encouraged. Even in 1957, with socialist construction in full swing, Mao considered:

> The contradiction between the working class and the national bourgeoisie comes under the category of contradictions among the people… In the concrete conditions of China, this antagonistic contradiction between the two classes, if properly handled, can be transformed into a non-antagonistic one and be resolved by peaceful methods.[71]

The reform strategy has been undeniably successful in terms of alleviating poverty and modernising the country. Economist Arthur Kroeber notes that workers' wages have increased continuously, pointing out that, in 1994, a Chinese factory worker could expect to earn a quarter of what their counterpart in Thailand was earning; just 14 years later, the Chinese worker was earning 25 percent more than the Thai worker.[72] Jude Woodward writes that per capita income in China doubled in the decade from 1980, "whereas it took Britain six decades to achieve the same after the Industrial Revolution in the late eighteenth century and America five decades after the Civil War."[73]

The combination of planning and ever-rising productivity has created a vast surplus, which has been used partly to "orchestrate a massive, sustained programme of infrastructure construction, including roads, railways, ports, airports, dams, electricity generation and distribution facilities, telecommunications, water and sewage systems, and housing, on a proportional scale far exceeding that of comparable developing countries, such as India, Indonesia, Pakistan and Bangladesh."[74]

The fundamental difference between the Chinese system and capitalism is that, with capital in control, it would not be possible to prioritise the needs of the working class and peasantry; China would not have been able to achieve the largest-scale poverty alleviation in history. Deng understood this:

> Ours is an economically backward country with a population of one billion. If we took the capitalist road, a small number of people in certain areas would quickly grow rich, and a new bourgeoisie would emerge along with a number of millionaires — all of these people amounting to less than one per cent of the population — while the overwhelming majority of the people would remain in poverty, scarcely able to feed and clothe themselves. Only the socialist system can eradicate poverty.[75]

In adapting its strategy in accordance with new realities and a sober assessment of the past, the CPC was following the same principle it had always stood for: to seek truth from facts and to develop a reciprocal relationship between theory and practice. In Mao's words, "the only yardstick of truth is the revolutionary practice of millions of people."[76] The CPC's experience in practice was that "having a totally planned economy hampers the development of the productive forces to a certain extent."[77] And this experience is largely consistent with that of other socialist states. Roland Boer observes:

> While a largely planned economy immediately after a successful communist revolution is a necessity — with its nationalisations, collectivisation, and crushing or transformation of the former bourgeois-landlord owners of the means of production – it leads after a few decades to new contradictions that stifle economic efficiency and improvement.[78]

China's leaders conjectured that a combination of planning and markets would "liberate the productive forces and speed up economic growth." This hypothesis has been proven correct by material reality, and has thereby made a historic contribution to humanity's collective understanding of socialist construction.

## No Great Wall

*Reform and opening up* wasn't purely a correction of earlier mistakes; it was also – perhaps mainly – a response to changing objective circumstances; specifically, a more favourable international environment resulting from the restoration of China's seat at the United Nations (1971) and the rapprochement between China and the US. Thomas Orlik, chief economist at Bloomberg Economics, notes that, "when Deng Xiaoping launched the reform and opening process, friendly relations with the United States provided the crucial underpinning. The path for Chinese goods to enter global markets was open."[79] So too was the door for foreign capital, technology, and expertise to enter China – first from Hong Kong and Japan, then the West. Zhou Enlai reportedly commented at the time of then-US Secretary of State Henry Kissinger's historic visit to Beijing in 1971 that "only America can help China to modernise."[80] Even allowing for Zhou's legendary diplomatic eloquence, this statement nevertheless contains an important kernel of truth.

Mao and Zhou had seen engagement with the US as a way to break China's isolation. The US leadership saw engagement with China as a way to perpetuate and exacerbate the division between China and the Soviet Union. (Everyone was triangulating; for its part, the Soviet leadership was hoping to work with the US to undermine and destabilise China.[81]) Regardless of the complex set of intentions, one key outcome of the US-China rapprochement in the early 1970s was that a favourable external environment was created in which a policy of 'opening up' could feasibly be pursued.

Deng was also not the first to recognise that the productive forces were undergoing historic changes in the West and that China would have to catch up. Zhou Enlai noted that "new developments in science are bringing humanity to a new technological and industrial revolution... We must conquer these new heights in science to reach advanced world standards."[82] Indeed it was Zhou who first conceptualised the *Four Modernisations* that Deng made the cornerstone of his strategy. In early 1963, Zhou stated: "If we want to build a powerful socialist country, we must modernise agriculture, industry, national defence, science and technology."[83] Again in January 1975 – in his last major speech – he talked of the urgent need to take advantage of the more peaceful and stable international context and "accomplish the comprehensive modernisation of agriculture, industry, national defence and science and technology before the end of the century, so that our national economy will be advancing in the front ranks of the world."[84]

The economic take-off of the post-1978 period "would not have been possible without the economic, political and social foundations that had been built up in the preceding period", in the words of the late Egyptian Marxist Samir Amin.[85] Even with the disruption caused by the Cultural Revolution, the early period of socialist construction achieved "progress on a scale which old China could not achieve in hundreds or even thousands of years."[86] This is universally understood among Chinese communists. Prominent economist Hu Angang writes that, by 1978, all children received an education, adult illiteracy had fallen from 80 percent to 33 percent, and basic healthcare was available to everyone. Industry had been built up from almost nothing. Meanwhile, "China succeeded in feeding one-fifth of the world's population with only 7 percent of the world's arable land and 6.5 percent of its water. China's pre-1978 social and economic development cannot be underestimated."[87]

This can be usefully compared with the same time period in India, which following independence from the British Empire in 1947 was in a similarly parlous state, with a life expectancy of 32. At the end of the pre-reform period in China, ie 1978, India's life expectancy had increased to 55, while China's had increased to 67. As John Ross elucidates, "this sharply growing difference was not because India had a bad record – as an increase of 22 years in life expectancy over a 31-year period graphically shows. It is simply that China's performance was sensational – life expectancy increasing by 32 years in a 29-year chronological period."[88]

Xi Jinping has observed that, although the two major phases of the People's Republic of China are different in many ways, "they are by no means separated from or opposed to each other. We should neither negate the pre-reform phase in comparison with the post-reform phase, nor the converse."[89]

The two major phases are both consistent with the CPC's guiding philosophy and raison d'être. Both have played an invaluable role in China's continuing transformation from a divided, war-torn, backward and phenomenally poor country in which "approximately one of every three children died within the first year of birth"[90] to a unified, peaceful, advanced and increasingly prosperous country which is blazing a trail towards a more developed socialism.

In each stage of its existence, the CPC has sought to creatively apply and develop Marxism according to the prevailing concrete circumstances; always seeking to safeguard China's sovereignty, maintain peace, and build prosperity for the masses of the people. Through many twists and turns, this has been a constant of a hundred years of Chinese Revolution.

## NOTES

1 Mao Zedong 1937, *On Contradiction*, Marxist Internet Archive, accessed 23 January 2023, <https://www.marxists.org/reference/archive/mao/selected-works/volume-1/mswv1_17.htm>
2 Agnes Smedley. *The Great Road: The Life and Times of Chu Teh*. United Kingdom: Monthly Review Press, 1972, p.vii
3 Cited in William Hinton. *Fanshen: A Documentary of Revolution in a Chinese Village*. New York: Monthly Review Press, 2008, p477
4 Israel Epstein. *From Opium War to Liberation*. Beijing: New World Press, 1956, p65
5 ibid, p67
6 Han Suyin. *Eldest Son: Zhou Enlai and the Making of Modern China*. London: Pimlico, 1994, p39
7 Alternatively romanised as Kuomintang (KMT)
8 Vladimir Lenin 1912, *Democracy and Narodism in China*, Marxist Internet Archive, accessed 23 January 2023, <https://www.marxists.org/archive/lenin/works/1912/jul/15.htm>.
9 Graham Hutchings. *China 1949: Year of Revolution*. London: Bloomsbury Academic, 2020, p17
10 Edgar Snow. *Red Star over China*. London: Grove Press UK, 2018, p98
11 Mao Zedong 1940, *On New Democracy*, Marxist Internet Archive, accessed 23 January 2023, <https://www.marxists.org/reference/archive/mao/selected-works/volume-2/mswv2_26.htm>
12 Hinton, *op cit*, p.xxiv
13 Han, *op cit*, p178
14 Snow, *op cit*, p185
15 Cited in Snow, *ibid*, p276
16 Hutchings, *op cit*, p44
17 *Xi urges efforts to carry forward great founding spirit of CPC and Yan'an Spirit*, Xinhua, accessed 26 January 2023, <https://english.news.cn/20221028/4d048ab7d53b4eb5b5a06da2def453ce/c.html>.
18 Mao, *On New Democracy*, op cit
19 *ibid*
20 Snow, *op cit*, p103
21 Mao Zedong 1940, *On the People's Democratic Dictatorship*, Marxist Internet Archive, accessed 24 January 2023, <https://www.marxists.org/reference/archive/mao/selected-works/volume-4/mswv4_65.htm>.
22 Hutchings, op cit, p270
23 Rebecca E Karl. *Mao Zedong and China in the Twentieth-Century World: A Concise History*. Durham North Carolina: Duke University Press, 2010, p87
24 Steve Yui-Sang Tsang. *Cold War's Odd Couple: The Unintended Partnership between the Republic of China and the UK*, 1950-1958, 2021, p6

25 Hutchings, op cit, p268
26 *Statement Issued by the President, 27 June 1950,* The Office of the Historian, accessed 24 January 2023, <https://history.state.gov/historicaldocuments/frus1950v07/d119>.
27 Mao Zedong 1953, *Combat Bourgeois Ideas in the Party,* Marxist Internet Archive, accessed 24 January 2023, <https://www.marxists.org/reference/archive/mao/selected-works/volume-5/mswv5_32.htm>.
28 Cited in Li Mingjiang. *Mao's China and the Sino-Soviet Split: Ideological Dilemma.* Routledge Contemporary China Series 79. London ; New York: Routledge, 2012, p55.
29 Rebecca E. Karl. *China's Revolutions in the Modern World: A Brief Interpretive History.* London ; New York: Verso, 2020, p129
30 Vijay Prashad. *The Poorer Nations: A Possible History of the Global South.* London; New York: Verso, 2012, p199.
31 Karl, *op cit,* p129
32 Ji Chaozhu. *The Man on Mao's Right: From Harvard Yard to Tiananmen Square, My Life inside China's Foreign Ministry.* New York: Random House, 2008, p195.
33 Liu Mingfu. *The China Dream: Great Power Thinking & Strategic Posture in the Post-American Era.* New York, NY: CN Times Books, 2015, p18.
34 Han, *op cit,* p271
35 Alexander Pantsov, and Steven I. Levine. *Deng Xiaoping: A Revolutionary Life.* Oxford: Oxford University Press, 2015, p196
36 Ji, *op cit,* p212
37 Utsa Patnaik 2011, *Revisiting Alleged 30 Million Famine Deaths during China's Great Leap,* MR Online, accessed 24 January 2023, <https://mronline.org/2011/06/26/revisiting-alleged-30-million-famine-deaths-during-chinas-great-leap/>.
38 Cited in Pantsov and Levine, *op cit,* p234
39 *Circular of the Central Committee of the Communist Party of China on the Great Proletarian Cultural Revolution (16 May 1966),* Marxist Internet Archive, accessed 24 January 2023, <https://www.marxists.org/subject/china/documents/cpc/cc_gpcr.htm>.
40 Mao Zedong 1966, *A Letter To The Red Guards Of Tsinghua University Middle School,* Marxist Internet Archive, accessed 24 January 2023, <https://www.marxists.org/reference/archive/mao/selected-works/volume-9/mswv9_60.htm>.
41 *Decision of the Central Committee of the Chinese Communist Party Concerning the Great Proletarian Cultural Revolution (8 August 1966),* Marxist Internet Archive, accessed 24 January 2023, <https://www.marxists.org/subject/china/peking-review/1966/PR1966-33g.htm>.
42 Li, *op cit,* p134
43 Han, *op cit,* p327
44 Odd Arne Westad. *The Global Cold War: Third World Interventions and the*

*Making of Our Times*. 1st pbk. ed. Cambridge ; New York: Cambridge University Press, 2007, p163

45 Han, *op cit*, p253

46 Ji, *op cit*, p333

47 Alexander Pantsov and Steven I. Levine. *Mao: The Real Story*. First Simon&Schuster paperback edition. New York: Simon & Schuster Paperbacks, 2013, p518

48 Han, *op cit*, p387

49 *Resolution on certain questions in the history of our party since the founding of the People's Republic of China (27 June 1981)*, Marxist Internet Archive, accessed 24 January 2023, <https://www.marxists.org/subject/china/documents/cpc/history/01.htm>.

50 *ibid*

51 Karl, *Mao Zedong and China in the Twentieth-Century World, op cit*, p119

52 This theme is discussed at length in my book *The End of the Beginning: Lessons of the Soviet Collapse*. New Delhi: Leftword Books, 2019.

53 Deng Xiaoping 1979, *Uphold the four cardinal principles*, China Daily, accessed 26 January 2023, <https://www.chinadaily.com.cn/china/19thcpcnationalcongress/2010-10/15/content_29714546.htm>

54 Roland Boer. *Socialism with Chinese Characteristics: A Guide for Foreigners*. Singapore: Springer, 2021, p108

55 Isabella Weber. *How China Escaped Shock Therapy: The Market Reform Debate*. Routledge Studies on the Chinese Economy. Abingdon, Oxon ; New York, N.Y: Routledge, 2021, p154

56 *Resolution on certain questions in the history of our party since the founding of the People's Republic of China (27 June 1981), op cit*

57 John Ross 2019, *70 years of China's social miracle*, Socialist Economic Bulletin, accessed 24 January 2023, <https://www.socialisteconomicbulletin.net/2019/09/70-years-of-chinas-social-miracle/>.

58 Deng Xiaoping 1978, *Emancipate the mind, seek truth from facts and unite as one in looking to the future*, China Daily, accessed 24 January 2023, <http://www.chinadaily.com.cn/china/19thcpcnationalcongress/2010-10/15/content_29714549.htm>.

59 Deng Xiaoping 1984, *Building a Socialism with a Specifically Chinese Character*, China.org.cn, accessed 24 January 2023, <http://www.china.org.cn/english/features/dengxiaoping/103371.htm>.

60 Deng Xiaoping 1979, *China's Goal Is To Achieve Comparative Prosperity By the End of the Century*, Marxist Internet Archive, accessed 24 January 2023, <https://www.marxists.org/reference/archive/deng-xiaoping/1979/87.htm>.

61 Jeffrey Sachs. *The Ages of Globalization: Geography, Technology, and Institutions*. New York: Columbia University Press, 2020, p179

62 Justin Yifu Lin. *Demystifying the Chinese Economy*. Cambridge:

Cambridge University Press, 2012, p6
63 *ibid*, p153
64 Cited in Pantsov and Levine, *Deng Xiaoping, op cit*, p337
65 Deng Xiaoping 1982, *We shall concentrate on economic development*, China.org.cn, accessed 24 January 2023, <http://www.china.org.cn/english/features/dengxiaoping/103383.htm>.
66 Tony Saich and Benjamin Yang. *The Rise to Power of the Chinese Communist Party: Documents and Analysis*. United States: Taylor & Francis, 2016.
67 Karl Marx. *Capital: A Critique of Political Economy. V. 3*: Penguin Classics. London ; New York, N.Y: Penguin Books in association with New Left Review, 1981, p368
68 Deng Xiaoping 1985, *Reform is the only way for China to develop its productive forces*, China Daily, accessed 24 January 2023, <http://www.chinadaily.com.cn/china/19thcpcnationalcongress/2010-10/21/content_29714522.htm>.
69 Xi Jinping 2013, *Uphold and Develop Socialism with Chinese Characteristics*, National People's Congress of the People's Republic of China, accessed 24 January 2023, <http://www.npc.gov.cn/englishnpc/c23934/202005/b04ff09d057b4c2d92fca94ca3fc8708.shtml>.
70 Vladimir Lenin 1921, *Report On The Substitution Of A Tax In Kind For The Surplus Grain Appropriation System*, Marxist Internet Archive, accessed 24 January 2023, <https://www.marxists.org/archive/lenin/works/1921/10thcong/ch03.htm>.
71 Mao Zedong 1957, *On the correct handling of contradictions among the people*, Marxist Internet Archive, accessed 24 January 2023, <https://www.marxists.org/reference/archive/mao/selected-works/volume-5/mswv5_58.htm>.
72 Arthur R. Kroeber. *China's Economy: What Everyone Needs to Know*. New York, NY: Oxford University Press, 2016, p173
73 Jude Woodward. *The US vs China: Asia's New Cold War?* Geopolitical Economy. Manchester: Manchester University Press, 2017, p42
74 Peter Nolan. *Understanding China: The Silk Road and the Communist Manifesto*. Routledge Studies on the Chinese Economy 60. London ; New York: Routledge, Taylor & Francis Group, 2016, p2
75 Deng Xiaoping 1987, *China can only take the socialist road*, China Daily, accessed 24 January 2023, <https://www.chinadaily.com.cn/china/19thcpcnationalcongress/2010-10/25/content_29714437.htm>.
76 Mao, *On New Democracy, op cit*
77 Deng Xiaoping 1985, *There is no fundamental contradiction between socialism and a market economy*, China Daily, accessed 24 January 2023, <http://www.chinadaily.com.cn/china/19thcpcnationalcongress/2010-10/21/content_29714520.htm>.
78 Boer, *op cit*, p128

79 Thomas Orlik. *China: The Bubble That Never Pops*. Oxford: Oxford University Press, 2020, p149
80 Han, *op cit*, p376
81 See for example *Memorandum by the President's Assistant for National Security Affairs (Kissinger) for the President's File. June 23, 1973*, Office of the Historian, accessed 24 January 2023, <https://history.state.gov/historicaldocuments/frus1969-76v15/d131>.
82 Han, *op cit*, p251
83 Cited in Boer, *op cit*, p141
84 Zhou Enlai 1975, *Report on the Work of the Government*, Marxist Internet Archive, accessed 24 January 2023, <https://www.marxists.org/reference/archive/zhou-enlai/1975/01/13.htm>.
85 Samir Amin. *Beyond US Hegemony: Assessing the Prospects for a Multipolar World*. United Kingdom: Zed Books, 2013, p23
86 Deng Xiaoping 1979, *Uphold the four cardinal principles*, China Daily, accessed 25 January 2023, <https://www.chinadaily.com.cn/china/19thcpcnationalcongress/2010-10/15/content_29714546.htm>.
87 Hu Angang. *China in 2020: A New Type of Superpower.* United States: Brookings Institution Press, 2012, p27
88 John Ross. *China's Great Road: Lessons for Marxist Theory and Socialist Practices*. Glasgow: Praxis Press, 2021, p19
89 Xi Jinping. *The Governance of China*. First edition. Beijing: Foreign Languages Press, 2014, p61
90 Hutchings, *op cit*, p7

Xian: tradition and modernity

# 2

# Neither Washington nor Beijing?

A newcomer to politics would likely assume that members of the global left support the People's Republic of China. It is after all led by a communist party, with Marxism as its guiding ideology. During the period since the Communist Party of China came to power in 1949, the Chinese people have experienced an unprecedented improvement in their living standards and human development. Life expectancy has increased from around 35 to over 78[1] years. Literacy has increased from an estimated 20 percent[2] to 97 percent.[3] The social and economic position of women has improved beyond recognition (one example being that, before the revolution, the vast majority of women received no formal education whatsoever, whereas now a majority of students in higher education institutions are female). Extreme poverty has been eliminated. China is becoming the pre-eminent world leader in tackling climate change.

Such progress is evidently consistent with traditional left-wing values; what typically attracts people to Marxism is precisely that it seeks to provide a framework for solving those problems of human development that capitalism has shown itself incapable of satisfactorily addressing. Capitalism has driven historic innovations in science and technology, thereby laying the ground for a future of shared prosperity; however, its contradictions are such that it inevitably generates poverty alongside wealth; it cannot but impose itself through division, deception and coercion; everywhere it marginalises, alienates, dominates and exploits. Seventy years of Chinese socialism, meanwhile, have broken the inverse correlation between wealth and poverty. Even though China suffers from high levels of inequality; even though China has some extremely rich people; life for ordinary workers and peasants has continuously improved, at a remarkable rate and over an extended period.

Yet support for China within the left in countries such as Britain and the US is in fact a fairly marginal position. The bulk of Marxist groups in those countries consider that China is not a socialist country; indeed some believe it to be "a rising imperialist power in the world system that oversees the exploitation of its own population ... and increasingly exploits Third World countries in pursuit of raw materials and outlets for its exports."[4] Some consider the China-led *Belt and Road Initiative* to be an example of "feverish global expansionism".[5] The Alliance for Worker's Liberty, with characteristic crudeness, describe China as being "functionally little different from, and in any case not better than, a fascist regime,"[6] every bit as imperialist as the US and politically much worse.

The growing confrontation between the US and China is not, on these terms, an attack by an imperialist power on a socialist or independent developing country, but rather "a classic confrontation along imperialist lines".[7] "The dynamics of US-China rivalry is an inter-imperial rivalry driven by inter-capitalist competition," writes Ho-fung Hung in the popular left-wing journal *Jacobin*.[8] The assumption here is that China is "an emerging imperialist power that is seeking to assert itself in a world dominated by the established imperialist power of the US".[9] If that is the case, those that ground their politics in anti-imperialism should not support either the US or China; rather they should "build a 'third camp' that makes links and solidarity across borders"[10] and adopt the slogan *Neither Washington nor Beijing, but international socialism."*

To many, this is an attractive idea. We don't align with oppressors anywhere; our only alignment is with the global working class. Eli Friedman eloquently presents this grand vision in Jacobin: "Our job is to continually and forcefully reaffirm internationalist values: we take sides with the poor, working classes, and oppressed people of every country, which means we share nothing with either the US or Chinese states and corporations."[11]

## We've been here before: Neither Washington nor Moscow

This notion of opposing both sides in a cold war – refusing to align with either of the two major competing powers and instead forming an independent 'third camp' – has surprisingly deep roots. Prominent US Trotskyist Max Shachtman described the third camp in 1940 as "the camp of proletarian internationalism, of the socialist revolution, of the struggle for the emancipation of all the oppressed."[12] During the original Cold War, in particular in Britain, a significant proportion of the socialist movement rallied behind the slogan *Neither Washington nor Moscow*, withholding their support from a Soviet Union they considered to be state capitalist and/or imperialist.

Then as now, the third camp position drew theoretical justification from the strategy promoted by Lenin and the Bolsheviks in relation to World War I. The communist movement in the early 1910s recognised that a war between the two major competing imperialist blocs (Germany on one side, and Britain and France on the other) was near-inevitable. At the 1912 conference of the Second International in Basel, Switzerland, the assembled organisations vowed to oppose the war, to refuse to align themselves with any component part of the international capitalist class, and to "utilise the economic and political crisis created by the war to arouse the people and thereby to hasten the downfall of capitalist class rule."[13] Rather than rallying behind the German, British, French or Russian ruling classes, workers were called on to "oppose the power of the international solidarity of the proletariat to capitalist imperialism."

When war eventually broke out in July 1914, the Bolsheviks stuck to this internationalist position. Lenin wrote regarding the warring imperialist blocs:

> One group of belligerent nations is headed by the German bourgeoisie. It is hoodwinking the working class and the toiling masses by asserting that this is a war in defence of the fatherland, freedom and civilisation, for the liberation of the peoples oppressed by tsarism... The other group of belligerent nations is headed by the British and the French bourgeoisie, who are hoodwinking the working class and the toiling masses by asserting that they are waging a war for the defence of their countries, for freedom and civilisation and against German militarism and despotism.[14]

Further:

> Neither group of belligerents is inferior to the other in spoliation, atrocities and the boundless brutality of war; however, to hoodwink the proletariat ... the bourgeoisie of each country is trying, with the help of false phrases about patriotism, to extol the significance of its 'own' national war, asserting that it is out to defeat the enemy, not for plunder and the seizure of territory, but for the 'liberation' of all other peoples except its own.

However, the majority of the organisations that had signed up to the Basel Manifesto just two years earlier now crumbled in the face of pressure, opting to support their 'own' ruling class's war efforts. Lenin condemned the prominent Marxist leaders in Germany, Austria and France for holding views that were "chauvinist, bourgeois and liberal, and in no way socialist."[15] This bitter strategic dispute was a catalyst to a split in the global working class movement. The Second International was disbanded in 1916, and the Third International (widely known as the Comintern) was established in 1919 with its headquarters in Moscow. A century later this rift – described by Lenin in his famous article *Imperialism and the Split in Socialism*[16] – remains a fundamental dividing line in the international left. Broadly speaking, one side consists of a reformist left inclined towards parliamentarism and collaboration with the capitalist class; the other side consists of a revolutionary left inclined towards an independent, internationalist working class line.

The theorists of *Neither Washington nor Moscow* in the 1940s insisted that the Cold War was analogous to the European inter-imperialist conflict of the 1910s; that the US-led bloc and the Soviet-led bloc were competing imperialist powers and that it was impermissible for socialists to ally with either of them. The characterisation of the Soviet Union as imperialist was highly controversial within the global left at the time, but prominent socialist thinkers led by Tony Cliff of the Socialist Review Group (the precursor to the Socialist Workers Party) argued strongly that "the logic of accumulation and expansion" drove the Soviet leadership to take part in "external global military competition".[17] Given Soviet imperialism and state capitalism, "nothing short of a socialist revolution, led by the working class, would be able to transform this situation".[18]

The third camp has apparently survived the storm generated by the collapse of the Soviet Union and simply pitched its tent a few thousand kilometres southeast; *Neither Washington nor Moscow* has reappeared as *Neither Washington nor Beijing*. Once again invoking the spirit of the Bolsheviks, several prominent left organisations call on the working class in the West to oppose both the US and China; to fight imperialism in all its forms; to support workers' struggle everywhere to bring down capitalism. If their assumptions are correct – if the New Cold War is indeed analogous to the situation prevailing in Europe before WWI, if China is an imperialist country, if the Chinese working class is ready to be mobilised in an international revolutionary socialist alliance – then perhaps their conclusion is also correct. I argue in this chapter that these assumptions are *not* correct, that China is not an imperialist country; that China is in fact a threat to the imperialist world system, and that the correct position for the left to take with regard to the New Cold War is to resolutely oppose the US and to support China.

## Is China imperialist?

The position of opposing both the US and China relies mainly on the premise that China is imperialist, and that the New Cold War is an inter-imperialist war – a war in which "both belligerent camps are fighting to oppress foreign countries or peoples."[19] If China can be shown *not* to be an imperialist power, and if the New Cold War can be shown *not* to be an inter-imperialist struggle, then the slogan *Neither Washington nor Beijing* should be rejected.

What is imperialism? One definition is "the policy of extending the rule or authority of an empire or nation over foreign countries, or of acquiring and holding colonies and dependencies."[20] Although vague, this incorporates the core concept of *empire*, hinted at by the word's etymology.

In his classic work *Imperialism: The Highest Stage of Capitalism* – the first serious study of the phenomenon from a Marxist perspective – Lenin states that, reduced to its "briefest possible definition", imperialism can be considered simply as "the monopoly stage of capitalism".[21] Lenin notes that such a concise definition is necessarily inadequate, and is only useful to the extent that it implies the presence of five "basic features":

1. Capitalism has developed to a level where, in the main branches of production, the only viable businesses are those that have been able to concentrate a huge quantity of capital, thereby forming monopolies.
2. The emergence of a "financial oligarchy" – essentially banks – as the driving force of the economy.
3. Export of capital (foreign investment) as an important engine of growth.
4. The formation of "international monopolist capitalist associations which share the world among themselves", the equivalent of the modern multinational company.
5. The world's territory has been completely divided up among the capitalist powers; markets and resources around the globe have been integrated into the capitalist world system.

A century later, Lenin's definition remains a useful and relevant description of the capitalist world. Indeed in some important ways it is more apt than ever, given the further concentration of capital and the domination of "generalised monopolies ... which exert their control over the productive systems of the periphery of global capitalism."[22]

However, a few months after the publication of *Imperialism: The Highest Stage of Capitalism,* a new variable appeared in global politics, in the form of a socialist camp. The socialist group of countries (which at its peak comprised the bulk of the Eurasian land mass) disrupted the imperialist system in a number of ways: most obviously, it directly withdrew the socialist countries from that system; it offered support to colonial and anti-imperialist liberation movements, accelerating their victory; and it offered aid and favourable trading relations to formerly colonised states that would otherwise have little other option than to subject themselves to neocolonial domination. The arrival of socialist state power in Europe and Asia was, therefore, an unprecedented boon for the cause of national sovereignty around the world. At the same time and in equal measure, it was a setback for the imperialist world system.

No longer is the world so cleanly divided into imperialist and oppressed nations as it was before 1917. As such, Lenin's five features of imperialism can't simply be used as a checklist for answering the question of whether any given country is imperialist. We have to answer the questions: does this country impose its hegemony – military, political or economic – over other countries? Is it engaged in a process of domination guided by economic interests? Does it, in Samir Amin's words, leverage "technological development, access to natural resources, the global financial system, dissemination of information, and weapons of mass destruction" in order to dominate the planet and prevent the emergence of any state or movement that could impede this domination?[23]

If it can be proven that China seeks to dominate foreign markets and resources; that it uses its growing economic strength to affect political decisions in poorer countries; that it engages in wars (overt or covert) to secure its own interests; it would then be reasonable to conclude that China is indeed an imperialist country.

## Crossing the Rubicon: at what point could China have become imperialist?

If China is an imperialist power, when did it become one? At the time Lenin was writing, China was unambiguously in the group of oppressed countries, having been stripped of a large part of its sovereignty by the colonial powers over the course of the preceding 80 years. One of the world-historic successes of the Chinese Revolution was to end that domination and to establish the national independence of the Chinese people.

The People's Republic of China rejected the capitalist model and set out on the journey towards communism – an economic system envisioned by Marx as "an association of free men, working with the means of production held in common, and expending their many different forms of labour-power in full self-awareness as one single social labour force."[24] Jumping directly from semi-feudal conditions such as existed in pre-revolutionary China to a communist system of production relations isn't feasible, and what was established in China in the 1950s was a mixed economy, with publicly-owned industry and massive land reform as its key features. Feudalism was comprehensively dismantled – another historic step forward, and one that remains incomplete in most other parts of the Global South. This mixed economy – which oscillated 'left' (with accelerated collectivisation and a heavy emphasis on moral incentives) and 'right' (with the limited use of market mechanisms) – was anything but imperialist. By no reasonable metric was it an example of monopoly capitalism; China's "export of capital" was limited largely to foreign aid projects in Africa, most famously the Tazara Railway linking Tanzania and Zambia, which aside from enabling regional development, broke Zambia's dependency on apartheid-ruled territories

(Rhodesia, South Africa, Mozambique).[25]

Following the death of Mao Zedong in 1976, the economic reformers among the revolutionary leadership won the debate about how to move the revolution forward, and China embarked upon a course of *Socialism with Chinese Characteristics* – leveraging market mechanisms, the profit motive, and foreign investment (within a context of central planning and heavy regulation) in order to rapidly develop the productive forces and pave the way for a better quality of life for hundreds of millions of Chinese people. Private business became increasingly important, and parts of the economy took on an essentially capitalist character. But again, not even the most hardline third-campist could consider China in the 1980s and 1990s an imperialist country. It exported precious little capital; rather, it was the recipient of enormous volumes of foreign capital, from Japan, Taiwan, Hong Kong, the US and Europe. In a controlled, limited and strategic way, China opened itself up to exploitation *by* the imperialist powers so as to develop its technological capacity and insert itself into global value chains.

So inasmuch as China is imperialist, this must be a phenomenon of the last 20 years, in which period China's sustained GDP growth has resulted in it becoming the largest economy in the world (in purchasing power parity (PPP) terms) and a technological powerhouse. Certainly China has its fair share of monopolies that deploy extraordinary quantities of capital. Outgoing FDI has increased by an order of magnitude, albeit starting from a very small base. The number of Chinese firms operating globally has grown at an estimated 16 percent a year since 2010.[26] China's foreign direct investment outflows stand at around 145 billion USD, slightly less than Germany and Japan, slightly more than the UK.[27] In terms of FDI outflows ratio to GDP (ie the importance of capital export to the national economy as a whole), the value for China is 0.7 percent – a similar level to Italy, and far less than Ireland, Canada, Japan and Sweden. It would be difficult to make a case for labelling China imperialist on the basis of its foreign investment alone.

In a long piece for *Counterfire*, Dragan Plavšić poses the question of whether China is a socialist force for good or an imperial superpower in the making. Concluding the latter, he claims that China's global expansion is "merely the latest example of a road well-travelled by other major economies such as Britain, Germany and the US, as they too expanded beyond their national limits in order to take competitive advantage of global trade and investment opportunities." Moreover, "the competitive logic that motivated them is not qualitatively different from the one motivating China today."[28]

Competition demands relentless innovation, which tends to reduce the role of human labour in the production process. In Marxist terms, that means reducing the ratio of *variable capital* to *constant capital* – spending relatively less on human labour power and relatively more on machinery, materials, fuel, and so on.[29] Given that variable capital is, ultimately, the component of capital that creates new value, the declining proportion of variable capital leads to a tendency of the rate of profit to fall.[30] Historically, the capitalist class has sought to compensate for declining rates of profit with ferocious expansion, capturing new markets and lowering the costs of production. This is the economic engine at the heart of imperialism.

The problem with Plavšić's analysis is that the "well-travelled road" taken by Britain, Germany and the US is no longer open. By the time Lenin was writing – a century ago – the world was already "completely divided up, so that in the future only redivision is possible". That is, country A can only dominate country B by displacing country C; the means for this process is war and military conquest. Since China's record remains remarkably peaceful, it's evident that inasmuch as China has a path to becoming an imperialist power, it is by no means the "well-travelled" one. Noam Chomsky, by no measure an ideological adherent of the CPC, pokes fun at the idea that China would become an aggressive military power on the order of the US, "with 800 overseas military bases, invading and overthrowing other governments, or committing terrorist acts... I think this will not, and cannot, happen in China... China is not assuming the role of an aggressor with a large military budget, etc."[31]

Further, the structure of the Chinese economy is such that it doesn't impel the domination of foreign markets, territories, resources and labour in the same way as free market capitalism does. The major banks – which obviously wield a decisive influence over how capital is deployed – are majority-owned by the state, responsible primarily not to shareholders but to the Chinese people. The key industries are dominated by state-owned companies and subjected to heavy regulation by a state that doesn't have private profit maximisation as its primary objective. The economist Arthur Kroeber describes China as "an economy where the state remains firmly in command, not least through its control of 'commanding heights' state enterprises, but where market tools are used to improve efficiency."[32] In summary, the Chinese economy fulfils much the same function now as it did in 1953, when Mao described it as existing "not chiefly to make profits for the capitalists but to meet the needs of the people and the state".[33]

Li Zhongjin and David Kotz assert that while "China's capitalists have the same drive toward imperialism of capitalists everywhere," this drive is restrained by a CPC government which "has no need to aim for imperial domination to achieve its economic aims." While capitalists are represented within the CPC, there is "no evidence that capitalists now control the CPC or can dictate state policy"; hence "the Chinese capitalist class lacks the power to compel the CPC to seek imperial domination."[34]

As such, the prospect of foreign domination does not have the same gravitational pull on the Chinese economy as it did/does on the economies of Britain, the US, Japan and others. Nor do the objective conditions exist for China to establish even an informal empire without direct military confrontation with the existing imperialist powers. The CPC was serious when it declared at its 17th Party Congress in 2007 that China "will never seek to engage in hegemony or empire expansion."[35] This was reiterated by Xi Jinping in his work report to the 20th Party Congress in 2022: "No matter what stage of development it reaches, China will never seek hegemony or engage in expansionism."[36] The Chinese government actively positions itself in the Global South, as a socialist country that stands in solidarity with the developing world, and this outlook structures its foreign policy.

Nevertheless, China stands accused of imperialist behaviour on several fronts, notably its economic relationship with Africa, its economic relationship with Latin America, its vast *Belt and Road* infrastructure programme, and its behaviour in the South China Sea. I will address each of these.

## China and Africa

### A brief timeline

After the establishment of the People's Republic of China in 1949, the Chinese leadership moved quickly to create bonds of solidarity between China and the African liberation movements. China was a leading supporter of the Algerian war of liberation and an early supporter of the South African struggle against white minority rule. Nelson Mandela recounts in *Long Walk to Freedom* that he encouraged Walter Sisulu, then secretary-general of the African National Congress, to visit China in 1953 in order to "discuss with the Chinese the possibility of supplying us with weapons for an armed struggle."[37] The links made during this trip laid the ground for the establishment in the early 1960s of a Chinese military training programme for the newly-founded uMkhonto we Sizwe - the ANC's armed wing. As an aside, two currently serving African heads of state received military training in China in the 1960s, at a time when their people were fighting for liberation: Eritrean president Isaias Afwerki and Zimbabwean president Emmerson Mnangagwa.

Chinese premier Zhou Enlai conducted a landmark tour of ten African nations between December 1963 and January 1964, during which he consolidated China's anti-imperialist solidarity with some of the leading post-colonial African states. A few years later, China provided the financing and knowhow for the construction of the Tazara Railway, which runs 1,860km from Dar es Salaam, the then Tanzanian capital and seaport, to central Zambia. Built with the primary purposes of fomenting economic development and helping Zambia to break its economic dependence on the apartheid states of Rhodesia and South Africa, the Tazara has been described as "the first infrastructure project conceived on a pan-African scale".[38] It remains an enduring symbol of China's friendship with independent Africa.

Well into the 1980s, dozens of large state farms were built in Africa as part of the Chinese aid programme – in Tanzania, Zimbabwe, Mali, Congo

Brazzaville, Guinea and elsewhere. Deborah Brautigam notes that, however, "during the 1970s and 1980s, the Chinese aid program shifted to emphasise much smaller demonstration farms, working with local farmers to teach rice farming and vegetable cultivation."[39]

In the 1980s and 90s, partly reflecting shifting priorities in China and partly in response to data indicating that many of the aid-constructed projects were no longer working very well (if at all), China started to put its engagement with Africa on a more commercial footing, focusing on mutually beneficial deals and joint ventures. China has since become Africa's largest trading partner, with a total trade volume of $254 billion in 2021,[40] well ahead of the US-Africa figure of $64 billion.[41]

In addition to trade, China also provides vast low-cost loans for infrastructure projects, with Chinese banks now accounting for around a fifth of all lending to Africa.[42] A 2018 article in the Guardian notes that "some 40 percent of the Chinese loans paid for power projects, and another 30 percent went on modernising transport infrastructure. The loans were at comparatively low interest rates and with long repayment periods." The article continues: "Chinese infrastructure projects stretch all the way to Angola and Nigeria, with ports planned along the coast from Dakar to Libreville and Lagos. Beijing has also signalled its support for the African Union's proposal of a pan-African high-speed rail network."[43]

## Imperialism doesn't look like this

Chinese investment in, and trade with, Africa is stimulating development, industrialisation, technological know-how and modernisation. Chinese investment has made possible a fast-expanding infrastructure network that will underpin African economic development for generations to come. This includes railways, schools, hospitals, roads, ports, factories and airports, along with "new tarmac roads linking major regional hubs, including the various townships with proper connection to large cities".[44]

Thanks in no small part to Chinese finance and expertise, Ethiopia in 2015 celebrated the opening of the first metro train system in sub-Saharan Africa,[45] along with Africa's first fully electrified cross-border railway line, the Ethiopia-Djibouti electric railway.[46] The African Union headquarters in Addis Ababa was funded by the Chinese government as a gift to the AU.[47] China is also building the headquarters of the Economic Community of West African States (Ecowas) in Abuja, Nigeria,[48] and in 2022 gifted a new parliament building to the government of Zimbabwe.[49] The new headquarters of the Africa Centers for Disease Control and Prevention (Africa CDC), again funded by China, was opened in January 2023.[50]

US-based academic Joel Wendland-Liu observes that "electrification projects in several countries such as DR Congo, Ghana, and other sub-Saharan African countries, along with considerable successes in railway projects in East Africa and Angola, are moving the needle on the relation between poor infrastructure and low growth rates."[51]

Nonetheless, in recent years there has been a seemingly endless stream of articles about Chinese imperialism in Africa. Western journalists and politicians tell us that China has become a new colonial power; that China is attempting to dominate African land and resources; that Africa is becoming entangled in a Beijing-devised debt trap; that Chinese investment in Africa only benefits China.

Deborah Brautigam, Professor of Political Economy and Director of the China Africa Research Initiative at Johns Hopkins University's School of Advanced International Studies, has done extensive research on the question of China's engagement with Africa. On the basis of this research, she has been able to authoritatively debunk some of the most popular myths. For example in response to the trope that Chinese companies only employ Chinese workers, Brautigam notes: "Surveys of employment on Chinese projects in Africa repeatedly find that three-quarters or more of the workers are, in fact, local." Meanwhile, "Africans are being invited to Chinese universities. China is offering scholarships. When Africans are thinking about technology and skills, they are thinking of China as a valid option."[52]

Regarding the so-called debt trap, Brautigam's research team found that:

> China had lent at least $95.5 billion between 2000 and 2015. That's a lot of debt. Yet by and large, the Chinese loans in our database were performing a useful service: financing Africa's serious infrastructure gap. On a continent where over 600 million Africans have no access to electricity, 40 percent of the Chinese loans paid for power generation and transmission. Another 30 percent went to modernising Africa's crumbling transport infrastructure... On the whole, power and transport are investments that boost economic growth. And we found that Chinese loans generally have comparatively low interest rates and long repayment periods.

Indeed the reluctance of Western development banks to take on risky loans means there's major demand for Chinese loans. And China tends to be more flexible with debt relief, restructuring and cancelling unsustainable payments.[53]

A 2022 report by the charity Debt Justice found that "African governments owe three times more debt to Western banks, asset managers and oil traders than to China."[54] The study found that only 12 percent of Africa's external debt was owed to Chinese lenders, and furthermore that interest rates on Chinese loans were typically around half those on Western private loans. "The average interest rate on private sector loans is 5 per cent, compared to 2.7 per cent on loans from Chinese public and private lenders."

Regarding accusations of a 'land grab', Brautigam writes that the various stories about wealthy Chinese buying up large tracts of African land in order to grow food for China "turned out to be mostly myths... China is not a dominant investor in plantation agriculture in Africa, in contrast to how it is often portrayed."[55]

Western establishment figures enthusiastically embrace the idea of China being an imperialist power, for the obvious reasons that it diverts attention from their own imperialism and helps promote disunity and mistrust within the Global South. Hillary Clinton says China is engaged in a "new colonialism" in Africa.[56] John Bolton believes China is using "predatory practices" to stunt Africa's growth.[57] Yet these ideas are not exclusive to the professional defenders of imperialism. Adrian Budd, writing in *Socialist Review* (purveyors of finest Third Camp ideology since 1950), states unequivocally that China is imperialist and complains that "Chinese investment in Africa, long dominated by Western imperialism, was $36 billion in 2016 against the US's $3.6 billion, Britain's $2.4 billion and France's $2.1 billion."[58]

But there's no equals sign between investment and imperialism – Angola is not an imperialist power in Portugal, in spite of its extensive investments there.[59] China's investments in Africa are welcomed in the recipient countries, because they serve to address critical gaps in infrastructure and finance. Deals are conducted on the basis of sovereignty and equality, without coercion. Progressive Greek economist and former government minister Yanis Varoufakis notes that "the Chinese are non-interventionist in a way that Westerners have never managed to fathom... They don't seem to have any military ambitions... Instead of going into Africa with troops, killing people like the West has done... they went to Addis Ababa and said to the government, 'we can see you have some problems with your infrastructure; we would like to build some new airports, upgrade your railway system, create a telephone system, and rebuild your roads.'"[60] Varoufakis – who prefaces his remarks by noting that he is by no means a supporter of the CPC – posits that the reason for this offer was not pure charity but rather to build trust with the Ethiopian government so as to be well positioned to be awarded oil contracts. Nonetheless, it is a fundamentally different approach to doing business than that adopted by Europeans and North Americans over the course of centuries.

Chinese loans are not conditional on countries imposing austerity or privatisation. Indeed the availability of alternative sources of funding means that debtor countries are not forced to accept the unfair terms that have been imposed by Western financial institutions for so long. As former South African minister of trade and industry Rob Davies put it, China's expanding presence in Africa "can only be a good thing ... because it means that we don't have to sign on the dotted line whatever is shoved under our noses any longer ... We now have alternatives and that's to our benefit."[61]

Martin Jacques addresses this issue in his book *When China Rules the World*:

> Chinese aid has far fewer strings attached than that of Western nations and institutions. While the IMF and the World Bank have insisted, in accord with their Western-inspired ideological agenda, on the liberalisation of foreign trade, privatisation and a reduced role for the state, the Chinese stance is far less restrictive and doctrinaire."

Jacques points out that the Chinese emphasis on respect for sovereignty is "a principle they regard to be inviolable and which is directly related to their own historical experience during the 'century of humiliation'".[62]
The expanding infrastructure investment is enabling *development* of countries that have been forcibly *underdeveloped* by the imperialist powers.[63] For example, Chiponda Chibelu notes that "in the last decade, African countries have largely turned to China to help them build and expand their digital infrastructure," having "received little support from Western governments for technology infrastructure."[64] China is actively encouraging the Information and Communication (ICT) revolution in Africa.

Meanwhile Chinese companies are investing in green development projects throughout the continent – and indeed the world. China has been the top investor in clean energy for nine out of the last ten years, according to the Frankfurt School of Finance and Management.[65] The Chinese Academy of Sciences is heavily involved in supporting research projects in Africa, including agronomic research aimed at ending food shortages.[66] Tens of thousands of African students attend universities in China, which now offers "more university scholarships to African students than the leading western governments combined".[67] Mohamed Hassan, president of the World Academy of Sciences, says that China is "doing better than any other country for Africa" when it comes to training scholars.[68]

Overall, rising Chinese investment and trade has been welcomed by African countries and is playing an important role in the continent's development. As the Zambian economist Dambisa Moyo writes, "the motivation for the host countries is not complicated: they need infrastructure, and they need to finance projects that can unlock economic growth... This is the genius of the China strategy: every country gets what it wants... China, of course, gains access to commodities, but host countries get the loans to finance infrastructure developmental programs in their economies, they get to trade (creating incomes for their domestic citizenry), and they get investments that can support much-needed job creation."[69]

China has adhered firmly to its 'five-no' approach as outlined by President Xi at the 2018 Beijing Summit of the Forum on China-Africa Cooperation: "No interference in African countries' internal affairs; no imposition of our will on African countries; no attachment of political strings to assistance to Africa; and no seeking of selfish political gains in investment and financing cooperation with Africa."[70] Africa has known imperialism, and it doesn't look like this.

So China's engagement with Africa bears very little resemblance to the "well-travelled road" of Britain, France, Portugal, Belgium, Germany and the US. Under European colonialism and neocolonialism, Africa remained in much the same state as was described by Marx in 1867: "A new and international division of labour springs up, one suited to the requirements of the main industrial countries, and it converts one part of the globe into a chiefly agricultural field of production for supplying the other part, which remains a pre-eminently industrial field."[71] As Liberia's former Minister of Public Works W Gyude Moore writes, under European colonialism "there has never been a continental-scale infrastructure building program for Africa's railways, roads, ports, water filtration plants and power stations"; meanwhile "China has built more infrastructure in Africa in two decades than the West has in centuries."[72]

On this question, the Senegalese-American musician Akon demonstrates a far greater insight than the third campists when he states that "no one has done more to benefit Africa than the Chinese."[73]

## China and Latin America

Most Latin American countries won their formal independence from Spanish and Portuguese colonialism in the 19th century, but they found themselves in the shadow of an incipient North American imperialism. The Monroe Doctrine, first articulated by President James Monroe in 1823, denounced European colonialism and interference in the Western Hemisphere, not on the basis of anti-colonial principle but with a view to buttressing US hegemonic designs. Since that time, the US has tended to consider Latin America as its 'backyard' – a collection of countries subjected to the control (direct or indirect) of Washington.[74]

Eduardo Galeano wrote that the transition from colonialism to neocolonialism made little difference to Latin America's position within the global capitalist economy. "Everything from the discovery until our times has always been transmuted into European – or later, United States – capital, and as such has accumulated on distant centres of power. Everything: the soil, its fruits and its mineral-rich depths, the people and their capacity to work and to consume, natural resources and human resources."[75]

Galeano's words were written half a century ago, but they still ring true. The US continues with its hegemonic strategy in relation to Latin America; a strategy which seeks to make the region's land, natural resources, labour and markets subservient to the needs of US monopoly capital. The US has shown a consistent interest in Mexican labour, in Chilean copper, in Brazilian land; but it has been indifferent to the needs of the people of these countries for development, for a decent standard of living, for social justice. And when the US fails to get what it wants through quiet pressure and economic coercion, it does not hesitate to use force, for example supporting coups against the elected governments of Bolivia,[76] Peru[77] and Venezuela,[78] or imposing illegal sanctions on Nicaragua[79] and Cuba.[80]

As a result, Latin America continues to suffer significant underdevelopment in many areas. The emergence of China as a major investor and trading partner is therefore proving to be indispensable for the region's economic progress.

In the last two decades, economic links between Latin America and the People's Republic of China have been expanding at a dizzying rate. Bilateral trade in 2000 was just 12 billion USD (1 percent of Latin American's total trade); now it stands at 430 billion USD.[81] In the same time period, China's foreign direct investment in Latin America has increased by a factor of five.[82]

Since the launch of the Belt and Road Initiative (BRI) in 2013, 21 of the 33 countries in the Latin American and Caribbean region have signed up to the China-led global infrastructure development strategy. Infrastructure projects have been a particular focus for Chinese firms.

Chinese investment has been widely recognised across the region for its positive economic and social impact, particularly in terms of facilitating government projects to reduce poverty and inequality. Kevin Gallagher, in his important book *The China Triangle*, writes that "Venezuela has been actively spending public funds to expand social inclusion to the country's poor. The country ... was able to fund such expenditures given the high price of oil in the 2000s – and due to the joint fund with China."[83]

Chinese firms have also been investing heavily in infrastructure projects in Latin America, as well as becoming the continent's largest creditor and lead trading partner. Max Nathanson observes that "Latin American governments have long lamented their countries' patchy infrastructure" and that China has "stepped in with a solution: roughly $150 billion loaned to Latin American countries since 2005."[84] The emergence of Chinese economic involvement in Latin America inspired then-US Secretary of State Rex Tillerson – not widely known for his boundless anti-imperialist spirit – to accuse China of being a "new imperial power ... using economic statecraft to pull the region into its orbit."[85]

However, China's role in Latin America is not considered to be 'imperialist' by the representatives of the working class and oppressed masses in that continent. For example, the late Hugo Chávez visited China six times over the course of his 13 years as President of Venezuela and was a strong proponent of China-Venezuela relations. He considered China to be a key partner in the struggle for a new world, memorably stating: "We've been manipulated to believe that the first man on the moon was the most important event of the 20th century. But no, much more important things happened, and one of the greatest events of the 20th century was the

Chinese revolution."[86]

The Chávez government and its successor have always encouraged Chinese economic engagement with Venezuela, and have never considered it to be imperialist. On the contrary, Chávez considered that an alliance with China constituted a bulwark *against* imperialism – a "Great Wall against American hegemonism."[87] Chinese financing has been crucial for development projects in energy, mining, industry, technology, communications, transport, housing and culture,[88] and has thus played a key role in the improvement in the living conditions of the Venezuelan poor over the last two decades. Kevin Gallagher writes that Venezuela's unprecedented anti-poverty programmes were made possible by a combination of "the high price of oil in the 2000s and … the joint fund with China."[89] Across the continent, the "China Boom" from 2003-13 "helped erase the increases in inequality in Latin America that accrued during the Washington Consensus period."[90]

A crucial difference between Chinese and Western investment – between Latin America's "China Boom" and the Washington Consensus – is that "when Chinese banks do come, they do not impose policy conditionalities of any kind, in keeping with their general foreign policy of nonintervention."[91] Rather, Chinese investors treat borrower countries as equals and work to design mutually beneficial deals. Since Chinese loans don't come with punishing conditions of austerity and privatisation, Latin American governments have been able to leverage China's investment and purchase of primary commodities to spend at an unprecedented rate on reducing poverty and inequality.

Chávez spoke plainly about the difference between China and the imperialist powers: "China is large but it's not an empire. China doesn't trample on anyone, it hasn't invaded anyone, it doesn't go around dropping bombs on anyone."[92] This dynamic continues. Comparing the attitude taken towards Venezuela by the US and China, then Foreign Minister Jorge Arreaza stated that "our country is under permanent attack and aggression from the United States of America… Thank God humanity can count on the People's Republic of China to guarantee peace or at least less conflict." Arreaza described the trade and investment deals between China and Venezuela as being set up in a "just, fair and equal manner."[93]

Fidel Castro – no slouch in the anti-imperialist department – thoroughly rejected the notion that China was an imperialist power. "China has objectively become the most promising hope and the best example for all Third World countries … an important element of balance, progress and safeguard of world peace and stability."[94] China's assistance and friendship has proven invaluable to socialist Cuba; China is now the island's second largest trading partner and its main source of technical assistance.[95]

China also established strong relations with Bolivia under the government of Evo Morales. Speaking at an event of the *No Cold War* campaign, Bolivian journalist Ollie Vargas talked about China's role in launching Bolivia's first telecoms satellite: "Bolivia is a small country, it doesn't have the expertise to launch a rocket into space, so it worked with China to launch the satellite which now provides internet and phone signal to all corners of the country, from the Amazon to the Andes, and here in the working class areas of the big cities."[96] Vargas said that the project had been a positive model of mutually beneficial cooperation, as China brought expertise and investment but it didn't seek to take ownership of the final product; the satellite belongs to the Bolivian people.

As with Africa, accusations of Chinese imperialism in Latin America don't stand up to scrutiny. China trades with Latin America; China invests in Latin America; but China is not attempting to dominate Latin America or compromise its sovereignty.

## Belt and Road

The Belt and Road Initiative (BRI) is a global infrastructure development strategy proposed by China in 2013. Unprecedented in scope, the BRI seeks to revive the original Silk Road – a vast trading network that arose during the Han Dynasty (206 BCE – 220 CE) and which connected China with India, Central Asia and further afield. The BRI seeks to promote global economic integration and cooperation via the construction of vast numbers of roads, railways, bridges, factories, ports, airports, energy infrastructure and telecommunications systems, all of which will enable deeper integration of markets and more efficient allocation of resources.

As of 2022, 150 countries and 32 international organisations have signed cooperation agreements to join the BRI.[97] BRI investment projects "are estimated to add over USD 1 trillion of outward funding for foreign infrastructure" in the ten years from 2017.[98]

The basic economic motivation of the BRI is to drive growth through expanding cooperation and coordination across borders. As Chinese economist Justin Yifu Lin puts it, "the greater the division of labour, the higher the economy's productivity. But the division of labour is limited by market size. So the larger the market, the more specialised the labour."[99]

Politically, the project fits into China's longstanding approach of using economic integration to increase the cost (and thereby reduce the likelihood) of confrontation. Peter Nolan writes that "China is in a position to make use of its rich experience in domestic infrastructure construction in order to make a major contribution to the development of the Silk Road in Central and Southeast Asia." A key political byproduct of this is "stimulating harmonious relations between the countries."[100]

China is uniquely well placed to be the driving force of such a project, given its size, its location, and the nature of its economy. The Portuguese politician and academic Bruno Maçães observes that the essentially planned nature of the Chinese economy, with the state "firmly in charge of the financial system", has enabled China to act quickly and decisively, directing immense financial resources towards BRI projects.[101] Chinese engineering expertise is already opening up some of the most difficult terrains in the world for roads and railways, for example.

Ashley Smith and Kevin Lin, writing in the Democratic Socialists of America (DSA)'s *Socialist Forum*, consider that the BRI is "unmistakably imperialist", picking items out of the *Imperialism, the Highest Stage of Capitalism* grab bag in order to prove their case. China is attempting to "export its vast surplus capacity, secure raw materials for its booming economy, and find new markets for its products."[102] They claim that the BRI is locking entire countries into "dependent development", even "de-industrialising some countries like Brazil and reducing all to serving the needs of Chinese capitalism."

This latter critique is more Mike Pompeo than Vladimir Lenin, and connects to an emerging New Cold War policy of blaming all economic problems on China. It's certainly the case that more open markets render some businesses unviable, but overall China's emergence as Brazil's largest trading partner has been beneficial for the people of both countries. Indeed Brazil's foreign minister under Lula from 2003-10, Celso Amorim, considered the blossoming China-Brazil relationship to be at the heart of a "reconfiguration of the world's commercial and diplomatic geography."[103]

If the BRI truly seeks to impose "dependent development", it's perhaps surprising that nearly every country in the Global South has signed up to it – including 43 out of 46 countries in sub-Saharan Africa.[104] Surely not *all* turkeys are voting for Christmas? In reality, most countries are highly favourable towards the BRI because it offers exactly what they need, and exactly what global imperialism has been impeding for centuries: development. For example, just 43 percent of people in Africa have access to electricity.[105] The road and rail networks are badly underdeveloped. Hundreds of years of a European 'civilising mission' in Africa have brought all of the misery of modern capitalism with very little of the progress.

Belt and Road projects are establishing an essential framework for economic development and are thereby creating the conditions for formerly colonised countries to *break out of dependency*, to evade the economic coercion perpetrated by the US and its allies. The larger part of the reason that the Washington Consensus – the imposition of 'shock doctrine' economics – has been broken is the availability of alternative financing, particularly from Chinese or China-led development banks; even the IMF and World Bank have had to scale back their loan conditionalities, as debtor countries now have better options. Kevin Gallagher notes that, for example, Latin American leaders "have been reluctant to further bind their economies to Washington Consensus policies – in large part because they believe they have an alternative in China."[106]

While much noise has been made in the West in relation to "debt trap diplomacy" along the Belt and Road, the actual situation is that "virtually every study that looks at the terms of developing country debt sees developed country lending as more onerous than that of China."[107] Responding to accusations that China had created a Belt and Road 'debt trap' in Pakistan, the Chinese ambassador noted that 42 percent of Pakistan's debt is to multilateral institutions and that Chinese preferential loans only constitute 10 percent.[108] Writing in The Atlantic, Deborah Brautigam and Meg Rithmire debunk the debt trap narrative, forensically examining its canonical example: that of the Hambantota port in Sri Lanka.[109] Brautigam and Rithmire comment that the idea of a cynical China hoodwinking naïve governments in the Global South "wrongfully portrays both Beijing and the developing countries it deals with"; indeed it contains an element of racism, the idea that the majority of countries in Africa, Asia and Latin America are lining up to be bamboozled by a Chinese colonialism that's so cunning as to not even require gunboats.

The BRI unquestionably promotes globalisation, but globalisation and imperialism are not the same thing. The original Silk Road was "the epicentre of one of the first waves of globalisation, connecting eastern and western markets, spurring immense wealth, and intermixing cultural and religious traditions. Valuable Chinese silk, spices, jade, and other goods moved west while China received gold and other precious metals, ivory, and glass products."[110] This is evidently a form of globalisation, but without the domination and coercion that characterise imperialism. The development of trade, building of infrastructure and expansion of friendly cooperation are all in the interests of the peoples of the participating countries. To compare such a process to imperialism as practised by Western Europe, North America and Japan is an insult to the hundreds of millions throughout Africa, Asia, the Middle East, Latin America and the Caribbean that have endured the misery of colonial and neocolonial subjugation. The Western powers are certainly concerned about the Belt and Road, given its "practical significance of shifting the world's centre of gravity from the Atlantic to the Pacific", in the words of Henry Kissinger.[111] But that ought not to be anything for socialists to be afraid of.

## South China Sea

China's "military expansionism" in the South China Sea is another oft-cited example of Chinese imperialism. China claims sovereignty over the bulk of the South China Sea, and in recent years has stepped up its naval operations and its construction of artificial islands in the area. Chinese claims overlap in several places with those of Brunei, Indonesia, Malaysia, the Philippines and Vietnam.

Amitai Etzioni points out that China's claims in the South China Sea, while extensive and ambitious, are not particularly unusual. For example, "Canada, Russia, Denmark, and Norway have made overlapping claims to the North Pole and the Arctic Ocean, and have conducted exploratory expeditions and military exercises in the region to strengthen their positions."[112] Even in the South China Sea itself, other countries put forward ambitious claims and engage in military construction. Jude Woodward observed that China's island-building was carried out largely in response to the actions taken by other states in the region: "In its actions on these disputed islands, China can with justice argue that it has done no more than others... It [is] rarely mentioned that Taiwan has long had an airstrip on Taiping, Malaysia on Swallow Reef, Vietnam on Spratly Island and the Philippines on Thitu."[113]

China's interest in the South China Sea islands isn't new, nor is it linked to the discovery of natural resources in or around those islands, as is often claimed.[114] These are largely uninhabitable islands that have been important stopping points for Chinese ships for at least 2,000 years; China has regarded the islands as its own since the time of the Han Dynasty.

The purpose of China's assertion of sovereignty over much of the South China Sea has nothing to do with "expansionism" and everything to do with ensuring its economic and military security. Robert Kaplan writes that the South China Sea is "uniquely crucial" for China's interests – "as central to Asia as the Mediterranean is to Europe".[115] Its bases at sea have no impact on shipping or ordinary peaceful activities, but are aimed at reducing its strategic vulnerability and preventing any attempt by hostile powers to impose a blockade. Given the continued US militarisation of the region, and its open attempt to create a Pacific alliance against China, this is more than just a hypothetical issue. For example, the only major shipping route from the South China Sea to the Indian Ocean is through the Malacca Strait; if the US were allowed the unadulterated control of the oceans that it seeks, it would be in a position to quickly cut off China's energy supplies.

Peter Frankopan writes:

> China's present and future depends on being able to ensure that it can get what it needs, safely, securely and without interruption – and ensuring that those who are keen to manage or curtail economic growth are prevented from being able to threaten routes to and from markets elsewhere in the world.[116]

Concerns about Chinese expansionism in the Pacific are misplaced and hypocritical, given the rights asserted by the US, Britain, France and others in the region. Under the United Nations Convention on the Law of the Sea (UNCLOS), passed in 1992 – but which, notably, the United States has refused to sign – each nation is awarded an Exclusive Economic Zone (EEZ) of 200 nautical miles around its territory. An EEZ accords special rights regarding the exploration and use of marine resources, including energy production from water and wind. Peter Nolan observes that, under this system, China's undisputed EEZ is just under a million square kilometres.[117] Meanwhile France has 10 million, the US 10 million, and the UK 6 million square kilometres' EEZ, the result of persisting colonial outposts. Britain's overseas territory includes the Falklands (Malvinas), South Sandwich Islands, British Virgin Islands, Cayman Islands, Monserrat, British Indian Ocean Territory and the Pitcairns – all many thousands of miles away from Britain. The Pitcairn Islands, a group of four volcanic islands in the South Pacific, with a combined human population of 70, provide Britain with a similar Pacific EEZ to that of China – which has a population of 1.4 billion. Inasmuch as there's a pressing issue of maritime colonialism that we should take a stand on, this is surely a far stronger candidate than China's claims.

There are several thorny longstanding territorial issues in the South China Sea, which will take time and goodwill to resolve. They can only be resolved primarily by the countries in the region themselves. The increasing US-led militarisation of the region, the deliberate stoking of relatively dormant disputes, and the 'freedom of navigation' patrols – totally unnecessary given that "more than 100,000 vessels pass through the South China Sea every year [and in] no single case has freedom of navigation been affected"[118] – only serve to escalate tensions, increase China's perceived threat level, and delay resolution. Indeed the US's actions (fully supported by Britain,[119] needless to say) are creating one of the most complex and fragile flashpoints in the world today. To complain of Chinese expansionism in the South China Sea is to wade into dangerous waters precisely on the side of US hegemonism. The key demand for the peace movement and for anti-imperialists must be for an end to US-led militarisation of the region, along with support for peaceful dialogue between the countries with competing territorial claims (an example of this is the negotiating framework for a code of conduct in the South China Sea agreed by China and ASEAN in 2017).[120]

## Multipolarity is a prerequisite for socialist advance

The slogan *Neither Washington nor Beijing, but international socialism* is an emphatic statement that the global working class can't hope to advance towards socialism by associating itself with either the US or China; that the rivalry between the two is inter-imperialist in character; that both countries promote a model of international relations designed solely to further their own hegemonic interests.

I have made a detailed case above that China is *not* imperialist; indeed China's foreign policy is a component of the struggle *against* imperialism, and creates space for global socialist advance.

In the 1950s and 60s, revolutionary China pursued an unambiguously revolutionary anti-imperialist foreign policy, providing crucial support for liberation movements in Vietnam, Algeria, Mozambique, Zimbabwe and elsewhere.[121] Just a year after the declaration of the PRC, the Chinese People's Volunteer Army crossed the Yalu River in order to aid the people of

Korea against the genocidal war launched by the US and its allies.[122] Three million Chinese fought in that war, and an estimated 180,000 lost their lives. Although the fierce ideological dispute between China and the Soviet Union led to China taking some objectively reactionary positions (most notably in Angola and Afghanistan), the guiding principle of Chinese foreign policy was militant anti-imperialism.

In the early 1970s, after over two decades of intense hostility, a window of opportunity opened for improved China-US relations. This laid the ground for China to regain its seat at the United Nations in 1971 and, at the end of the decade, the establishment of formal diplomatic relations with the US. With the start of the economic reform in 1978, China urgently sought foreign investment from, and trade with, Southeast Asia, Japan and the US. The need to create a favourable business environment led to the adoption of a "good neighbour policy", which included dialling down support for communist-led armed struggle in Malaysia, Burma, Thailand, the Philippines and elsewhere. Deng Xiaoping's recommendation to "hide our capabilities and bide our time" meant, in essence, China minding its own business and focussing on its internal development.

Over the last 20-plus years, and the last decade in particular, however, China has become more active in its foreign policy, with a strong focus on multipolarity: "a pattern of multiple centres of power, all with a certain capacity to influence world affairs, shaping a negotiated order."[123] Such a world order is specifically non-hegemonic; it aims to transition from a US-dominated unipolar world order to a more equal system of international relations in which big powers and regional blocs cooperate and compete. The interdependence between the different powers, and their comparable levels of strength, increases the cost and risk of conflict, thereby promoting peace. In the words of Columbia University professor Jeffrey Sachs, this is "a multipolar world in which each region has its own issues and role in global politics" and where "no country and no single region can any longer determine the fate of others."[124]

Although the multipolar narrative doesn't make explicit reference to anti-imperialism, it's clear that a multipolar world implies the negation of the US hegemonist project for military and economic control of the planet. As such, its basic character is anti-imperialist, which is why it is treated with such contempt in US policy circles; it represents a world that looks very different from "global American leadership", a world where the US is no longer "without peer in its ability to project power around the world."[125]

As discussed above, the very fact that China exists as a source of investment and finance is a major boost to the countries of the developing world (and indeed parts of Europe), which no longer have to accept punishing austerity and privatisation as conditions for emergency loans. Jenny Clegg writes that "developing countries as a whole may find, in the opportunities created by China's rise, more room for flexibility to follow their own mix of state and market, and even to explore the socialist experiments they were forced to abandon by the International Monetary Fund (IMF) in the 1980s."[126] This is an important point. Multipolarity opens a path for greater sovereignty for developing countries; it breaks the stranglehold of the imperialist core (US, Europe, Japan) over the periphery and, in so doing, "provides the framework for the possible and necessary overcoming of capitalism", in the memorable words of Samir Amin.[127] Through forums such as BRICS (an international alliance of five major emerging economies: Brazil, Russia, India, China and South Africa), FOCAC (Forum on China-Africa Cooperation), China-CELAC (Forum of China and the Community of Latin American and Caribbean States) and others, China is strongly promoting South-South cooperation and helping to advance the interests of the developing world in general.

Clegg notes that "what is at stake with China's rise is ... a real choice over the future model of the international order: the US strategic goal of a unipolar world to uphold and extend existing patterns of exploitation, or a multipolar and democratic one for a more equitable, just and peaceful world."[128] For the left to issue a plague on both these houses would be nothing short of a farce.

## 'Neither Washington Nor Beijing' in reality means support for Washington

Humanity knows from bitter experience and lived reality what a system of imperialism looks like. Modern imperialism takes the form of a US-led military and economic system incorporating hundreds of military bases; a strategy of military encirclement; unilateral sanctions against dozens of countries; multiple wars of regime change and proxy wars; destabilisation campaigns; nuclear threats; economic coercion, and more. It is clearly absurd to put an equals sign between this and the reality of China's foreign policy.

The basic character of global politics in the current era is not that of inter-imperialist rivalry between the US and China, but rather a struggle between the US-led push for its continued hegemony and the China-led push for a multipolar world order. If Marxists do indeed "point out and bring to the front the common interests of the entire proletariat, independently of all nationality,"[129] they should support the movement towards multipolarity, which provides greater opportunities for peace and development, and a more favourable context for humanity's advance towards socialism. China is leading this movement, and the US is leading the opposition to it.

If there existed a thriving political movement to the left of the Chinese Communist Party which sought to continue China's progressive global strategy but to reverse the post-Mao market reforms and transition to a system of worker-run cooperatives (for example), Western leftists would have to assess the relative merits of supporting such a movement in its struggle against the CPC-led government. But this is sheer fantasy.

Opposition to the CPC in China comes primarily from pro-Western pro-neoliberal elements that seek to undermine socialism and roll back the project of multipolarity. Meanwhile, Chinese workers and peasants by and large support the government, and why shouldn't they? In the four decades from 1981, the number of people in China living in internationally-defined absolute poverty fell from 850 million to zero.[130] Living standards have consistently improved, at all levels of society. Wages are rising, social welfare is improving. According to an extensive study conducted by the Kennedy School of Government at Harvard University, 93 percent of Chinese people are satisfied with their central government.[131] Even former MI6 director of operations and intelligence Nigel Inkster grudgingly admits that "if anything, objective evidence points to growing levels of popular satisfaction within China about their government's performance."[132] The basic conditions that inspire people to rise up against their government simply do not prevail.

Regardless of what one thinks of Socialism with Chinese Characteristics, anyone on the left must support China against US-led imperialist attacks and the New Cold War. The prominent Belgian Trotskyist economist Ernest Mandel was by no means a supporter of Soviet socialism, but he insisted firmly that the Soviet Union must be defended against imperialism. Reflecting on Tony Cliff's *Neither Washington nor Moscow* line, he wrote: "Why, if it is conceivable to defend the SPD [German Social Democratic Party] against fascism, despite its being led by the Noskes, the assassins of Karl Liebknecht and Rosa Luxemburg, is it 'inconceivable' to defend the USSR against imperialism?"[133]

Let the latter-day third-campists answer the same question in relation to China.

## NOTES

1 Du Qiongfang 2022, *Chinese life expectancy increased to 78.2 years over past decade thanks to childbearing, population policies*, Global Times, accessed 6 January 2023, <https://www.globaltimes.cn/page/202209/1274894.shtml>.

2 A. John Jowett 1989. *Patterns of literacy in the People's Republic of China.* GeoJournal 18, 417 – 427. https://doi.org/10.1007/BF00772696

3 *Adult literacy rate in China from 1982 to 2018*, Statista, accessed 6 January 2023, <https://www.statista.com/statistics/271336/literacy-in-china/>.

4 Ashley Smith 2019, *The Bitter Fruit of Trump's China-bashing*, Socialist Worker, accessed 6 January 2023, <https://socialistworker.org/2019/02/24/the-bitter-fruit-of-trumps-china-bashing>.

5 Dragan Plavšić 2020, *The China question*, Counterfire, accessed 6 January 2023, <https://www.counterfire.org/articles/analysis/21808-the-china-question>.

6 Martin Thomas 2019, *Neither Washington nor Beijing, but international socialism!*, Workers' Liberty, accessed 6 January 2023, <https://www.workersliberty.org/story/2019-08-29/neither-washington-nor-beijing-international-socialism>.

7 Plavšić, *op cit*

8 Ho-Fung Hung 2020, *The US-China Rivalry Is About Capitalist Competition*, Jacobin, accessed 15 January 2023, <https://www.jacobinmag.com/2020/07/us-china-competition-capitalism-rivalry>.

9 Dragan Plavšić 2020, *China: a socialist force for good or an imperial superpower in the making? An historical evaluation*, Counterfire, accessed 6 January 2023, <https://www.counterfire.org/articles/analysis/21612-china-a-socialist-force-for-good-or-an-imperial-superpower-in-the-making-an-historical-evaluation-long-read>.

10 Ben Towse 2020, *Neither Washington nor Beijing: The Left Must Stand With the Uighurs*, Novara Media, accessed 6 January 2023, <https://novaramedia.com/2020/08/05/neither-washington-nor-beijing-the-left-must-stand-with-the-uighurs/>.

11 Eli Friedman 2020, *Socialists Should Side With Workers – Not the Chinese or American Ruling Class*, Jacobin, accessed 6 January 2023, <https://jacobinmag.com/2020/04/china-united-states-new-cold-war-nationalism-socialists>.

12 Max Shachtman 1940, *The Soviet Union and the World War*, New International, accessed 6 January 2023, <https://www.marxists.org/archive/shachtma/1940/04/ussrwar.htm>.

13 *Manifesto of the International Socialist Congress at Basel* (1912), Marxist Internet Archive, accessed 6 January 2023, <https://www.marxists.org/history/international/social-democracy/1912/basel-manifesto.htm>

14 Vladimir Lenin 1914, *The War and Russian Social-Democracy*, Marxist Internet Archive, accessed 6 January 2023, <https://www.marxists.org/archive/lenin/works/1914/sep/28.htm>.
15 *ibid*
16 Vladimir Lenin 1916, *Imperialism and the Split in Socialism*, Marxist Internet Archive, accessed 6 January 2023, <https://www.marxists.org/archive/lenin/works/1916/oct/x01.htm>.
17 David Bush 2018, *Neither Washington Nor Moscow: origins and applying it today*, Counterfire, accessed 6 January 2023, <https://www.counterfire.org/articles/opinion/19399-neither-washington-nor-moscow>.
18 Sheila McGregor 2002, *Neither Washington nor Moscow*, International Socialism, accessed 6 January 2023, <https://www.marxists.org/history/etol/newspape/isj2/2002/isj2-097/mcgregor.htm>.
19 Lenin, cited in Shachtman *op cit*
20 Dictionary.com, *imperialism*, accessed 6 January 2023, <https://www.dictionary.com/browse/imperialism>.
21 Vladimir Lenin 1916, *Imperialism, the Highest Stage of Capitalism* (chapter 7), Marxist Internet Archive, accessed 6 January 2023, <https://www.marxists.org/archive/lenin/works/1916/imp-hsc/ch07.htm>
22 Samir Amin. *The Implosion of Contemporary Capitalism*, Monthly Review Press, New York, 2013, p.1
23 *ibid*, p32
24 Karl Marx. *Capital: A Critique of Political Economy. V. 1*: Penguin Classics. London ; New York, NY: Penguin Books in association with New Left Review, 1981, p171
25 Chen Xi 2019, *TAZARA documentary reaffirms China-Africa relations*, Global Times, accessed 6 January 2023, <https://www.globaltimes.cn/content/1169284.shtml>.
26 McKinsey Global Institute 2019, *China and the world: Inside the dynamics of a changing relationship*, McKinsey, accessed 6 January 2023, <https://www.mckinsey.com/featured-insights/china/china-and-the-world-inside-the-dynamics-of-a-changing-relationship#>.
27 *Leading countries worldwide in 2020 and 2021, by Foreign Direct Investment (FDI) outflows*, Statista, accessed 6 January 2023, <https://www.statista.com/statistics/273931/largest-direct-investors-worldwide/>.
28 Plavšić, *China: a socialist force for good or an imperial superpower in the making?, op cit*
29 Josh Sykes 2022, *Red Theory: Constant and variable capital*, FightBack News, accessed 6 January 2023, <https://www.fightbacknews.org/2022/8/14/red-theory-constant-and-variable-capital>.
30 Michael Roberts 2021, *The rate and the mass of profit*, The Next Recession, accessed 6 January 2023, <https://thenextrecession.wordpress.com/2021/08/25/the-rate-and-the-mass-of-profit/>.

31 Noam Chomsky 2010, *Noam Chomsky in China (partial transcript)*, The Noam Chomsky Website, accessed 6 January 2023, <https: / / chomsky.info / 20100822 / >.

32 Arthur R. Kroeber. *China's Economy: What Everyone Needs to Know.* New York, NY: Oxford University Press, 2016, p225

33 Mao Zedong 1953, *On state capitalism*, Marxist Internet Archive, accessed 15 January 2023, <https: / / www.marxists.org / reference / archive / mao / selected-works / volume-5 / mswv5_30.htm>.

34 Li Zhongjin and David M. Kotz 2020, *Is China Imperialist? Economy, State, and Insertion in the Global System*, American Economic Association, accessed 6 January 2023, <https: / / www.aeaweb.org / conference / 2021 / preliminary / paper / e4D3fNd3> (PDF).

35 Cited in Liu Mingfu. *The China Dream: Great Power Thinking & Strategic Posture in the Post-American Era*. New York, NY: CN Times Books, 2015. Kindle edition.

36 Xi Jinping 2022, *Full text of the report to the 20th National Congress of the Communist Party of China*, Xinhua, accessed 6 January 2023, <https: / / english.news.cn / 20221025 / 8eb6f5239f984f01a2bc45b5b5db0c51 / c.html>.

37 Nelson Mandela. *Long Walk To Freedom Vol 1: 1918-1962*. United Kingdom: Little, Brown Book Group, 2009, Kindle location 2765

38 Nick Van Mead 2018, *China in Africa: win-win development, or a new colonialism?*, The Guardian, accessed 9 January 2023, <https: / / www.theguardian.com / cities / 2018 / jul / 31 / china-in-africa-win-win-development-or-a-new-colonialism>.

39 Deborah Brautigam. *Will Africa Feed China?* Oxford ; New York: Oxford University Press, 2015, p38

40 Anna Fleck 2022, *China – Africa Trade Hits Record Highs in 2021*, Statista, accessed 9 January 2023, <https: / / www.statista.com / chart / 27880 / trade-between-china-and-africa / >.

41 *Trade in Goods with Africa*, US Census Bureau, accessed 9 January 2023, <https: / / www.census.gov / foreign-trade / balance / c0013.html>.

42 Kathrin Hille and David Pilling 2022, *China applies brakes to Africa lending*, Financial Times, accessed 9 January 2023, <https: / / www.ft.com / content / 64b4bcd5-032e-4be5-aa3b-e902f5b1345e>.

43 Nick Van Mead 2018, *China in Africa: win-win development, or a new colonialism?*, The Guardian, accessed 9 January 2023, <https: / / www.theguardian.com / cities / 2018 / jul / 31 / china-in-africa-win-win-development-or-a-new-colonialism>.

44 Istvan Tarrosy and Zoltán Vörös 2018, *China and Ethiopia, Part 1: The Light Railway System*, The Diplomat, accessed 9 January 2023, <https: / / thediplomat.com / 2018 / 02 / china-and-ethiopia-part-1-the-light-railway-system / >.

45 Lidz-Ama Appiah 2015, *Ethiopia gets the first metro system in sub-*

*Saharan Africa*, CNN, accessed 9 January 2023, <https://edition.cnn.com/2015/10/14/tech/addis-ababa-light-rail-metro/index.html>.

46 *Ethiopia-Djibouti electric railway line opens* (2016), BBC News, accessed 9 January 2023, <https://www.bbc.co.uk/news/world-africa-37562177>.

47 *African Union opens Chinese-funded HQ in Ethiopia* (2012), BBC News, accessed 9 January 2023, <https://www.bbc.co.uk/news/world-africa-16770932>.

48 Mohammed Momoh 2022, *After African Union, China sets eyes on $32m Ecowas headquarters*, The East African, accessed 9 January 2023, <https://www.theeastafrican.co.ke/tea/rest-of-africa/china-to-build-32m-ecowas-head-office-4049094>.

49 Jevans Nyabiage 2022, *Chinese firm prepares to hand over new US$140 million parliament to Zimbabwe*, SCMP, accessed 9 January 2023, <https://www.scmp.com/news/china/diplomacy/article/3183959/chinese-firm-prepares-hand-over-new-us140-million-parliament>.

50 *Chinese-aided Africa CDC headquarters project approaches completion* (2022), Xinhua, accessed 9 January 2023, <https://english.news.cn/20221227/887b23ff99314affae172802c9a1c79a/c.html>.

51 Joel Wendland-Liu 2022, *Africa, China, and U.S. imperialism*, Communist Party USA, accessed 9 January 2023, <https://www.cpusa.org/article/africa-china-and-u-s-imperialism/>.

52 Deborah Brautigam 2018, *U.S. politicians get China in Africa all wrong*, Washington Post, accessed 9 January 2023, <https://www.washingtonpost.com/news/theworldpost/wp/2018/04/12/china-africa/>.

53 Alonso Soto 2020, *Africa Seen Getting More Debt Relief From China Than Bondholders*, Bloomberg, accessed 9 January 2023, <https://www.bloomberg.com/news/articles/2020-06-18/africa-seen-getting-more-debt-relief-from-china-than-bondholders>.

54 *African governments owe three times more debt to private lenders than China*, Debt Justice, accessed 9 January 2023, <https://debtjustice.org.uk/press-release/african-governments-owe-three-times-more-debt-to-private-lenders-than-china>.

55 Deborah Brautigam 2018, *U.S. politicians get China in Africa all wrong*, Washington Post, accessed 9 January 2023, <https://www.washingtonpost.com/news/theworldpost/wp/2018/04/12/china-africa/>.

56 Flavia Krause-Jackson 2011, *Clinton Chastises China on Internet, African 'New Colonialism'*, Bloomberg, accessed 9 January 2023, <https://www.bloomberg.com/news/articles/2011-06-11/clinton-chastises-china-on-internet-african-new-colonialism->.

57 David Pilling 2018, *Bolton accuses China and Russia of 'predatory practices' in Africa*, Financial Times, accessed 9 January 2023, <https://

www.ft.com / content / 6645a26a-ff08-11e8-ac00-57a2a826423e>.

58 Adrian Budd 2018, *China, the US and imperialism*, Socialist Review, accessed 9 January 2023, <http: / / socialistreview.org.uk / 431 / china-us-and-imperialism>.

59 Claire Gatinois 2014, *Portugal indebted to Angola after economic reversal of fortune*, The Guardian, accessed 9 January 2023, <https: / / www.theguardian.com / world / 2014 / jun / 03 / portugal-economy-bailout-angola-invests>.

60 *Yanis Varoufakis on Chinese 'Imperialism'* (2020), YouTube, accessed 9 January 2023, <https: / / www.youtube.com / watch?v=03l3Ra4bL_A>.

61 Jamil Anderlini 2010, *Pretoria defends China's Africa policy*, Financial Times, accessed 9 January 2023, <https: / / www.ft.com / content / 302f88ca-af8a-11df-a172-00144feabdc0>.

62 Martin Jacques. *When China Rules the World: The End of the Western World and the Birth of a New Global Order. 2. ed*. New York, NY: Penguin Books, 2012, p425

63 Walter Rodney. *How Europe Underdeveloped Africa*. New edition. Brooklyn: Verso, 2018.

64 Chiponda Chimbelu 2019, *Investing in Africa's tech infrastructure. Has China won already?*, Deutsche Welle, accessed 15 January 2023, <https: / / www.dw.com / en / investing-in-africas-tech-infrastructure-has-china-won-already / a-48540426>.

65 Charlie Campbell 2019, *China Is Bankrolling Green Energy Projects Around the World*, Time, accessed 9 January 2023, <https: / / time.com / 5714267 / china-green-energy / >.

66 Antoaneta Roussi 2019, *Chinese investments fuel growth in African science*, Nature, accessed 9 January 2023, <https: / / www.nature.com / immersive / d41586-019-01398-x / index.html>.

67 Andrew Jack 2020, *China surpasses western government African university scholarships*, Financial Times, accessed 9 January 2023, <https: / / www.ft.com / content / 4b2e6c1c-83cf-448a-9112-477be01d2eee>.

68 Roussi, *op cit*

69 Dambisa Moyo. *Winner Take All: China's Race for Resources and What It Means for Us*. London: Penguin, 2013, p85

70 Kirsty Needham 2018, *China waives debt, promises 'no imposition of will' on African nations*, Sydney Morning Herald, accessed 9 January 2023, <https: / / www.smh.com.au / world / asia / china-waives-debt-promises-no-imposition-of-will-on-african-nations-20180904-p501nr.html>.

71 Marx, *op cit*, p578

72 W. Gyude Moore 2020, *China has built more infrastructure in Africa in two decades than the West has in centuries*, Pearls and Irritations, accessed 9 January 2023, <https: / / johnmenadue.com / w-gyude-

moore-china-has-built-more-infrastructure-in-africa-in-two-decades-than-the-west-has-in-centuries/>.
73 *Akon: No Country in the World Has Done More Good for Africa than China* (2020), YouTube, accessed 9 January 2023, <https://www.youtube.com/watch?v=YtStkSHgQiA>.
74 Alexander Main 2018, *Is Latin America Still the US's "Backyard"?*, CEPR, accessed 10 January 2023, <https://www.cepr.net/is-latin-america-still-the-us-s-backyard/>.
75 Eduardo Galeano. *Open Veins of Latin America: Five Centuries of the Pillage of a Continent*. 25th anniversary ed. New York: Monthly Review Press, 1997, p190
76 Mark Weisbrot 2020, *Silence reigns on the US-backed coup against Evo Morales in Bolivia*, The Guardian, accessed 10 January 2023, <https://www.theguardian.com/commentisfree/2020/sep/18/silence-us-backed-coup-evo-morales-bolivia-american-states>.
77 Vijay Prashad and José Carlos Llerena Robles 2022, *Early evidence suggests U.S. may have pushed for coup in Peru*, People's World, accessed 10 January 2023, <https://www.peoplesworld.org/article/early-evidence-suggests-u-s-may-have-pushed-for-coup-in-peru/>.
78 Julian Borger 2002, *US 'gave the nod' to Venezuelan coup*, The Guardian, accessed 10 January 2023, <https://www.theguardian.com/world/2002/apr/17/usa.venezuela>.
79 Chuck Kaufman 2020, *Sanctions Kill! End US Sanctions on Nicaragua*, Alliance for Global Justice, accessed 10 January 2023, <https://afgj.org/nicanotes-sanctions-kill-end-us-sanctions-on-nicaragua>.
80 Ramona Wadi 2021, *The Illegal US Blockade on Cuba Hinders the Island's Economic Development*, Politics Today, accessed 10 January 2023, <https://politicstoday.org/the-illegal-us-blockade-on-cuba-hinders-the-islands-economic-development/>.
81 John Polga-Hecimovich 2022, *China's evolving economic footprint in Latin America*, GIS Reports, accessed 10 January 2023, <https://www.gisreportsonline.com/r/chinas-economic-power-grows-in-latin-america/>.
82 Ciara Nugent and Charlie Cambell 2021, *The U.S. and China Are Battling for Influence in Latin America, and the Pandemic Has Raised the Stakes*, Time, accessed 10 January 2023, <https://time.com/5936037/us-china-latin-america-influence/>.
83 Kevin Gallagher. *The China Triangle: Latin America's China Boom and the Fate of the Washington Consensus*. New York, NY: Oxford University Press, 2016, p85
84 Max Nathanson 2018, *How to Respond to Chinese Investment in Latin America*, Foreign Policy, accessed 10 January 2023, <https://foreignpolicy.com/2018/11/28/how-to-respond-to-chinese-investment-in-latin-america/>.

85 Tan Huileng 2018, *China says Rex Tillerson is demonstrating US 'disdain' and 'paranoia'*, CNBC, accessed 10 January 2023, <https://www.cnbc.com/2018/02/04/china-hits-back-at-rex-tillerson-over-comments-that-latam-does-not-need-new-imperial-powers.html>.

86 2006, *Chávez praises China as he starts 6-day visit*, New York Times, accessed 10 January 2023, <https://www.nytimes.com/2006/08/23/business/worldbusiness/23iht-ven.html>.

87 Jonathan Watts 2006, *Chávez says China deal 'great wall' against US*, The Guardian, accessed 10 January 2023, <https://www.theguardian.com/world/2006/aug/25/venezuela.china>.

88 Ewan Robertson 2014, *Venezuela Receives US$18 Billion of Chinese Financing, Signs 38 Accords*, Venezuela Analysis, accessed 10 January 2023, <https://venezuelanalysis.com/news/10800>.

89 Gallagher, *op cit*, p85

90 *ibid*, p182

91 *ibid*, p82

92 Charlie Devereux 2012, *China Bankrolling Chavez's Re-Election Bid With Oil Loans*, Bloomberg, accessed 10 January 2023, <https://www.bloomberg.com/news/articles/2012-09-25/china-bankrolling-chavez-s-re-election-bid-with-oil-loans>.

93 *Venezuelan Minister attacks US during China visit*, Yahoo News, accessed 10 January 2023, <https://news.yahoo.com/venezuelan-minister-attacks-us-during-china-visit-095756733.html>.

94 Ajit Singh 2017, *China Is Most Promising Hope for Third World: Fidel*, Telesur, accessed 10 January 2023, <https://www.telesurenglish.net/opinion/China-Is-Most-Promising-Hope-for-Third-World-Fidel-20171128-0017.html>.

95 Bradley J. Murg and Rasheed J. Griffith 2020, *Sino-Cuban Relations: No 'New Cold War' in Havana*, The Diplomat, accessed 10 January 2023, <https://thediplomat.com/2020/12/sino-cuban-relations-no-new-cold-war-in-havana/>.

96 *Ollie Vargas – International Peace Forum* (2020), YouTube, accessed 10 January 2023, <https://www.youtube.com/watch?v=O64aIw2usSQ>.

97 *Belt and Road 2022 in numbers*, People's Daily, accessed 11 January 2023, <http://en.people.cn/n3/2023/0106/c90000-10192784.html>.

98 *The Belt and Road Initiative in the global trade, investment and finance landscape* (2018), OECD Business and Finance Outlook, accessed 11 January 2023, <https://www.oecd-ilibrary.org/sites/bus_fin_out-2018-6-en/index.html?itemId=/content/component/bus_fin_out-2018-6-en>.

99 Justin Yifu Lin. *Demystifying the Chinese Economy*. Cambridge: Cambridge University Press, 2012, p23

100 Peter Nolan. *Understanding China: The Silk Road and the Communist Manifesto*. Routledge Studies on the Chinese Economy 60. London ;

New York: Routledge, Taylor & Francis Group, 2016, p4
101 Bruno Maçães. *Belt and Road: A Chinese World Order.* London: Hurst & Company, 2018, p49
102 Ashley Smith and Kevin Lin 2020, *Neither Washington Nor Beijing: Socialists, Inter-Imperial Rivalry, and Hong Kong,* Socialist Forum, accessed 11 January 2023, <https://socialistforum.dsausa.org/issues/winter-2020/neither-washington-nor-beijing-socialists-inter-imperial-rivalry-and-hong-kong/>.
103 Hal Brands 2011, *Evaluating Brazilian Grand Strategy under Lula,* Comparative Strategy, 30:1, 28-49, DOI: 10.1080/01495933.2011.545686
104 *Countries of the Belt and Road Initiative (BRI),* Green Finance & Development Center, accessed 11 January 2023, <https://greenfdc.org/countries-of-the-belt-and-road-initiative-bri/>.
105 Nirav Patel 2019, *Figure of the week: Electricity access in Africa,* Brookings, accessed 11 January 2023, <https://www.brookings.edu/blog/africa-in-focus/2019/03/29/figure-of-the-week-electricity-access-in-africa/>.
106 Gallagher, *op cit,* p233
107 Brad Glosserman 2020, *'Debt trap' diplomacy is a card China seldom plays in Belt and Road initiative,* Japan Times, accessed 11 January 2023, <https://www.japantimes.co.jp/opinion/2020/09/01/commentary/debt-trap-diplomacy-bri-china/>.
108 Maçães, *op cit,* p156
109 Deborah Brautigam and Meg Rithmire 2020 *The Chinese 'Debt Trap' Is a Myth,* The Atlantic, accessed 11 January 2023, <https://www.theatlantic.com/international/archive/2021/02/china-debt-trap-diplomacy/617953/>.
110 James McBride et al 2020, *China's Massive Belt and Road Initiative,* CFR, accessed 11 January 2023, <https://www.cfr.org/backgrounder/chinas-massive-belt-and-road-initiative>.
111 Robert Delaney 2017, *Kissinger urges greater cooperation with China as 'the world's centre of gravity' shifts,* South China Morning Post, accessed 11 January 2023, <https://www.scmp.com/news/china/policies-politics/article/2112957/kissinger-urges-us-boost-cooperation-beijing-massive>.
112 Amitai Etzioni. *Avoiding War with China: Two Nations, One World.* Charlottesville: University of Virginia Press, 2017, p111
113 Jude Woodward. *The US vs China: Asia's New Cold War?* Geopolitical Economy. Manchester: Manchester University Press, 2017, p177
114 For example: Howard French 2015, *What's behind Beijing's drive to control the South China Sea?,* The Guardian, accessed 12 January 2023, <https://www.theguardian.com/world/2015/jul/28/whats-behind-beijings-drive-control-south-china-sea-hainan>.
115 Robert D. Kaplan. *Asia's Cauldron: The South China Sea and the End of a*

*Stable Pacific*. New York: Random House, 2014, p71

116 Frankopan, Peter. *The New Silk Roads: The Present and Future of the World*. United Kingdom: Bloomsbury Publishing, 2018, p83

117 Peter Nolan 2013, *Imperial Archipelagos*, New Left Review, accessed 12 January 2023, <https: / / newleftreview.org / issues / ii80 / articles / peter-nolan-imperial-archipelagos>.

118 Liu Xiaoming 2016, *Who is really behind the tensions in the South China Sea?*, Financial Times, accessed 12 January 2023, <https: / / www.ft.com / content / 147a3ff6-12d2-11e6-91da-096d89bd2173>.

119 Richard Heydarian 2021, *'Global Britain' takes aim at China in South China Sea*, Asia Times, accessed 12 January 2023, <https: / / asiatimes.com / 2021 / 01 / global-britain-takes-aim-at-china-in-south-china-sea / >.

120 Christian Shepherd and Manuel Mogato 2017, *ASEAN, China adopt framework for crafting code on South China Sea*, Reuters, accessed 12 January 2023, <https: / / www.reuters.com / article / us-asean-philippines-southchinasea-idUSKBN1AM0AY>.

121 China's support for liberation movements is well documented in several books. One recommendation is: Jeremy Friedman. *Shadow Cold War: The Sino-Soviet Competition for the Third World*. The New Cold War History. Chapel Hill: University of North Carolina Press, 2015.

122 Qi Dexue 2020, *China's 70th Anniversary of the War to Resist U.S. Aggression and Aid Korea*, Qiao Collective, accessed 12 January 2023, <https: / / www.qiaocollective.com / en / articles / 70th-anniversary-korean-war>.

123 Jenny Clegg. *China's Global Strategy: Towards a Multipolar World*. London ; New York : New York: Pluto Press ; Distributed in the United States of America exclusively by Palgrave Macmillan, 2009, p13

124 Jeffrey Sachs 2023, *The New World Economy*, Jeff Sachs, accessed 12 January 2023, <https: / / www.jeffsachs.org / newspaper-articles / febj7gnedfemn5b2wh46pbwarye53f>.

125 Konstantin Kakaes 2019, *The limits of Chinese military power*, MIT Technology Review, accessed 12 January 2023, <https: / / www.technologyreview.com / 2019 / 10 / 24 / 290 / the-limits-of-chinese-military-power / >.

126 Clegg, *op cit*, p226

127 Samir Amin. *Beyond US Hegemony? Assessing the Prospects for a Multipolar World*. New York: World Book Pub. ; Sird ; UKZN Press ; Zed Books ; Distributed in the USA exclusively by Palgrave Macmillan, 2006, p149

128 Clegg, *op cit*, p11

129 *Marx and Engels: Manifesto of the Communist Party: Chapter 2* (1848), Marxist Internet Archive, accessed 13 January 2023, <https: / / www.marxists.org / archive / marx / works / 1848 / communist-manifesto / ch02.htm>

130 Yuan Yang and Nian Liu 2020, *Inside China's race to beat poverty,* Financial Times, accessed 15 January 2023, <https://www.ft.com/content/b818aece-4cd7-4c99-8b62-e52ae4aa1b21>.

131 Alex Lo 2020, *Beijing enjoys greater legitimacy than any Western state,* South China Morning Post, accessed 15 January 2023, <https://www.scmp.com/comment/opinion/article/3093825/beijing-enjoys-greater-legitimacy-any-western-state>.

132 Nigel Inkster. *The Great Decoupling: China, America and the Struggle for Technological Supremacy*. Hurst Publishers, 2021, p107

133 Ernest Mandel 1990, *A theory which has not withstood the test of facts,* Marxist Internet Archive, accessed 15 January 2023, <https://www.marxists.org/archive/mandel/1990/xx/theory.html>.

# 3

# Will China suffer the same fate as the Soviet Union?

> We should think of China's communist regime quite differently from that of the USSR: it has, after all, succeeded where the Soviet Union failed. (Martin Jacques)[1]

THIS chapter addresses the reasons for the collapse of the Soviet Union, and seeks to understand whether the People's Republic of China is vulnerable to the same forces that undermined the foundations of European socialism. What lessons can be drawn from the Soviet collapse? Has capitalism won? What future does socialism have in the world? Is there any escape for humanity from brutal exploitation, inequality and underdevelopment? Is there a future in which the world's billions can truly exercise their free will, their humanity, liberated from poverty and alienation?

The conclusions I draw are that China is following a fundamentally different path to that of the Soviet Union; that it has made a serious and comprehensive study of the Soviet collapse and rigorously applied what it has learnt; that the People's Republic of China remains a socialist country and the driving force towards a multipolar world; that, in spite of the rolling back of the first wave of socialist advance, Marxism remains as relevant as ever; and that, consequently, socialism has a bright future in the world.

## Maintaining the legitimacy of the CPC through highly effective governance and improvement in living standards

> The Chinese experience since 1978 shows that a developing country must take the improvement of people's standard of

> living as its top priority… With this belief, China has done its utmost to improve people's standard of living and achieved remarkable results in poverty eradication. (Zhang Weiwei)[2]

In the aftermath of the collapse of the Soviet Union and the European people's democracies between 1989 and 1991, many senior officials in China worried that the reform process could get out of hand. The Soviet leaders had attempted reform via *glasnost* and *perestroika*, and their experiments had ended in disaster. Wasn't this a cautionary message for the CPC to return to the model of comprehensive state ownership and strictly centralised economic control?

Deng Xiaoping's insight was that the key economic factor undermining the Soviet Union wasn't its limited experiment with market forms but its failure to deliver improvements in people's living standards. Economic stagnation from the mid-1970s onwards meant that people's basic expectations for a better life weren't being met. This – along with an ongoing ideological decay – served to sap popular confidence in the superiority of the socialist system, a process catalysed by the West's elaborate and sophisticated system of anti-communist propaganda. When it came to defending socialism from attack, it turned out to be very difficult to mobilise the masses.

Deng understood that the Communist Party's legitimacy would only be maintained by eliminating poverty and improving people's living conditions. Therefore on his famous Southern Tour in 1992, he pointed out that internal and external circumstances were particularly favourable for pursuing economic reform, and on that basis urged boldness rather than caution.

> Since we have the necessary domestic conditions and a favourable international environment, and since under the socialist system we have the advantage of being able to concentrate our forces on a major task, it is now both possible and necessary for us to bring about, in the prolonged process of modernisation, several periods of rapid growth with good economic returns. We must have this ambition.[3]

He explained that economic development was particularly important in the light of fast growth in other East and Southeast Asian countries: "The economies of some of our neighbouring countries and regions are growing faster than ours. If our economy stagnates or develops only slowly, the people will make comparisons and ask why."[4]

As long as the CPC maintained political control, as long as the crucial parts of the economy (the 'commanding heights') continued to be publicly owned, markets and foreign investment would benefit China. Attracted by the huge, well-educated and hardworking labour force, foreign companies would invest in China, thereby increasing China's capital and technical know-how, creating a virtuous cycle that would allow China to rise up the value chain and provide vastly improved living conditions to its population.

This determined focus on improving people's day-to-day wellbeing echoes Mao Zedong almost 60 years earlier:

> All the practical problems in the masses' everyday life should claim our attention. If we attend to these problems, solve them and satisfy the needs of the masses, we shall really become organisers of the well-being of the masses, and they will truly rally round us and give us their warm support.[5]

It should be uncontroversial to say that the economic strategy adopted in the period of *Reform and opening up* (1978 onwards) has been highly successful. China's per capita income in 1979 was 210 USD. Much of the rural population lived below the poverty line. Per capita food production had grown a total of just 10 percent from 1952. Chen Yun, the lead economist of the Deng era, warned in 1979:

> Our country has more than 900 million people, 80 percent are peasants. The revolution has been won for 30 years and the people are demanding improvements in their lives. Have there been improvements? Yes. But many places still do not have enough to eat, this is a big problem.[6]

The PRC had fallen a long way behind the 'East Asian miracle' zone (Japan, South Korea, Taiwan, Hong Kong, Singapore, Thailand, Malaysia and Indonesia) in terms of living standards. Justin Yifu Lin writes that the post-Mao leadership "had to improve national economic performance and make its people as rich as their neighbours, or it might lose support and its legitimacy for rule."[7]

In the following decades, the number of people in China living in 'absolute poverty' (as defined by the World Bank) fell from 840 million to zero, as discussed at length in the next chapter. Wages have increased continuously. Between 1988 and 2008, average per capita income grew by 229 percent, ten times the global average of 24 percent.

Although inequality has emerged as a serious problem, practically all Chinese people are substantially better off than they were 40 years ago in terms of nutrition, housing, clothing, access to services, and ability to travel. Consumer goods that were previously considered luxuries – such as washing machines, refrigerators, heated shower units, air conditioners, colour televisions, computers – can now be found in almost every home.

In the 2000s, the government re-established a comprehensive social security programme, including universal health insurance, minimum nine-year free compulsory education, pensions, subsidised housing, and income support. Workers' wages are increasing at a faster rate than GDP, and as a result the income gap is starting to narrow.

Human Development Index (HDI) is a useful compound metric comprising life expectancy, educational level and per capita income. In HDI terms, China has risen from 0.407 in 1980 to 0.768 in 2021 (for calibration purposes, Norway is at the top of the charts with 0.962 and South Sudan at the bottom with 0.386). China's increase in HDI makes it the only country to have moved from the *low* to the *high* HDI category – leap-frogging *medium* – since the UN Development Program first began studying global HDI trends in 1990.[8] The requirement for the *very high* HDI group is 0.800 – it's likely China will get there before the end of this decade.

Chinese productivity and innovation levels are gradually catching up with the most advanced capitalist countries, as the government's huge investment in science and technology reaps rewards. Veteran science writer Philip Ball notes:

> The patronising old idea that China ... can imitate but not innovate is certainly false now. In several scientific fields, China is starting to set the pace for others to follow. On my tour of Chinese labs in 1992, only those I saw at the flagship Peking University looked comparable to what you might find at a good university in the west. Today the resources available to China's top scientists are enviable to many of their western counterparts.[9]

Whereas Soviet infrastructure was starting to crumble by the 1980s, modern Chinese infrastructure is world-class. Indeed, the quality of roads, trains, airports, ports and buildings in major Chinese cities is now noticeably higher than in global cities like New York and London.

The continuously improving economic situation and corresponding improvement in people's quality of life has led to strong popular support for the government and for Chinese socialism. The Pew Research Centre reports that President Xi Jinping enjoys a confidence rating of 94 percent,[10] which compares favourably with US President Joe Biden's approval rating of 40 percent.[11] In 2014, 89 percent of Chinese rated their economy 'good', compared with 64 percent for India and 40 percent for the US.[12] British academic Peter Nolan writes that, "under Communist Party rule, China has experienced the most remarkable era of growth and development in modern history."[13] Because of that, the Chinese government enjoys tremendous popular support and legitimacy, and its rule can be expected to continue for a long time to come.

## Why has Chinese economic reform succeeded when the Soviet reform failed?

> The vastly different results of the Russian and Chinese reforms are demonstrative of the critical importance of choosing the right reform strategies and paths. (Hu Angang)[14]

The late Italian Marxist historian Domenico Losurdo noted that, in the 1930s and 40s, the Soviet 'command economy' had worked extremely well: "The rapid development of modern industry was interwoven with the construction of a welfare state that guaranteed the economic and social rights of citizens in a way that was unprecedented."[15]

However, after the period of frenetic building of socialism, followed by World War II, followed by reconstruction, came "the transition from great historical crisis to a more 'normal' period" in which "the masses' enthusiasm and commitment to production and work weakened and then disappeared." In its final few years, "the Soviet Union was characterised by massive absenteeism and disengagement in the workplace: not only did production development stagnate, but there was no longer any application of the principle that Marx said drove socialism — remuneration according to the quantity and quality of work delivered."

From the mid-1970s onwards, the Soviet economy entered a period of slow economic growth, just at the point when the major capitalist countries were starting to leverage developments in technology and management to achieve major steps forward in productivity. Jude Woodward notes:

> From 20 per cent of the size of the US economy in 1944, the Soviet economy peaked at 44 per cent that of the US by 1970 ($1,352 billion to $3,082 billion) but had fallen back to 36 per cent of the US by 1989 ($2,037 billion to $5,704 billion). It never came near challenging the economic weight of the US.[16]

Losurdo contends that China in the late 1970s faced very similar problems:

> The China that arose from the Cultural Revolution resembled the Soviet Union to an extraordinary degree in its last years of existence: the socialist principle of compensation based on the amount and quality of work delivered was substantially liquidated, and disaffection, disengagement, absenteeism and anarchy reigned in the workplace.[17]

China had made remarkable progress in terms of life expectancy, land ownership, social equality, education and mass empowerment since the birth of the People's Republic in 1949, yet by the late 1970s it was still a long way from being an advanced country. Hundreds of millions of people in the villages faced food insecurity and poor housing conditions.

Being a poor country with a tremendous responsibility to meet the immediate needs of its huge population, China lacked the resources to invest heavily in research and development, and the resulting low productivity meant that it couldn't guarantee an adequate standard of living to its people. Cut off from the global marketplace, it wasn't able to quickly learn from others or benefit from an ever-more globalised division of labour. There was a shortage of capital, a low level of technological development, and a lack of incentives for production and innovation. Much as with the Soviet Union in its later decades, China's planning system continued to be overly reliant on voluntarism and 'moral incentives' to raise production. The history of socialist economics over the last century indicates that such an approach suffers from diminishing returns and can't be sustained forever.

This is the context in which *Reform and Opening Up* was adopted in the late 1970s. Superficially, the reform strategy pursued by China from 1978 shares some similarity with the various attempts at economic reform in the Soviet Union, particularly the set of policies introduced by the Gorbachev leadership under the umbrella of *perestroika*. However, there are profound differences between the Chinese and Soviet approaches that help to explain the unquestionable success of one and the comprehensive failure of the other.

China's approach to reform was extremely cautious and pragmatic, "based on a step-by-step, piecemeal and experimental approach. If a reform worked it was extended to new areas; if it failed then it was abandoned."[18] All reforms had to be tested in practice, all results had to be analysed, and all analysis had to inform future experiments. Chen Yun stated in 1980 that:

> the steps must be steady, because we shall encounter many complicated problems. So do not rush… We should proceed with experiments, review our experience from time to time, and correct mistakes whenever we discover them, so that minor mistakes will not grow into major ones.[19]

Many key reform concepts came from the grassroots. "We processed their ideas and raised them to the level of guidelines for the whole country. Practice is the sole criterion for testing truth."[20]

Reform in China was patient, incremental and results-oriented, whereas "Gorbachev made the fatal mistake of trying to do too much, too fast."[21] Gorbachev's reforms were implemented in a heavy-handed, top-down way, without leveraging the ideas and creativity of the masses or attempting to collate feedback. Given that the project was presented as a form of 'democratisation', it's ironic that it was carried out in a profoundly undemocratic manner. The leadership didn't mobilise the existing, proven structures of society (the soviets and the Communist Party), but sought to bypass and weaken them.

> Instead of relying on the most pragmatic elements of the party and state officialdom in restructuring of the country, Gorbachev tried to build up new political forces and movements while gradually diminishing the power of the party and of centralised state structures.[22]

The media was put to work – not to unite the people behind a programme of development but to vilify the Communist Party. The economic programme was incoherent and subject to sudden changes in direction. The result was, in the words of veteran Russian communist Gennady Zyuganov, "a parade of political arrogance, demagoguery, and dilettantism, which gradually overwhelmed and paralysed the country."[23]

The Chinese and Soviet economies in the 1970s both suffered from a stifling over-centralisation. China's reform process addressed this imbalance in a gradual manner, in which "the relaxation of restrictions on private capital development was combined with state control and planned and state-led heavy investment."[24] In the Soviet Union, by contrast, the planning agencies were simply dismantled overnight, creating chaos throughout the economy.

Deng exhorted China's reformers to "cross the river by feeling the stones". On his famous Southern Tour in 1992, he summed up this method of experimentation:

> Are securities and the stock market good or bad? Do they entail any dangers? Are they peculiar to capitalism? Can socialism make use of them? We allow people to reserve their judgement, but we must try these things out. If, after one or two years of experimentation, they prove feasible, we can expand them. Otherwise, we can put a stop to them and be done with it.[25]

Although China's reform process served to introduce market forces into the economy, the whole process was carried out under the tight control of the government and took place within the context of a planned economy. The level of marketisation that has taken place in China is an order of magnitude greater than what took place in the Soviet Union; however, China has also maintained stronger macroeconomic control. Even now, after more than four decades of economic reform, "the state remains firmly in command" of the Chinese economy. Kroeber observes:

> The government will pursue reforms that increase the role of the market in setting prices, but will avoid reforms that permit

> the market to transfer control of assets from the state to the private sector.[26]

Cambridge University professor Peter Nolan, by no means a cheerleader for centrally-planned economies, writes: "The comparison of the experience of China and Russia's reforms confirms that, at certain junctures and in certain countries, effective planning is a necessary condition of economic success."[27] Nolan points out that the Chinese state took the lead in conducting large-scale experiments and analysing the results; protecting domestic industry from the sudden appearance of foreign goods; supporting the growth of the state-owned enterprises to a level where they could become competitive in the global marketplace; investing in social and economic infrastructure (transport, healthcare, education, transport, power generation); and coordinating the different parts of the reform programme.

In their valuable study of the reasons for the Soviet collapse, David Kotz and Fred Weir observe that there was hardly any privatisation in the Chinese reform process – state enterprises were kept under state ownership and control.

> There was no sudden price liberalisation – state enterprises continued to sell at controlled prices. Central planning was retained for the state sector of the economy. Rather than slashing state spending, various levels of government poured funds into improving China's basic economic infrastructure of transportation, communication, and power. Rather than tight monetary policy, ample credit was provided for expansion and modernisation. The state has sought to gradually develop a market economy over a period of decades, and the state has actively guided the process.[28]

Similarly Isabella Weber, author of *How China Escaped Shock Therapy*, notes that whereas Russia's sudden abandonment of planning led to "severe economic decline and deindustrialization", China's reforms "laid the institutional and structural foundations for its economic ascent under tight political control by the party and the state."[29]

Contrasting Russia's embrace of neoliberal economics with China's hybrid approach, Weber notes that between 1990 and 2017, Russia's share of world GDP almost halved, while China's share increased close to sixfold.[30] She considers that this disparity is the result of China having rejected the neoliberal economists' prescriptions for 'big bang' price reform:

> Instead of liberalising all prices in one big bang, the state initially continued to plan the industrial core of the economy and set the prices of essential goods while the prices of surplus

> output and nonessential goods were successively liberalised. As a result, prices were gradually determined by the market.[31]

China's reform approach is thus "the opposite of shock therapy". Whereas the purpose of the neoliberal state is to "fortify the market", "the Chinese state uses the market as a tool in the pursuit of its larger development goals."[32]

The result was a far more effective programme of economic reform than that which took place in the Soviet Union from 1985-91 or in post-Soviet Russia from 1991 onwards.

If "the proof of the pudding is in the eating", then Chinese dessert has proven itself to be far tastier and more nutritious than its Soviet counterpart. *Perestroika* turned a sluggish economy into a failing one. By 1991, the last year of the USSR's existence, the economy was contracting at a rate of 15 percent per year. Gorbachev's blind faith in the inherent corrective power of the market turned out to be misplaced; investment collapsed. "Net fixed investment declined at the astounding rate of 21 per cent in 1990 and an estimated 25 per cent in 1991."[33]

In China, GDP growth increased from around 4 percent in the 1970s to nearly 10 percent in the period from 1978 to 1992. Since 1978, China's economy has grown more than any other country; it also tops the list for growth of per capita GDP, which has risen from $156 in 1978 to over $12,000 at the time of writing.[34]

## China is not weakening Communist Party rule or attacking its own history

> If China allowed bourgeois liberalisation, there would inevitably be turmoil. We would accomplish nothing, and our principles, policies, line and development strategy would all be doomed to failure. (Deng Xiaoping)[35]

In both China and the Soviet Union, market-oriented economic reform meant breaking with past policy to some degree. A major difference is that in the Soviet Union, this change of policy was accompanied by a concerted attempt to undermine the legitimacy of the Communist Party and the confidence of the people in their history.

In 1986, Gorbachev and his advisers came up with the concept of *glasnost* – 'openness' – to encapsulate policies of greater government transparency, wider political discussion and increased popular participation. The idea seemed unobjectionable to begin with, but glasnost soon became a battle cry for an all-out attack on the legitimacy of Communist Party rule and a powerful weapon in the hands of class forces hostile to socialism.

Faced with significant opposition to their economic proposals within the Communist Party, and lacking a base among the masses, Gorbachev's team increasingly looked to 'liberal reformers' for support – people who supported perestroika and wanted it to be accompanied by a transition towards a European-style parliamentary political system. These reformers encouraged Gorbachev to engineer a quiet coup in the name of democracy, ending the Communist Party's leading role in the government by dismantling the Supreme Soviet and replacing it with a Congress of People's Deputies. Representatives to this latter body were directly elected, but the selection of candidates was heavily manipulated in favour of pro-perestroika, pro-western Gorbachev loyalists. Prominent Chinese academics Cheng Enfu and Liu Zixu observe:

> In the name of promoting young cadres and of reform, Gorbachev replaced large numbers of party, political and military leaders with anti-CPSU and anti-socialist cadres or cadres with ambivalent positions. This practice laid the foundations, in organisational and cadre selection terms, for the political 'shift of direction.'[36]

Yegor Ligachev, a high-ranking Soviet official who witnessed all this first hand, supports this conclusion:

> What happened in our country is primarily the result of the debilitation and eventual elimination of the Communist Party's leading role in society, the ejection of the party from major policymaking, its ideological and organisational unravelling.[37]

The political transformation was supported by a thoroughgoing media campaign denigrating Soviet history, vastly exaggerating the excesses and mistakes of the Stalin period, and even attacking the Soviet Union's role in the Second World War. Things went so far that Cuban leader Fidel Castro was prompted to comment in 1989:

> Without a strong, disciplined and respected party, it's impossible to develop a revolution or a truly socialist rectification. It isn't possible to carry out such a process by slandering socialism, destroying its values, discrediting the party, demoralising the vanguard, renouncing its leading role, ending social discipline, sowing chaos and anarchy all around. This might foster a counter-revolution, but not revolutionary changes... It's repugnant that many in the USSR itself are dedicating themselves to destroying historic feats and extraordinary merits of that heroic people.[38]

The Communist Party had been the major vehicle for promoting the needs and ideas of the Soviet working class; once it was sidelined, the workers had no obvious means of organising in defence of their interests. This opened up a space for a pro-capitalist minority to dominate political power and, ultimately, break up the country and dismantle socialism.

The Chinese leadership understood that the People's Republic of China could not survive without the continued leadership of the Communist Party, and this is a key lesson that it has learned from the collapse of the Soviet Union. Xi Jinping has opined that:

> one important reason for the disintegration of the Soviet Union and the collapse of the CPSU is the complete denial of the history of the Soviet Union, and the history of the CPSU, the denial of Lenin and other leading personalities, and historical nihilism confused the people's thoughts.[39]

There was no appetite whatsoever for transplanting the political ideas of the European bourgeoisie onto Chinese soil. According to Zhang Weiwei, who worked as an interpreter for Deng Xiaoping, Deng was completely focused on the main task: improving people's livelihoods. Any political reform should be conducted not for its own sake but only to the extent that it served the overall goal.

> He believed that copying the Western model and placing political reform on the top of the agenda, like the Soviets were doing at the time, was utterly foolish. In fact, that was exactly Deng's comment on Gorbachev after their meeting: 'This man may look smart but in fact is stupid.'[40]

In a changing economic environment, where private capital was being accumulated and a new class of entrepreneurs emerging, continued Communist Party rule was essential to guarantee that development benefitted the masses and that the new owners of capital didn't become politically dominant. Moreover, political stability was an absolute requirement for successful economic reform.

In practically every important speech on China's development path from 1978 until his death in 1997, Deng insisted on what he termed the Four Cardinal Principles: 1) Defend the socialist road; 2) Maintain the people's democratic dictatorship; 3) Maintain the leadership of the party; and 4) Adhere to Marxism-Leninism and Mao Zedong Thought. He was extremely clear regarding the importance of a workers' state:

> What kind of democracy do the Chinese people need today? It can only be socialist democracy, people's democracy, and not

> bourgeois democracy... Personal interests must be subordinated to collective ones, the interests of the part to those of the whole, and immediate to long-term interests. In other words, limited interests must be subordinated to overall interests, and minor interests to major ones... It is still necessary to exercise dictatorship over all these anti-socialist elements... The fact of the matter is that socialism cannot be defended or built up without the dictatorship of the proletariat."[41]

Further:

> Collapse is easy, but construction is difficult. If we don't nip bourgeois liberalization in the bud, we may find ourselves in trouble... One of the basic concepts of Marxism is that the socialist system must be defended by the dictatorship of the proletariat... History has proved that a new, rising class that has just taken power is, generally speaking, weaker than the opposing classes. It must therefore resort to dictatorship to consolidate its power. Democracy is practised within the ranks of the people and dictatorship over the enemy. This is the people's democratic dictatorship. It is right to consolidate the people's power by employing the force of the people's democratic dictatorship.[42]

The CPC has not followed the Soviet example of attacking its own history. Although the post-Mao Chinese leadership made serious criticisms of certain policies (in particular the Great Leap Forward and the Cultural Revolution), it has never come anywhere close to repudiating Mao and undermining the basic ideological and historical foundations of Chinese socialism. No Chinese Wall has been constructed between the Mao-era and the post-Mao era; the two phases are inextricably linked, and are both "pragmatic explorations in building socialism conducted by the people under the leadership of the Party."[43]

> We will forever keep Chairman Mao's portrait on Tiananmen Gate as a symbol of our country, and we will always remember him as a founder of our Party and state... We will not do to Chairman Mao what Khrushchev did to Stalin (Deng Xiaoping).[44]

The CPSU leadership suffered a crisis of legitimacy of its own creation. Gorbachev and his colleagues attacked and weakened the organs of working class rule. They colluded in the transfer of political power to anti-socialist forces. In China, however, as Martin Jacques points out, "the rule of the Communist Party is no longer in doubt: it enjoys the prestige that one would expect given the transformation that it has presided over."[45]

## Four decades of peaceful development

> The last thing China wants is war. China is very poor and wants to develop; it can't do that without a peaceful environment. Since we want a peaceful environment, we must cooperate with all of the world's forces for peace. (Deng Xiaoping)[46]

The necessity of maintaining peaceful relations with the imperialist world has been a preoccupation of socialist states from 1917 onwards. All socialist leaderships – those of Lenin, Stalin, Mao Zedong, Ho Chi Minh, Kim Il Sung and Fidel Castro included – have pursued 'peaceful coexistence' to the extent that it has been possible.

The importance of international peace for China's development was implicitly recognised by Mao in the early 1970s, when Henry Kissinger's visit to Beijing opened the way for normalisation of ties, expansion of bilateral trade, and, in 1979, the establishment of diplomatic relations between China and the US. From that time until recently, China has managed to maintain peaceful and broadly cooperative, mutually beneficial relations with the capitalist world, albeit with the complexities and contradictions that form an inevitable part of such a relationship.

Peaceful coexistence has required compromises, one of which has been China relinquishing a direct leadership role in the global transition to socialism. The Soviet Union took on a heavy responsibility as the global centre of progressive forces, giving extensive practical solidarity to socialist states, national liberation movements and progressive governments around the world – including vast economic support to the People's Republic of China between 1949 and 1959; military and economic support to the people's democracies of Eastern Europe, to Cuba, Vietnam, Afghanistan, Angola, Nicaragua, Korea, Ethiopia and elsewhere; training, aid and weapons to the ANC in South Africa, Frelimo in Mozambique, SWAPO in South West Africa (now Namibia), PAIGC in Guinea Bissau, and others.

In addition to direct aid, the Soviet role as the protector of the progressive world – and its position as one of two 'superpowers' – meant that it felt forced to devote an extraordinary portion of its resources to military development. The figures vary wildly, but Russian-American historian Alexander Pantsov estimates that "at the start of Gorbachev's perestroika, in 1985, the Soviets were spending 40 percent of their budget on defence." Indeed Pantsov goes so far to conclude that "the economy of the USSR collapsed under the burden of military expenditures".[47] Certainly this was the objective of Ronald Reagan's 'full-court press' strategy in the early 1980s – vastly increasing US military expenditure, forcing the USSR to follow suit and thereby deepening its economic difficulties.

Former US Secretary of Defense Robert McNamara makes it clear that the US was following a deliberate strategy of using an arms race to weaken the Soviet Union and to damage its reputation.

"The Soviet Union came out of the Second World War with a brilliant military victory… It had three priorities following the war: 1. Renewing the country's infrastructure completely so the Soviet people could reach the promise of communism; 2. Rebuilding and renewing the country's defence in the face of the stalking capitalist world; 3. Gaining new friends in the world, especially in Eastern Europe and the Third World."

He gleefully predicts that "if the United States succeeds in engaging the Soviet Union in an arms race, then all these plans would go out the window… If the Soviet Union is dragged into an arms race and a massive portion of its budget, 40 percent if possible, is allocated to this purpose, then a lesser amount would be left for improving the people's lives, and therefore, the dream of communism, which so many people are awaiting around the world, would be postponed."[48]

The Soviet Union had long stuck to a system of *strategic parity* in nuclear weapons development, sparing no effort to keep up with – but not surpass – the US. As long as it had the ability to retaliate against any US-initiated nuclear strike, it could basically guarantee that such a strike wouldn't take place. But the economic burden was enormous. In a capitalist society, the arms industry is a highly profitable field of investment; creating demand for weapons is a boon for private capital. In a socialist society with a primary accountability to working people, arms manufacturing means diverting human and material resources away from basic needs.

This was not a situation of the Soviet Union's making, but one that was forced on it by a US-led imperialist bloc hell-bent on undermining the socialist world. Indeed, the Soviet leaders routinely proposed multilateral disarmament and a thawing of the Cold War. Boris Ponomarev, chief of the International Department of the CPSU Central Committee from 1955 to 1986, wrote:

> The US has taken the initiative all along in developing and perfecting nuclear weapons and their delivery vehicles ever since the advent of the atom bomb. Each time the USSR was forced to respond to the challenge to strengthen its own defences, to protect the countries of the socialist community and to keep its armed forces adequately equipped with up-to-date weaponry. But the Soviet Union has been and remains the most consistent advocate of the limitation of the arms race, a champion of disarmament under effective international control.[49]

Furthermore, by the late 1970s, the western powers were engaged in a massive 'rollback' operation, supporting rebellions against progressive governments in Angola, Afghanistan, Nicaragua, Mozambique, South Yemen and elsewhere. Vijay Prashad writes that the CIA and the Pentagon "abandoned the idea of the mere 'containment' of communism in favour of using military force to push back against its exertions".[50] All the states under attack had an urgent need for military and civilian aid, which the Soviet Union had little choice but to provide.

The peak of this 'hot' Cold War was in Afghanistan, where the leftist People's Democratic Party of Afghanistan (PDPA) government pleaded with the Soviet leaders to help them quell an Islamic fundamentalist rebellion that was generously funded and armed by the US. The first Soviet troops crossed the border into Afghanistan on 25 December 1979. The scope of their mission was limited: try to restore unity within the PDPA, help the Afghan Army gain the upper hand against the uprising, and come home soon.

> The aim was not to take over or occupy the country. It was to secure the towns and the roads between them, and to withdraw as soon as the Afghan government and its armed forces were in a state to take over the responsibility for themselves.[51]

The intervention turned out to be much more difficult, complex and prolonged than the Soviets had imagined. Their Afghan allies were divided and often demoralised; meanwhile their enemies were armed with sophisticated weaponry, had significant support among the rural population, were fuelled by a vehement hatred of the Russians, and were able to leverage Afghanistan's mountainous territory to their advantage. The Red Army was not trained for a counter-insurgency war; the last major war it had fought was World War II. Norwegian historian Odd Arne Westad writes:

> From 1981 onwards the war turned into a bloody stalemate, in which more than one million Afghans died and at least 25,000 Soviets. In spite of well-planned efforts, the Red Army simply could not control the areas that were within their operational zones — they advanced into rebel strongholds, kept them occupied for weeks or months, and then had to withdraw as the Mujahedin concentrated its forces or, more often, because its opponents attacked elsewhere.[52]

The Red Army didn't lose any of its major battles in Afghanistan; it won control of hundreds of towns, villages and roads, only to lose them again when its focus moved elsewhere. The US deployed increasingly sophisticated weaponry to the rebel groups at just the right rate so as to prolong the war.

The Red Army began a phased withdrawal on 15 May 1988. It had not been defeated as such, but it had manifestly failed in its objectives of cementing PDPA rule and suppressing the rebellion. Meanwhile, the Soviet Union had expended vast economic, military and human resources. Thousands of young lives were lost. Soviet diplomatic clout had reached its nadir. The CPSU's popular legitimacy was damaged, just as had been hoped by US strategists: Zbigniew Brzezinski, who was US National Security Advisor at the time of the Soviet intervention, had talked specifically about "the opportunity of giving to the USSR its Vietnam war."[53]

Afghanistan and the arms race were by no means the sole – or even primary – factor in the Soviet Union's demise, but they certainly contributed.

China on the other hand has been able to enjoy a long period of peace. The Chinese People's Volunteer Army proved during the Korean War (the War to Resist America and Aid Korea) of 1950-53 that People's China was willing and able to defend itself from attack, and no doubt the US drew the appropriate lesson that any military operation against it would be highly risky.

The post-1978 leadership of the CPC realised that, by inserting China into the emerging global supply chains, China could become sufficiently important to the functioning of the global economy that the imperialist states would have to think very carefully about the wisdom of attacking or isolating it. Jude Woodward notes that China's rise has forced many countries to pursue good relations with it, even if they oppose its ideology.

> Rather developed neighbours such as South Korea or Taiwan are deeply economically engaged with China and do not want this derailed... Even America's European allies, notably Germany, France and Britain, were prepared to ignore US opinion on China when they signed up to the Asian Infrastructure Investment Bank.[54]

This could be thought of as a sort of strategic parity with Chinese characteristics, with a much lower price tag than its Soviet equivalent. Additionally, China's integration in the world economy has allowed it to be a part of "the unprecedented global technological revolution, offering a short cut for the country to accelerate its industrial transformation and upgrade its economic structure."[55]

In the relatively safe international environment constructed by the PRC government, China has been able to reduce its military spending from around 7 percent of GDP in 1978 to around 2 percent by the early 1990s (at which level it has remained),[56] allowing more resources to be devoted to improving living standards. Although its strategy doesn't allow it to play an active military role in the defence of friendly states and movements,

China's economic strength means that it is able to provide crucial support for progressive countries around the world, as discussed in the last chapter.

Deng in 1979 looked forward to a point in the future when China would be "a relatively wealthy country of the Third World with a per capita GNP of US $1,000", at which point "our people will enjoy a much higher standard of living than they do now" and "we could offer more assistance to the poor countries of the Third World."[57] This prediction has come true (and the target far surpassed), and China does indeed offer important assistance throughout Africa, Latin America, Central Asia, Southeast Asia, the Caribbean and the Pacific.

In the years since the Obama administration's 'Pivot to Asia' (2011 onwards), and particularly since Donald Trump's trade war – continued by Biden – and escalation in anti-China rhetoric, US-China relations have become increasingly tense, and the trajectory of mutually-beneficial cooperation starting in the early 1970s has been partially reversed. This escalating New Cold War, which aims to slow down China's rise and suppress the emergence of a multipolar system of international relations, is the subject of the final chapter of this book. Suffice to say here that the US is very unlikely to prevent China from reaching its goal of "building a great modern socialist country that is prosperous, strong, democratic, culturally advanced, harmonious and beautiful by 2049."[58]

## Conclusion

> So long as socialism does not collapse in China, it will always hold its ground in the world. (Deng Xiaoping)[59]

Many analysts in the West assumed that, following the collapse of European socialism, China and the other socialist countries would undergo a similar process of counter-revolution and that the "end of history" would be completed. Over three decades later, it's abundantly clear that China, Cuba, Vietnam, Laos and the Democratic People's Republic of Korea are not following that tragic trajectory.

China's reform process has been highly successful; the quality of life of its people continues to improve; it has emerged as a global leader in numerous key areas of science, technological innovation and environmental preservation; it is on the cusp of becoming a 'high income' country;[60] separatism is being effectively contained; and the Communist Party of China remains highly popular, with a membership of close to a hundred million.[61] In short, China is continuing to develop a form of socialism that is appropriate to its own conditions.

Chinese economists often talk of the "latecomers' advantage" in the world of technology, whereby "technological innovation and industrial upgrading can be achieved by imitation, import, and/or integration of existing technologies and industries, all of which implies much lower R&D costs."[62] There's a sense in which this idea applies to the world of politics as well. The USSR was the world's first socialist state, and as such its successes and mistakes constitute indispensable raw material for the study of socialist society. The CPC has been assiduous in learning from the Soviet demise in order to avoid suffering a similar fate. David Shambaugh, citing a study by the Chinese Academy of Social Sciences, sums up some of the key lessons the CPC has tried to absorb. These include "concentrating on economic development and continuously improving people's standard of living", "upholding Marxism as the guiding ideology", "strengthening party leadership", and "continuously strengthening efforts on party building – especially in the areas of ideology, image, organisation, and democratic centralism – in order to safeguard the leadership power in the hands of loyal Marxists."[63]

The issue of maintaining a workers' state and preventing the ascendance and dominance of pro-capitalist 'liberals' is arguably the most important lesson to be learned from the collapse of the USSR. Even with ongoing economic difficulties, it's perfectly conceivable that Soviet socialism could have survived if the top leadership hadn't effectively abandoned the project. In that sense, Gorbachev and his close collaborators bear significant responsibility for the Soviet demise. Allen Lynch, a researcher of Russian politics at the University of Virginia, speculates that, if Gorbachev's predecessor Yuri Andropov had lived longer (he died at the age of 69 after just one year as General Secretary of the CPSU), things might have been very different.

> Judging from Andropov's programmatic statements in 1982-83, as well as his long record at the summit of Soviet politics, there can be little doubt that he would not have countenanced anything remotely resembling Gorbachev's political reforms or that he would have hesitated to use force to stop public challenges to communist rule. Moreover, Andropov's networks in the Party, KGB, government and military were incomparably stronger than Gorbachev's and he might well have leveraged a viable coalition for piecemeal reform of the Soviet economy.[64]

The lessons from the collapse of the Soviet Union must be thoroughly learned by the remaining – and future – socialist states as well as the global working class as a whole. In the current stage of history, where these states constitute a minority and where they face a powerful ideological enemy that is determined to undermine them, these lessons are broadly applicable. They form a key part of the great legacy that the Soviet experience leaves to the global working class.

The Soviet project is by no means a historical relic; its experience is relevant and even crucial to contemporary politics. The heroic feats of the Soviet people live on in China, Vietnam, Cuba, Laos and Korea; in socialist-oriented and progressive states and movements around the world. Even in the territories of the former Soviet Union and the former socialist states in Europe, the memory of better times endures (not least in the considerable defence and retention of Soviet achievements, traditions and forms in Belarus). Their populations are starting, as Fidel Castro predicted they would, to regret the counter-revolution, to miss "those orderly countries, where everybody had clothes, food, medicine, education, where there was no crime and no mafia"; they are coming to "understand *en masse* the historic crime they committed in destroying socialism."[65]

The socialist project lives on in China, and becomes stronger every day. As quality of life gradually catches up with and outstrips that in the leading capitalist countries, and as China emerges as a global leader in science and technology and as a force for peace, multipolarity, sovereign development and environmental preservation, Chinese socialism will become widely recognised as a highly effective, innovative and adaptive branch of Marxism.

## NOTES

1 Martin Jacques. *When China Rules the World: The End of the Western World and the Birth of a New Global Order. 2. ed.* New York, NY: Penguin Books, 2012, p535

2 Zhang Weiwei. *The China Wave: Rise of a Civilizational State*. Hackensack, N.J: World Century, 2012, p96

3 Deng Xiaoping 1992, *Excerpts From Talks Given In Wuchang, Shenzhen, Zhuhai and Shanghai*, Marxist Internet Archive, accessed 27 January 2023, <https://www.marxists.org/reference/archive/deng-xiaoping/1992/179.htm>.

4 *ibid*

5 Mao Zedong 1934, *Be concerned with the well-being of the masses, pay attention to methods of work*, Marxist Internet Archive, accessed 27 January 2023, <https://www.marxists.org/reference/archive/mao/selected-works/volume-1/mswv1_10.htm>.

6 Cited in Isabella Weber. *How China Escaped Shock Therapy: The Market Reform Debate*. Routledge Studies on the Chinese Economy. Abingdon, Oxon ; New York, N.Y: Routledge, 2021, p159

7 Justin Yifu Lin. *Demystifying the Chinese Economy*. Cambridge: Cambridge University Press, 2012, p154

8 *China National Human Development Report Special Edition*, UNDP, accessed 27 January 2023, <https://www.undp.org/china/publications/national-human-development-report-special-edition>.

9 Philip Ball 2018, *China's great leap forward in science*, The Guardian, accessed 27 January 2023, <https://www.theguardian.com/science/2018/feb/18/china-great-leap-forward-science-research-innovation-investment-5g-genetics-quantum-internet>.

10 *Confidence in the Chinese President*, Pew Research Centre Global Indicators Database, accessed 27 January 2023, <https://www.pewresearch.org/global/database/indicator/69/country/cn/>.

11 Jason Lange 2023, *Biden's approval at 40%, near lowest of his presidency*, Reuters, accessed 27 January 2023, <https://www.reuters.com/graphics/USA-BIDEN/POLL/nmopagnqapa/>.

12 Kroeber, *op cit*, p198

13 Peter Nolan. *Understanding China: The Silk Road and the Communist Manifesto*. Routledge Studies on the Chinese Economy 60. London ; New York: Routledge, Taylor & Francis Group, 2016, p2

14 Hu Angang. *China in 2020: A New Type of Superpower*. The Thornton Center Chinese Thinkers Series. Washington, D.C: Brookings Institution Press, 2011, p28

15 Domenico Losurdo, "Has China Turned to Capitalism? Reflections on the Transition from Capitalism to Socialism", *International Critical Thought*, Volume 7, 2017: 15-31

16 Jude Woodward. *The US vs China: Asia's New Cold War? Geopolitical*

*Economy*. Manchester: Manchester University Press, 2017, p248
17 Losurdo, *op cit*
18 Jacques, *When China Rules the World*, p176
19 Cited in Hu Angang, *China in 2020*, p33
20 Deng 1992, *op cit*
21 David L. Shambaugh. *China's Communist Party: Atrophy and Adaptation*. Washington, D.C. : Berkeley: Woodrow Wilson Center Press ; University of California Press, 2008, p65
22 Vladislav Zubok. *A Failed Empire: The Soviet Union in the Cold War from Stalin to Gorbachev*. The New Cold War History. Chapel Hill: University of North Carolina Press, 2007, p307
23 Gennady Zyuganov. *My Russia: The Political Autobiography of Gennady Zyuganov*. Armonk, N.Y: M.E. Sharpe, 1997, p107
24 Michael Roberts 2017, *The Russian revolution: some economic notes*, The Next Recession, accessed 29 January 2023, <https://thenextrecession.wordpress.com/2017/11/08/the-russian-revolution-some-economic-notes/>.
25 Deng 1992, *op cit*
26 Kroeber, *op cit*, p225
27 Peter Nolan. *China's Rise, Russia's Fall: Politics, Economics and Planning in the Transition from Stalinism*. New York: St. Martin's Press, 1995, p312
28 David M. Kotz and Fred Weir. *Revolution from above: The Demise of the Soviet System*. London ; New York: Routledge, 1997, p197
29 Weber, *op cit*, p268
30 *ibid*, p2
31 *ibid*, p7
32 *ibid*, p3
33 Kotz and Weir, *op cit*, p97
34 *GDP per capita (current US$) – China*, World Bank, accessed 31 January 2023, <https://data.worldbank.org/indicator/NY.GDP.PCAP.CD?locations=CN>.
35 Deng Xiaoping 1989, *We Must Adhere To Socialism and Prevent Peaceful Evolution Towards Capitalism*, Marxist Internet Archive, accessed 30 January 2023, <https://www.marxists.org/reference/archive/deng-xiaoping/1989/173.htm>.
36 Cheng Enfu and Liu Zixu, "The Historical Contribution of the October Revolution to the Economic and Social Development of the Soviet Union—Analysis of the Soviet Economic Model and the Causes of Its Dramatic End", *International Critical Thought*, Volume 7, 2017: 297-308
37 Yegor Ligachev. *Inside Gorbachev's Kremlin: The Memoirs Of Yegor Ligachev*. United States: Taylor & Francis, 2018, p286
38 Fidel Castro 1989, *Discurso pronunciado por Fidel Castro Ruz en el acto de despedida de duelo a nuestros internacionalistas caídos durante el cumplimiento de honrosas misiones militares y civiles* (translated by Carlos

Martinez), Cuba.cu, accessed 30 January 2023, <http: / / www.cuba.cu / gobierno / discursos / 1989 / esp / f071289e.html>.

39 Cited in Jennifer M. Rudolph and Michael Szonyi, eds. *The China Questions: Critical Insights into a Rising Power*. Cambridge, Massachusetts: Harvard University Press, 2018, p23

40 Zhang Weiwei 2014, *My Personal Memories as Deng Xiaoping's Interpreter: From Oriana Fallaci to Kim Il-sung to Gorbachev*, HuffPost, accessed 30 January 2023, <https: / / www.huffpost.com / entry / deng-xiaoping-remembered_b_5706143>.

41 Deng Xiaoping 1979, *Uphold the Four Cardinal Principles*, Marxist Internet Archive, accessed 30 January 2023, <https: / / www.marxists.org / reference / archive / deng-xiaoping / 1979 / 115.htm>.

42 Deng 1992, *op cit*

43 Xi Jinping. *The Governance of China*. First edition. Beijing: Foreign Languages Press, 2014, p47

44 Deng Xiaoping 1980, *Answers to the Italian Journalist Oriana Fallaci*, Selected Works of Deng Xiaoping, accessed 30 January 2023, <https: / / dengxiaopingworks.wordpress.com / 2013 / 02 / 25 / answers-to-the-italian-journalist-oriana-fallaci / >.

45 Jacques, *op cit*, p277

46 Deng Xiaoping 1984, *We Regard Reform As A Revolution*, Marxist Internet Archive, accessed 30 January 2023, <https: / / www.marxists.org / reference / archive / deng-xiaoping / 1984 / 193.htm>.

47 Alexander Pantsov and Steven I. Levine. *Deng Xiaoping: A Revolutionary Life*. Oxford: Oxford University Press, 2015, p432

48 Cited in Bahman Azad. *Heroic Struggle, Bitter Defeat: Factors Contributing to the Dismantling of the Socialist State in the Soviet Union*. 1st ed. New York: International Publishers, 2000, p138

49 Boris Ponomarev. *Marxism-Leninism in Today's World, a Living and Effective Teaching: A Reply to Critics*. 1st English ed. Oxford ; New York: Pergamon Press, 1983, p53

50 Vijay Prashad. *The Poorer Nations: A Possible History of the Global South*. London ; New York: Verso, 2012, p112

51 Rodric Braithwaite. *Afgantsy: The Russians in Afghanistan 1979-89*. London: Profile Books, 2012, p123

52 Odd Arne Westad. *The Global Cold War: Third World Interventions and the Making of Our Times*. 1st pbk. ed. Cambridge ; New York: Cambridge University Press, 2007, p356

53 Zbigniew Brzezinski 1998, *Interview with Le Nouvel Observateur*, Marxist Internet Archive, accessed 31 January 2023, <https: / / www.marxists.org / history / afghanistan / archive / brzezinski / 1998 / interview.htm>.

54 Woodward, *op cit*, p251

55 Jenny Clegg. *China's Global Strategy: Towards a Multipolar World*. London ; New York : New York: Pluto Press , 2009, p129

56 *Military expenditure (% of GDP) – China,* World Bank, accessed 31 January 2023, <https: / / data.worldbank.org / indicator / MS.MIL.XPND.GD.ZS?locations=CN>.
57 Deng Xiaoping 1979, *China's Goal Is To Achieve Comparative Prosperity By the End of the Century,* Marxist Internet Archive, accessed 31 January 2023, <https: / / www.marxists.org / reference / archive / deng-xiaoping / 1979 / 87.htm>.
58 Xi Jinping 2021, *Leading CPC to strive for a better world,* Xinhua, accessed 31 January 2023, <http: / / www.xinhuanet.com / english / 2021-07 / 01 / c_1310036749.htm>.
59 Deng 1989, *op cit*
60 Li Xuanmin 2022, *China to become high-income country no later than the end of 2023: economists,* Global Times, accessed 31 January 2023, <https: / / www.globaltimes.cn / page / 202201 / 1250099.shtml>.
61 Guo Rui 2022, *China's Communist Party nears 97 million, with more younger and educated members,* South China Morning Post, accessed 31 January 2023, <https: / / www.scmp.com / news / china / politics / article / 3183669 / chinas-communist-party-grows-near-97-million-its-made-younger>.
62 Justin Yifu Lin 2013, *Advantage of being a latecomer,* China Daily, accessed 31 January 2023, <https: / / www.chinadaily.com.cn / business / 2013-08 / 07 / content_16877935.htm>.
63 Shambaugh, *op cit,* p77
64 Allen C. Lynch 2012, *Deng's and Gorbachev's Reform Strategies Compared,* Russia in Global Affairs, accessed 31 January 2023, <https: / / eng.globalaffairs.ru / articles / dengs-and-gorbachevs-reform-strategies-compared / >.
65 Fidel Castro 1995, *Discurso pronunciado por Fidel Castro Ruz en la recepción efectuada en el Palacio de la Reunificación. Ciudad Ho Chi Minh, Viet Nam* (translated by Carlos Martinez), Cuba.cu, accessed 30 January 2023, <http: / / www.cuba.cu / gobierno / discursos / 1989 / esp / f071289e.html>.

Xian: Muslim food district

# 4

# China's long war on poverty

In late 2020, the Chinese government announced that its goal of eliminating extreme poverty by 2021 (the centenary of the founding of the Communist Party of China) had been met. At the start of the targeted poverty alleviation programme in 2014, just under 100 million people were identified as living below the poverty line; seven years later, the number was zero.

To eradicate extreme poverty in a developing country of 1.4 billion people – which at the time of the founding of the People's Republic of China in 1949 was one of the poorest countries in the world, characterised by widespread malnutrition, illiteracy, foreign domination and technological backwardness – is without doubt "the greatest anti-poverty achievement in history", in the words of UN Secretary General Antonio Guterres.[1]

What does it mean to *not suffer extreme poverty* in China? The most easily measurable aspect is having a daily income higher than the World Bank-defined international poverty line of 1.90 USD per day. But according to the Chinese government's definition, a person can be considered to have left extreme poverty only if the "two assurances and three guarantees" have been met.[2] The two assurances are for adequate food and clothing; the three guarantees are for access to medical services, safe housing with drinking water and electricity, and at least nine years of free education. Meanwhile, the land ownership system in China means that the rural poor have rent-free access to land and housing – putting them in a very different category to the rural poor elsewhere in the world.

Hence ending extreme poverty is far more than simply ensuring that everyone's income is greater than the international poverty line; it means their overall basic needs are adequately met; that they enjoy sufficient access to food, clothing, housing, clean water, modern energy, education and healthcare. As Fudan University professor Zhang Weiwei has pointed out, "the concept of poverty in most other developing countries means lack of basics for life like food, electricity and housing. This is not the case with the poor or the poor regions of China."[3]

While the achievements of the targeted poverty alleviation program are unprecedented, the Communist Party of China's preoccupation with poverty alleviation begins not in 2013 but in 1921. The pursuit of common prosperity and ensuring the fundamental human rights of the Chinese people is a thread that runs throughout the history of the Chinese Revolution and of the People's Republic of China.

The Chinese communists' first major steps towards poverty alleviation were taken in the liberated zones, starting with the Jiangxi–Fujian Soviet in 1931. Under the prevailing social order, the Chinese peasantry (the vast majority of the population) endured atrocious conditions, regularly suffering famines. A century of foreign domination and warlord rule had only deepened the brutal inequality of the feudal system, with the peasantry having to provide both foot soldiers and grain surpluses.

Land reform was the starting point for addressing this monstrous poverty. In their classic book about the land reform process in a small village in Hebei, *Ten Mile Inn*, Isabel and David Crook describe the situation prevailing in 1937:

> Seventy percent of the people of the village lived in the most dire circumstances. For much of the year they subsisted on husks, wild herbs, and watery gruel 'so thin you could see the reflection of the moon in it'... Landlords and peasants alike were pitifully poor. Nevertheless there was a profound difference between them. In times of famine, it was the members of the poor families who died or emigrated, who were forced by poverty to kill or sell children whom they could not feed, who were driven by hunger to join the warlord armies, who were imprisoned for the nonpayment of taxes or lost their meagre property by default for nonpayment of debts.[4]

Land reform acquired different dimensions in different places and at different times, but its essence was "the uncompensated division of landlords' fields among the peasants and outright cancellation of all accumulated rural debt – that is, the destruction of feudalism."[5] Rural collectivisation in the liberated zones allowed for the entire village population to share both the work and the fruits of the land.

Village collectives established public health and education for the first time. Edgar Snow observed that for example, in the Chinese Soviets, "the

Reds attained a higher degree of literacy among the populace in three or four years than had been achieved anywhere else in rural China after centuries."[6]

William Hinton wrote in *Fanshen* about the extraordinary impact that the land reform process had on the rural poor, and particularly women: "For the first time in their lives they felt some measure of control over their destiny. They slept under their own roofs, walked on their own land, planted their own seed, looked forward to harvesting their own crops and, what was perhaps best of all, owed neither grain nor money to any man."[7]

This newly-democratised countryside would form the core support base for the Chinese Revolution in the ensuing decades. As Peng Dehuai (who would later become China's Defence Minister) commented, "tactics are important, but we could not exist if the majority of the people did not support us."[8] The social and economic progress was deeply intertwined with the military resistance against Japanese aggression and, later, the reactionary nationalist armies. Hinton observes that the CPC and its allies "mobilised tens of millions of hard-pressed peasants for resistance, and that resistance, by reaching out to all strata of society, laid the groundwork for the social revolution to come."[9]

During the war against Japanese aggression (1937-45), land expropriation in the liberated zones was paused in the interests of building the broadest possible united front to defend Chinese sovereignty. In this period, the CPC and its armies worked with village committees to reduce rents, reduce interest on loans, and mitigate some of the gross injustices of feudal life.

Following the declaration of the People's Republic of China in October 1949, the land reform programme that had been trialled in the liberated areas was expanded throughout the country. Within a few years, landlordism was eliminated and almost the entire peasantry was organised in collective farms. This was, in the words of Xi Jinping, "the most extensive and profound social reform in Chinese history."[10]

Bourgeois history tends to regard the period from 1949 until 1978 (the start of *Reform and Opening Up*) as a failure in economic terms. According to the standard narrative, the Chinese people discovered to their own cost that common ownership and equality run counter to human nature. And yet in terms of improving the wellbeing of the Chinese people, the period of initial socialist construction was an overwhelming success, in spite of setbacks, mistakes, excesses and an adverse external environment. So much is conceded even by Adrian Wood, principal economist on the team that compiled the first World Bank report on China in 1983, who commented that "the previous 30 to 40 years of Chinese development had been remarkably successful."[11]

The curse of famine had finally been lifted. There was unprecedented progress in public health, leading to an increase in life expectancy from 36 to 67 in the first three decades following liberation. It's true that life expectancy increased globally during this period, but in China's case the increase was particularly steep – from several years below the global average to several years above it. Access to education was universal, and young adult illiteracy was wiped out. China broke out of perennial underdevelopment, building a broad industrial base.

While poor in comparison with most people in the advanced capitalist countries, Chinese people lived significantly better than their counterparts in most other developing countries. In neighbouring India for example, the rural poor continued to face famine, widespread malnutrition, and lack of access to healthcare, education, modern energy and clean water.

Thus it is important to recognise that the period of initial socialist construction played an essential role in China's long march to end poverty.

## A bigger cake

The period of Reform and Opening Up, starting in 1978 with a set of economic policies introduced by the Deng Xiaoping leadership, is not typically discussed in terms of poverty alleviation. And yet it was conceived in precisely those terms: "to rid our country of poverty and backwardness."[12] Professor He Ganqiang of Nanjing University has described the basic goals of the reforms as: "release and develop the social productive forces, boost scientific development, and promote common prosperity for the people."[13]

China in 1978 was still very much a poor country. Thirty percent of the rural population – around 250 million people – lived below the poverty line. Millions experienced inadequate nutrition. While basic industrialisation had been achieved, productivity was still low, a long way behind the advanced capitalist countries. Per capita food production had only grown 10 percent since 1952, although its distribution was now of course far more equitable.[14] Conditions in the countryside were infinitely better than they had been before the revolution, as a result of land reform and the introduction of social welfare; however, the fast-track programme of industrialisation placed a heavy demand on the peasantry to provide a grain surplus that would subsidise the country's overall development.

Kang Bing, former deputy editor-in-chief of *China Daily*, wrote a moving personal account of his childhood growing up in Xi'an:

> Growing up in 1960s and 1970s, my childhood memory is closely connected with hunger. Unable to provide enough food to feed its ever-increasing population which almost doubled in about 30 years, the People's Republic had to adopt a food rationing system to ensure equal distribution of food… In my home city of Xi'an, the monthly quota for one urban resident was 100 grams of cooking oil, half a kilogram of meat, half a dozen eggs and 100 grams of sugar. As for milk, that was given only to families with newborns. Many families today consume the entire monthly quota of oil, meat, eggs and sugar in one

> day. Although the ration system ensured everybody had a share of the available food and prevented starvation deaths, it led to malnutrition among children, adolescents, adults and the elderly alike.[15]

Chen Yun, one of the CPC's foremost economic strategists from the early 1940s onwards, and a leading architect of Reform and Opening Up, warned in 1979:

> Our country has more than 900 million people, 80 percent are peasants. The revolution has been won for 30 years and the people are demanding improvements in their lives. Have there been improvements? Yes. But many places still do not have enough to eat, this is a big problem.[16]

Significant numbers in South China were migrating to Hong Kong in search of a better life. Prominent Chinese economist Justin Yifu Lin puts the case bluntly:

> By 1978 Japan had basically caught up with the United States, and South Korea and Taiwan, China, had narrowed the income gap with developed countries. China, although boasting a complete industrial system, an atomic bomb, and a man-made satellite, had a standard of living a far cry from that of the developed world. The new leadership had to improve national economic performance and make its people as rich as their neighbours, or it might lose support and its legitimacy for rule.[17]

The CPC leadership concluded that scientific and technological development was the crucial factor in pushing forward the evolution of the Chinese Revolution and raising the living standards of the people. To a considerable degree then, Reform and Opening Up was part of a longer-term strategy of *catching up* with the West. Mao himself placed great emphasis on the value of catching up:

> America has 170 million people, we have several times that number, plentiful resources, and a similar climate; catching up is possible. Should we catch up? Of course we should, or else what are you 600 million people doing? ... In another 50 or 60 years, we should be ahead of them. This is a responsibility, we have this many people, this much territory, this many resources, and a socialist society. If in 50 or 60 years you still can't catch up to America, what's the matter with you? You deserve

> to have your membership in the human race revoked![18]

Lenin wrote in his 1918 article *The Immediate Tasks of the Soviet Government* that "socialism calls for a conscious mass advance to greater productivity of labour compared with capitalism."[19] Yet three decades after the establishment of the PRC, China's labour productivity remained far behind that of the US. Part of the reason for this is that China had been cut off from technological developments in the capitalist world as a result of a near-total blockade imposed by the Truman administration. In the same article, Lenin had opined that "the possibility of building socialism depends exactly upon our success in combining the Soviet power and the Soviet organisation of administration with the up-to-date achievements of capitalism." But these up-to-date achievements of capitalism were beyond China's reach during the 1950s and 60s.

The improvement in relations with the US – starting with Henry Kissinger's secret visit to Beijing in 1971 and President Nixon's visit the following year – opened the way for China to acquire capital goods, attract investment and learn from the West's scientific, technological and managerial innovations. With the formal establishment of US-China bilateral relations in 1979 and the initiation of normal trade relations in 1980, China also gained access to a global market.

Concurrently, the Chinese leadership was developing a deeper understanding of the situation in the countryside and the need to urgently improve living standards. Isabella Weber writes in her 2021 book *How China Escaped Shock Therapy* that, somewhat ironically, many of the young economists pushing for reform in the rural economy were urban intellectuals that had been 'sent down' to the countryside during the Cultural Revolution:

> The experience of rural poverty was the starting point for a movement of young intellectuals who were dedicated to rural reform after their return to the urban centres.[20]

Xi Jinping, himself a 'sent-down youth' in the 1970s, made a similar point in 1990, while working as party secretary in Ningde, Fujian:

> Many Party members are sent to extremely remote, impoverished areas, where they learn about the people's suffering firsthand… Upon their return, Party members always say that they have developed more empathy for the people, and they feel a stronger sense of responsibility to serve them.[21]

Solving the problem of rural poverty was therefore the starting point for the reform process, which emphasised productivity, science and technology as means of generating greater social wealth. That process has been spectacularly successful in its poverty reduction aims. Indeed the UN Development Program in 2010 described China as having achieved "the most rapid decline in absolute poverty ever witnessed."[22]

Between 1978 and 2013, the number of people living below the World Bank threshold of absolute poverty dropped from 80 percent to 9 percent of the population.[23] While China's per capita GDP was approximately the same as India's in 1978, by 2020 it was five times higher. Per capita GDP figures are partially misleading here since, in the pre-reform era, many essential goods and services were provided freely to the population (hence the Chinese peasantry enjoyed a far higher standard of living than the Indian peasantry, in spite of having a similar income). Nonetheless, the vast majority of Chinese people experienced a dramatic improvement in living standards in the decades following the adoption of Reform and Opening Up.

Food production increased substantially, such that "China finally produced enough grain to abolish grain rationing altogether."[24] People also benefitted from a much more varied diet. In the 1980s, key consumer goods such as refrigerators and washing machines went from being relatively rare to being almost universal. The rate of access to clean water and modern energy also increased dramatically.

British economist John Ross judges that:

> the most comprehensive criteria for judging the overall impact of social and environmental conditions in a country is average life expectancy – as this sums up and balances the combined effect of all positive and negative economic, social, environmental, health, educational and other trends.[25]

Average life expectancy in China in 1975 was 62 – impressive for a large developing country at the time, certainly when compared with India's 49. However in the US it was 71. By 2022, China's average life expectancy had reached 78.2,[26] while in the US it was 76.4 (having dropped from a peak of 78.8 in 2019.[27]

Infant mortality rate is another important poverty indicator. Colin Mackerras notes that infant mortality in China "fell from 37.6 deaths per 1,000 live births around the late 1970s to 5.4 per 1,000 in 2020, just lower than the United States, where it was 5.69 per 1000 live births the same year."[28]

Arthur Kroeber writes that between 1988 and 2008, average per capita income in China grew by 229 percent – "ten times the global average of 24 percent, and far ahead of the rates for India (34 percent)."[29]

Thus it is beyond dispute that economic reforms have been tremendously impactful in terms of reducing poverty in China. What is also beyond dispute is that inequality has grown at a startling rate. While the cake is much bigger – China's GDP rose from 150 billion USD in 1978 to 17.7 trillion USD in

2021 – it has been divided very unequally.[30] But even the smallest slices are much larger than they were. The late Egyptian political scientist Samir Amin, who was by no means uncritical of Chinese socialism, pointed out that "the growth of income has been a reality for almost all the population even if that growth has been much higher for some than it has been for the others." Therefore in China, "growing inequality has been accompanied by reduction of poverty", unlike in the vast majority of countries of the Global South, where "growth – and in some cases significant high growth – has benefited only a minority."[31]

The Italian Marxist philosopher Domenico Losurdo made a profound analysis of the inequalities introduced as a result of China's market reforms. He pointed out that there are two types of inequality to consider: "1) inequality existing on the global scale between the most and least developed countries; and 2) the inequality existing within each individual country." Losurdo states that China's rise constitutes a most extraordinary contribution to the fight against global-scale inequality. He also points to the existence of an "absolute inequality that exists between life and death" which Chinese socialism has addressed with extraordinary success, "eliminating once and for all the absolute qualitative inequality inherent in starvation and the risk of starvation."[32]

None of which is to say that inequality in China is not a problem. It is a serious problem, and is recognised as such by China's government, which has been actively working to reduce inequality for the last two decades. Kroeber notes that since 2000, Beijing has launched:

> a host of policies specifically designed to reduce urban-rural inequality and inequalities between poor and rich regions. Programs to boost rural incomes have included: a relaxation of rules requiring farmers to grow grain, enabling them to increase production of more profitable cash crops; the easing and finally abolition of taxes and fees on agricultural production; a major push to build farm-to-market roads, helping farmers gain access to richer urban consumers; and stepped-up investments in food processing industries.[33]

All this has been combined with vast infrastructure development programmes, particularly in the poorer Western and Central regions. Kroeber observes that the urban-rural income gap started to shrink from 2009. In addition to the urban-rural gap, inequality between lower-income groups and higher-income groups has also been waning since 2010. Compulsory free 9-year education was established in 2007, and the rural cooperative medical insurance system was set up in 2003. The rural minimum living standard guarantee (dibao) programme, first introduced in Shanghai in 1993, is "one of the largest minimum income cash transfer schemes in the world."[34] These and other steps to restore a functioning social welfare system aim to address the inequality and unfairness associated with the market economy.

In sum, it should be clear that four decades of market reforms and the expansion of private capital, while introducing a level of inequality that would have been unimaginable in pre-1978 China, have nevertheless played an indispensable role in reducing poverty. Indeed, as mentioned above, eliminating poverty was the central motivating force of Reform and Opening Up. As Deng Xiaoping said in 1987: "to uphold socialism, a socialism that is to be superior to capitalism, it is imperative first and foremost to eliminate poverty."[35]

## Targeted poverty alleviation

At the 18th National Congress of the CPC in 2012, General Secretary Xi Jinping announced the two centenary goals: "realising a moderately prosperous society by the centenary of the CPC in 2021 and turning China into a prosperous, democratic, culturally advanced and harmonious modern socialist country by the centenary of the People's Republic of China in 2049."[36] The most important component of becoming a "moderately prosperous society" was to eliminate absolute poverty. Towards this goal, in 2014, China's government embarked upon the largest systematic poverty alleviation programme in history.

Researchers at the Tricontinental Institute have published a dossier about the targeted poverty alleviation programme, *Serve the People: The Eradication of Extreme Poverty in China*, based on extensive research, case studies and interviews, carried out by a small team on the ground in China. The dossier describes the four questions that guided implementation of the programme: "Who should be lifted out of poverty? Who carries out the work? What measures need to be taken to address poverty? How can evaluations be done to ensure that people remain out of poverty?"[37]

To help answer the first question, that is, to identify those living in extreme poverty, the dossier notes that 800,000 CPC cadres, community workers and volunteers were mobilised to "visit and survey every household across the country, identifying 89.62 million poor people in 29.48 million households and 128,000 villages." Having identified those living below the poverty line, the cadres worked with each family and community to identify specific measures to improve their situation.

As noted in the introduction to this chapter, the Chinese government's definition of extreme poverty is not based solely on income level, but also includes the *two assurances* (for adequate food and clothing) and *three guarantees* (access to medical services, safe housing with drinking water and electricity, and at least nine years of free education). As such, permanently ending extreme poverty is not a unidimensional problem that can be solved simply by transferring cash to poor families. To create family- and community-specific solutions to poverty has required an extraordinary level of mobilisation.

> Three million carefully selected cadres were dispatched to poor villages, forming 255,000 teams that reside there. Living in humble conditions for generally one to three years at a time, the teams worked alongside poor peasants, local officials, and volunteers until each household was lifted out of poverty... By 2015, all poor villages had a resident team, and every poor household had an assigned cadre to help in the process of being lifted, and more importantly, of lifting themselves out of poverty.[38]

The targeted poverty alleviation campaign used a wide array of methods. Millions of jobs were created through the development of local production units (with the corresponding access to funding, training, equipment and markets), and also through the innovative use of technology, for example using e-commerce to connect small rural businesses with China's vast online market. A report by China's State Council Information Office discusses the launch of e-commerce projects throughout the countryside:

> All 832 poor counties have been included in the initiative... The number of e-businesses in these counties grew from 1.32 million in 2016 to 3.11 million in 2020.[39]

As part of the poverty alleviation programme, many industries have been transferred from the urban coastal areas to the rural inland zones, with more than 300,000 industrial bases having been built in the last decade. The government "has facilitated the transfer of food processing, clothes manufacturing, and other labour-intensive industries from the east to the west. With the growth of such specialty industries, poor areas have gained economic momentum."[40] Thus while working to eliminate poverty, China is also making progress towards the vision outlined by Marx and Engels 150 years ago of "abolishing the antithesis between town and country".[41]

The poverty alleviation programme is also connected to China's bid to create an 'ecological civilisation', protecting ecosystems, reducing pollution and getting to net zero greenhouse gas emissions. For example, millions of people have been employed in the restoration and protection of forests and grasslands.[42]

Education also plays an important role in poverty alleviation, and in recent years several million teachers have been dispatched to the poorer Central and Western regions.[43] In the decade from 2010 to 2020, the average number of years of education for Chinese adults increased from nine to ten, and the number of people with tertiary education nearly doubled, from 8,930 to 15,467 per 100,000.[44] Remote learning techniques have also been widely deployed in impoverished areas, greatly aided by improvements in communications infrastructure: over 98 percent of poor villages now have access to optical fibre communications and 4G technology, up from less than 70 percent in 2017.[45]

The authors of the Tricontinental dossier note that, "for families who are living in extremely remote areas or exposed to frequent natural disasters, it is near impossible to break the cycle of poverty without moving to more habitable environments." As such, almost 10 million people were voluntarily relocated from remote zones to newly built urban communities, which included schools, hospitals, childcare facilities and cultural centres.

As noted at the beginning of the chapter, the targeted poverty alleviation programme succeeded in reducing the number of people living in absolute poverty from just under 100 million people to zero. As Xi Jinping observed:

> thanks to the sustained efforts of the Chinese people from generation to generation, those who once lived in poverty no longer have to worry about food or clothing or access to education, housing and medical insurance.[46]

What's more, the goal of eliminating extreme poverty was fulfilled while the country was concurrently battling a pandemic which has driven millions into poverty throughout the world. The success of this campaign should be considered as testament to China's socialist system: no state with a capitalist ruling class has ever made such a comprehensive and systematic effort to provide people's most basic human rights. The orientation of government policy towards the needs of the poor; the strong institutional and infrastructural framework; and the willingness of millions of cadre to participate in the campaign: all these are reflections of a vibrant Chinese socialism.

## Towards common prosperity

With the completion of the targeted poverty alleviation campaign and the accomplishment of the first centenary goal, China has scored an important victory; but the long war on poverty continues, and the second centenary goal has now come into sharper focus. Building a great modern socialist country in all respects implies taking on *relative* poverty, improving per capita GDP, revitalising rural areas, and reducing inequality between regions and groups. It is time for "making the cake bigger and better and sharing it fairly through rational institutional arrangements."[47]

In an article entitled *Making Solid Progress Toward Common Prosperity*, based on a speech at the 10th meeting of the Central Financial and Economic Affairs Commission on 17 August 2021, Xi Jinping explained that the success of the targeted poverty alleviation campaign had "created conditions conducive to bringing about prosperity for all," and that China was now advancing into "a historical stage in which we will make solid steps toward common prosperity."[48]

In a detailed analysis of the concept of *common prosperity*, British academic Michael Dunford notes that the phrase first appeared in an article in *People's Daily* on 25 September 1953, and was posed as a key goal of China's socialist construction.[49] Deng Xiaoping talked frequently about common prosperity, highlighting that the principle of "letting a few get rich first" was only a means of accelerating the advance of the entire population, and that the basic aims and structures of socialism should not be thrown out with the introduction of certain elements of capitalism:

> Wealth in a socialist society belongs to the people. To get rich in a socialist society means prosperity for the entire people. The principles of socialism are: first, development of production and second, common prosperity. We permit some people and some regions to become prosperous first, for the purpose of achieving common prosperity faster.[50]

Jiang Zemin also often invoked the idea of common prosperity: "We will ensure that our people will reap the benefit of continued economic growth and gradually achieve common prosperity."[51] In his report to the Eighteenth National Congress of the CPC, Hu Jintao described common prosperity as "the fundamental principle of socialism with Chinese characteristics", adding that the government must:

> adjust the pattern of national income distribution, tighten its regulation by secondary distribution and work hard to narrow income gaps so that all the people can share in more fruits of development in a fair way and move steadily toward common prosperity.[52]

Thus each generation of the leadership of the People's Republic of China has actively promoted the concept of common prosperity. However, with the completion of the targeted poverty alleviation programme, common prosperity becomes a major policy priority. In a speech given in January 2021 at a seminar for provincial and ministerial level officials on studying and implementing the guiding principles of the Fifth Plenary Session of the 19th CPC Central Committee, Xi Jinping said:

> Realising common prosperity is more than an economic goal. It is a major political issue that bears on our Party's governance foundation. We cannot allow the gap between the rich and the poor to continue growing… We cannot permit the wealth gap to become an unbridgeable gulf… We must be proactive about

> narrowing the gaps between regions, between urban and rural areas, and between rich and poor people. We should promote all-around social progress and well-rounded personal development, and advocate social fairness and justice, so that our people enjoy the fruits of development in a fairer way. We should see that people have a stronger sense of fulfilment, happiness, and security and make them feel that common prosperity is not an empty slogan but a concrete fact that they can see and feel for themselves.[53]

In the above-cited article, *Making Solid Progress Toward Common Prosperity,* Xi Jinping put forward various targets and timelines: to make "solid progress toward bringing prosperity to all", reducing income inequality by the end of the 14th five-year plan in 2025; ensuring equitable access to basic public services by 2035; and "basically achieving" common prosperity by 2049, with "gaps between individual incomes and actual consumption levels narrowed to an appropriate range." Xi called for an action plan to be formulated with these targets in mind. And since the Chinese government is not in the habit of making empty promises, the action plan should include "rational and workable systems of targets and methods of evaluation."

The renewed emphasis on common prosperity also sends a message about maintaining the primacy of the public sector of China's economy, since it is the role of the state-owned companies, government planning and macroeconomic regulation which ensures the country's overall economic activity serves the people as a whole. As the influential Chinese academic Cheng Enfu pointed out in 2014:

> If the public economy is not treated as dominant in the socialist economy, government's adjustment function will be weakened greatly, which will greatly hinder the implementation of the economic and social development strategy of the country and the country will lack the economic basis that will guarantee the fundamental interest of the masses and common prosperity.[54]

Hu Leming, Deputy Director of the Institute of Economics, Chinese Academy of Social Sciences, makes a similar point about the relationship between the public economy and the pursuit of common prosperity:

> Without the leading position of the public economy, there will be no solid economic basis and powerful material means and basis for governance by the Communist Party, nor for the whole socialist superstructure, and we will have no means to prevent growing income disparity and will not be able to realise common prosperity.[55]

Deng Xiaoping often insisted that "predominance of public ownership and common prosperity are the two fundamental socialist principles that we must adhere to."[56] The renewed emphasis on common prosperity is an important step in the ongoing attempts to "strike a proper balance between efficiency and fairness",[57] to impose limits on the influence of the owners of capital, to reassert the primacy of the state-owned economy and the interests of the working class, and to reiterate that the CPC will never "take the evil road of changing our flags and banners."[58]

While the common prosperity campaign is in its early stages, there have already been a number of important developments, including a regulatory crackdown on the private education sector,[59] a set of measures to prevent gaming addiction among children,[60] the imposition of stricter rent controls,[61] and several laws and regulations to protect the rights of workers in the "gig economy". Tech companies "must now sign labour contracts with their gig workers, and provide them with the insurance coverage of state-run insurers"[62]; furthermore, China's Trade Union Law has been revised to enable and encourage unionisation of gig economy workers.[63]

China's success in eliminating extreme poverty is "far from a full stop" and we can expect the Chinese party and government to continue "consolidating and expanding poverty alleviation achievements,"[64] deepening the campaign to end relative poverty and achieve common prosperity.

Meanwhile in the advanced capitalist countries, where the capitalist class is the ruling class, and where neoliberal economic theory has dominated for the last four decades, we are seeing an alarming rise in poverty and inequality. Rather than pursuing common prosperity, the US and its allies are drifting towards mass destitution. This disparity highlights that China's continuing achievements in poverty alleviation are a function of its socialist system. As Deng Xiaoping said in 1987, ultimately, "only the socialist system can eradicate poverty."[65]

## NOTES

1 Antonio Guterres 2019, *Helping 800 Million People Escape Poverty Was Greatest Such Effort in History, Says Secretary-General, on Seventieth Anniversary of China's Founding*, United Nations, accessed 14 February 2023, <https://www.un.org/press/en/2019/sgsm19779.doc.htm>.

2 Xi Jinping 2019, *Deliver the Two Assurances and Three Guarantees*, Qiushi, accessed 14 February 2023, <http://en.qstheory.cn/2022-02/23/c_705865.htm>.

3 Zhang Weiwei. *The China Horizon: Glory and Dream of a Civilizational State*. Hackensack, NJ: World Century, 2016, p16

4 Isabel and David Crook. *Ten Mile Inn: Mass Movement in a Chinese Village*. 1st ed. The Pantheon Asia Library. New York: Pantheon Books, 1979, p8

5 Israel Epstein. *From Opium War to Liberation*. Hong Kong: Joint Pub. (H.K.) Co., 1998, p123

6 Edgar Snow. *Red Star over China*. London: Grove Press UK, 2018, p186

7 William Hinton. *Fanshen: A Documentary of Revolution in a Chinese Village*. New York: Monthly Review Press, 2008, p155

8 Snow, *op cit*, p277

9 Hinton, *op cit*, p84

10 Xi Jinping 2022, *Full text of Xi Jinping's speech at ceremony marking centenary of Communist Youth League of China*, Xinhua, accessed 14 February 2023, <https://english.news.cn/20220512/1903fe24c27140f2a8cb051dc10a3f9e/c.html>.

11 Cited in Isabella Weber. *How China Escaped Shock Therapy: The Market Reform Debate*. Routledge Studies on the Chinese Economy. Abingdon, Oxon ; New York, N.Y: Routledge, 2021, p104

12 Deng Xiaoping 1978, *Emancipate the Mind, Seek Truth From Facts and Unite As One In Looking to the Future*, Marxist Internet Archive, accessed 14 February 2023, <https://www.marxists.org/reference/archive/deng-xiaoping/1978/110.htm>.

13 He Ganqiang 2012. *Promoting common prosperity through improving ownership relations in China*, International Critical Thought, 2:2, 156-170, DOI: 10.1080/21598282.2012.684279

14 Justin Yifu Lin. *Demystifying the Chinese Economy*. Cambridge: Cambridge University Press, 2012, p152

15 Kang Bing 2022, *Chinese people's journey from malnutrition to over-nutrition*, China Daily, accessed 14 February 2023, <http://epaper.chinadaily.com.cn/a/202201/05/WS61d4ea84a3108267e13211a7.html>.

16 Weber, *op cit*, p159

17 Lin, *op cit*, p153

18 Cited in Liu Mingfu. *The China Dream: Great Power Thinking & Strategic Posture in the Post-American Era*. New York, NY: CN Times Books, 2015, p17

19 Vladimir Lenin 1918, *The Immediate Tasks of the Soviet Government*, Marxist Internet Archive, accessed 14 February 2023, <https://www.marxists.org/archive/lenin/works/1918/mar/x03.htm>.
20 Weber, *op cit*, p157
21 Xi Jinping. *Up and out of Poverty: Selected Speeches in Fujian*. Beijing: Foreign Languages Press, 2016, p46
22 Cited in Neil Hirst. *The Energy Conundrum: Climate Change, Global Prosperity, and the Tough Decisions We Have to Make*. New Jersey: World Scientific, 2018, p68
23 Tings Chak et al 2021, *Serve the People: The Eradication of Extreme Poverty in China*, Tricontinental Institute, accessed 6 May 2022, <https://thetricontinental.org/studies-1-socialist-construction/>.
24 Ang Yuen Yuen. *How China Escaped the Poverty Trap*. Cornell Studies in Political Economy. Ithaca ; London: Cornell University Press, 2016, p95
25 John Ross. *China's Great Road: Lessons for Marxist Theory and Socialist Practices*. Glasgow: Praxis Press, 2021, p18
26 *China's average life expectancy rises to 78.2 years*, Xinhua, accessed 14 February 2023, <https://english.news.cn/20220712/3257b383c8444bcf9c0282c40a9b9383/c.html>.
27 Yuki Noguchi 2022, *American life expectancy is now at its lowest in nearly two decades*, NPR, accessed 14 February 2023, <https://www.npr.org/sections/health-shots/2022/12/22/1144864971/american-life-expectancy-is-now-at-its-lowest-in-nearly-two-decades>.
28 Colin Mackerras 2021, *Common prosperity should be valued in China and not disparaged by critics*, Pearls and Irritations, accessed 14 February 2023, <https://johnmenadue.com/common-prosperity-should-be-valued-in-china-and-not-disparaged-by-critics/>.
29 Arthur R. Kroeber. *China's Economy: What Everyone Needs to Know*. New York, NY: Oxford University Press, 2016, p198
30 The cake metaphor was popularised in: Xi Jinping 2013, *Align Our Thinking with the Guidelines of the Third Plenary Session of the 18th CPC Central Committee*, Qiushi, accessed 7 May 2022, <http://en.qstheory.cn/2020-10/14/c_607589.htm>.
31 Samir Amin 2018, *Interview: 'There is a structural crisis of capitalism'*, Frontline, accessed 14 February 2023, <https://frontline.thehindu.com/other/there-is-a-structural-crisis-of-capitalism/article10107168.ece>.
32 Domenico Losurdo 2017. *Has China Turned to Capitalism?—Reflections on the Transition from Capitalism to Socialism*, International Critical Thought, 7:1, 15-31, DOI: 10.1080/21598282.2017.1287585
33 Kroeber, *op cit*, p199
34 Jennifer Golan et al 2017, *Unconditional Cash Transfers in China: Who Benefits from the Rural Minimum Living Standard Guarantee (Dibao) Program?*, World Development, Volume 93, 2017, 316-336, <https://doi.

org/10.1016/j.worlddev.2016.12.011>

35 Deng Xiaoping 1987, *To Uphold Socialism We Must Eliminate Poverty*, China.org.cn, accessed 14 February 2023, <http://www.china.org.cn/english/features/dengxiaoping/103350.htm>.

36 Xi Jinping. *The Governance of China*. First edition. Beijing: Foreign Languages Press, 2014, p6

37 Chak et al, *op cit*

38 *ibid*

39 *Poverty Alleviation: China's Experience and Contribution* (2021), The State Council Information Office of the People's Republic of China, accessed 14 February 2023, <http://english.scio.gov.cn/whitepapers/2021-04/06/content_77380652_5.htm>.

40 *ibid*

41 Friedrich Engels 1873, *The Housing Question*, Marxist Internet Archive, accessed 14 February 2023, <https://www.marxists.org/archive/marx/works/subject/hist-mat/hous-qst/ch03b.htm>.

42 Lei Ming et al 2021, *Synthesize dual goals: A study on China's ecological poverty alleviation system*, Journal of Integrative Agriculture, 20:4, 1042-1059, <https://doi.org/10.1016/S2095-3119(21)63635-3>

43 See for example: *China to send 22,000-plus teachers to support poor areas*, Xinhua, accessed 14 February 2023, <https://www.xinhuanet.com/english/2020-06/10/c_139129092.htm>.

44 *Chinese increasingly likely to attend university, nearly all young adults are literate*, The Bank of Finland Institute for Emerging Economies, accessed 14 February 2023, <https://www.bofit.fi/en/monitoring/weekly/2021/vw202120_3/>.

45 *Internet empowers China's battle against COVID-19 as netizens near 1 bln*, Xinhua, accessed 14 February 2023, <http://www.news.cn/english/2021-02/03/c_139719149.htm>.

46 Xi Jinping 2022, *2022 New Year address by President Xi Jinping*, Ministry of Foreign Affairs of the People's Republic of China, accessed 14 February 2023, <https://www.fmprc.gov.cn/mfa_eng/wjdt_665385/zyjh_665391/202112/t20211231_10478096.html>.

47 *Foreign Ministry Spokesperson Wang Wenbin's Regular Press Conference on January 7, 2022*, Ministry of Foreign Affairs of the People's Republic of China, accessed 14 February 2023, <https://www.fmprc.gov.cn/mfa_eng/xwfw_665399/s2510_665401/2511_665403/202201/t20220107_10480006.html>.

48 Xi Jinping 2022, *Making Solid Progress Toward Common Prosperity*, Qiushi, accessed 14 February 2023, <http://en.qstheory.cn/2022-01/18/c_699346.htm>.

49 Michael Dunford 2021, *On Common Prosperity*, Friends of Socialist China, accessed 14 February 2023, <https://socialistchina.org/2021/10/17/on-common-prosperity/>.

50 Deng Xiaoping 1986, *Replies To the American TV Correspondent Mike Wallace*, Marxist Internet Archive, accessed 14 February 2023, <https://www.marxists.org/reference/archive/deng-xiaoping/1986/192.htm>.
51 Jiang Zemin 1997, *Speech by President Jiang Zemin of The People's Republic of China*, Asia Society, accessed 14 February 2023, <https://asiasociety.org/speech-president-jiang-zemin-peoples-republic-china>.
52 Hu Jintao 2012, *Full text of Hu's report at 18th Party Congress*, China Daily, accessed 14 February 2023, <https://www.chinadaily.com.cn/china/19thcpcnationalcongress/2012-11/18/content_29578562.htm>.
53 Xi Jinping 2021, *Understanding the New Development Stage, Applying the New Development Philosophy, and Creating a New Development Dynamic*, Quishi, accessed 14 February 2023, <http://en.qstheory.cn/2021-07/08/c_641137.htm>.
54 Cheng Enfu (ed). *Delving into the Issues of the Chinese Economy and the World by Marxist Economists*. Canut Int Publishers, 2020, p115
55 *ibid*, p125
56 Deng Xiaoping 1985, *Unity Depends On Ideals and Discipline*, Marxist Internet Archive, accessed 14 February 2023, <https://www.marxists.org/reference/archive/deng-xiaoping/1985/102.htm>.
57 Hu Jintao 2012, *Full text of Hu's report at 18th Party Congress*, China Daily, accessed 14 February 2023, <https://www.chinadaily.com.cn/china/19thcpcnationalcongress/2012-11/18/content_29578562.htm>.
58 *China party says no to political reform on eve of key meet* (2013), Reuters, accessed 14 February 2023, <https://www.reuters.com/article/china-politics-idUSL3N0IT0ZN20131108>.
59 Chang Che 2021, *After online tutoring, why is China cracking down on private schools?*, Sup China, accessed 14 February 2023, <https://supchina.com/2021/09/09/after-online-tutoring-why-is-china-cracking-down-on-private-schools/>.
60 John Letzing 2012, *What's behind China's video game restrictions?*, World Economic Forum, accessed 14 February 2023, <https://www.weforum.org/agenda/2021/09/what-s-behind-china-s-video-game-restrictions/>.
61 Pearl Liu and Lam Ka-sing 2021, *China to cap annual urban rent increases at 5 per cent to rein in runaway prices and make homes affordable to job seekers*, SCMP, accessed 17 May 2022, <https://www.scmp.com/business/money/money-news/article/3147047/china-cap-annual-urban-rent-increases-5-cent-rein-runaway>.
62 Masha Borak 2021, *Can China's drive to protect gig economy workers work by pressing Big Tech to give more?*, SCMP, accessed 14 February 2023, <https://www.scmp.com/tech/big-tech/article/3148590/can-chinas-drive-protect-gig-economy-workers-work-pressing-big-tech>.
63 Ding Xiangyu 2022, *China Revises Trade Union Law to Protect Gig Workers*, China Justice Observer, accessed 14 February 2023, <https://www.

chinajusticeobserver.com / a / china-revises-trade-union-law-to-protect-gig-workers>.

64 *Xinhua Commentary: Is China's poverty alleviation standard too low to deserve a victory?*, Xinhua, accessed 14 February 2023, <http: / / www.xinhuanet.com / english / 2021-02 / 26 / c_139770039.htm>.

65 Deng Xiaoping 1987, *China Can Only Take the Socialist Road*, Marxist Internet Archive, accessed 14 February 2023, <https: / / www.marxists.org / reference / archive / deng-xiaoping / 1987 / 23.htm>.

**Urumqi: public dancing**

# 5

# Manufacturing consent for the containment and encirclement of China

> If you're not careful, the newspapers will have you hating the people who are being oppressed, and loving the people who are doing the oppressing. (Malcolm X)

THE Western media is waging a systematic and ferocious propaganda war against China. In the court of Western public opinion, China stands accused of an array of terrifying crimes: conducting a genocide against Uyghur Muslims in Xinjiang; wiping out democracy in Hong Kong; militarising the South China Sea; attempting to impose colonial control over Taiwan; carrying out a land grab in Africa; preventing Tibetans and Inner Mongolians from speaking their languages; spying on the good peoples of the democratic world; and more.

Australian scholar Roland Boer has characterised these accusations as "atrocity propaganda – an old anti-communist and indeed anti-anyone-who-does-not-toe-the-Western-line approach that tries to manufacture a certain image for popular consumption." Boer observes that this propaganda serves to create an impression of China as a brutal authoritarian dystopia which "can only be a fiction for anyone who actually spends some time in China, let alone lives there."[1]

It's not difficult to understand why China would be subjected to this sort of elaborate disinformation campaign. This media offensive is part of the imperialist world's ongoing attempts to reverse the Chinese Revolution, to subvert Chinese socialism, to weaken China, to diminish its role in international affairs and, as a result, to undermine the global trajectory towards multipolarity and a future free from hegemonism. As journalist Chen Weihua has pointed out, "the reasons for the intensifying US propaganda war are obvious: Washington views a fast-rising China as a challenge to its primacy around the world." Furthermore, "the success of a country with a different political system is unacceptable to politicians in Washington."[2]

Propaganda wars can also be war propaganda. In this case, the war in question is the escalating US-led New Cold War.[3] The various slanders against China – particularly the most lurid accusations, such as that of genocide in Xinjiang – have much in common with the 2003 allegations regarding Iraq's weapons of mass destruction, or the 2011 allegation that the Libyan state under Muammar Gaddafi was preparing a massacre in Benghazi. These narratives are constructed specifically in order to mobilise public opinion in favour of imperialist foreign policy: waging a genocidal war against the people of Iraq; bombing Libya into the Stone Age; and, today, conducting a wide-ranging campaign of economic coercion, political subversion and military threats against the People's Republic of China.

In his book *Neo-Colonialism, the Last Stage of Imperialism,* Kwame Nkrumah, Pan-Africanist and first President of Ghana, discusses how "ideological and cultural weapons in the form of intrigues, manoeuvres and slander campaigns" were employed by the Western powers during the Cold War in order to undermine the socialist countries and the newly-liberated territories of Africa, Asia and Latin America:

> While Hollywood takes care of fiction, the enormous monopoly press, together with the outflow of slick, clever, expensive magazines, attends to what it chooses to call 'news'... A flood of anti-liberation propaganda emanates from the capital cities of the West, directed against China, Vietnam, Indonesia, Algeria, Ghana and all countries which hack out their own independent path to freedom.[4]

The mechanisms for such "intrigues, manoeuvres and slander campaigns" have changed little since Nkrumah's day. British media analysts David Cromwell and David Edwards explore the concept of the *propaganda blitz* – "fast-moving attacks intended to inflict maximum damage in minimum time." These media attacks are "communicated with high emotional intensity and moral outrage" and, crucially, give the appearance of enjoying consensus support among experts, academics, journalists and politicians.[5] This consensus "generates the impression that everyone knows that the claim is truthful."[6] Such a consensus is most powerful when it includes not only right-wing ideologues but also prominent leftist commentators. "If even celebrity progressive journalists – people famous for their principled stands, and colourful socks and ties – join the denunciations, then there must be something to the claims. At this point, it becomes difficult to doubt it."

When it comes to China, many such commentators are only too happy to oblige: British columnist Owen Jones for example, writing for *The Guardian*, has asserted that "despite the denials of the Chinese regime, the brutal campaign against the Uighurs in the Xinjiang region is real."[7] Jones backs his assertion up with links to two other *Guardian* articles, both of which rely on research provided by the Australian Strategic Policy Institute (ASPI) – a hawkish anti-China think tank funded by the Australian government, the US government and various multinational arms manufacturers (of which more below). That is, this self-described socialist relies on the same sources as the most extreme China hawks in Washington. Yet his public endorsement of anti-China slander, along with that of NATO-aligned commentators such as Paul Mason,[8] serves to create the impression that such slander is entirely credible, as opposed to being what it in fact is, namely yet another unhinged far-right conspiracy theory.

Although the various anti-China slanders clearly lack evidentiary support, they are nonetheless powerful, persuasive and sophisticated. It requires no great skill to persuade hardened reactionaries and anti-communists to take a hard line against China, but the propaganda war is carefully crafted such that it actively taps into progressive ideas and sentiments. The accusation of genocide is particularly potent: by accusing China of perpetrating a genocide against Uyghur Muslims in Xinjiang, imperialist politicians and journalists are able to mobilise legitimate sympathies with Muslims and national minorities, as well as invoking righteous indignation in relation to genocide. An emotional-intellectual environment is created in which to defend China against accusations of genocide is equivalent to being a Holocaust denier. Solidarity with China thus incurs a hefty psychological, and perhaps material and physical, cost.

## Manufacturing Consent

Edward Herman and Noam Chomsky's 1988 work *Manufacturing Consent: The Political Economy of the Mass Media* remains an authoritative and indispensable analysis of how the so-called free press works in the capitalist world. In particular, the book explores the connection between the economic interests of the ruling class and the ideas that are communicated via mass media. "The media serve, and propagandise on behalf of, the powerful societal interests that control and finance them. The representatives of these interests have important agendas and principles that they want to advance, and they are well positioned to shape and constrain media policy."[9]

Herman and Chomsky develop a *propaganda model*, in which a set of informal but entrenched 'filters' determine what media consumers read, watch and hear. These filters include:

- The ownership structure of the dominant mass-media firms. Media owners are members of the capitalist class, and they consistently privilege the interests of that class.
- Reliance on advertising revenue. Since most media operations can only survive, meet their costs and turn a profit if they carry advertising from large corporations, they must be sensitive to the political views of those corporations.
- Reliance on information "provided by government, business, and 'experts' funded and approved by these primary sources and agents of power."[10] The authors note that the Pentagon, for example, "has a public-information service that involves many thousands of employees, spending hundreds of millions of dollars every year and dwarfing not only the public-information resources of any dissenting individual or group but the aggregate of such groups."[11]
- A system of 'flak', or negative feedback, in response to news stories that don't conform to the values of those in power. This "may take the form of letters, telegrams, phone calls, petitions, lawsuits, speeches and bills before Congress, and other modes of complaint, threat, and punitive action."[12] With the advent of the internet – and particularly social media – methods of 'flak' have multiplied, and provide an important means of conditioning what information is consumed by the public.
- The pervasive ideological framework of anticommunism, which serves as "a national religion and control mechanism". Here the authors are referring specifically to the United States, but the point holds elsewhere in the West.

According to Herman and Chomsky's propaganda model, "the raw material of news must pass through successive filters, leaving only the cleansed residue fit to print."[13] The resulting news output serves to "inculcate and defend the economic, social, and political agenda of privileged groups that dominate the domestic society and the state."[14]

Western mainstream media coverage of China fits comfortably within this model. Almost without exception the major media operations – from Fox News to *The Guardian*, from the BBC to the *Washington Post* – present a narrative consistently hostile to China. For example, in relation to the 2019 protest movement in Hong Kong, the Western press was universal in its one-sided condemnation of the Hong Kong police and authorities, and in its effusive support for 'pro-democracy' protestors. Violence by the protestors – storming the parliament building, attacking buses, throwing petrol bombs, vandalising buildings and intimidating ordinary citizens – was either totally ignored or written off as the actions of a small minority, whereas the local Hong Kong government was subjected to an extraordinary level of scrutiny and condemnation. A *Guardian* editorial went so far as to state that "China is crushing any shred of resistance in Hong Kong, in breach of its promises to maintain the region's freedoms"[15] – unironically citing Chris Patten, the last (unelected like all his predecessors) British governor of Hong Kong, in support of its claim. It apparently didn't occur to the author to contrast the Hong Kong police's incredibly restrained response to the protests with the US police's shockingly violent repression of Black Lives Matter protests during the summer of 2020, which saw several fatalities at the hands of the US police, compared to precisely zero at the hands of their Hong Kong counterparts.[16]

No major Western news outlet seriously explored the violence of the protestors; nor did they mention the protest leaders' extensive links with some of the most reactionary US politicians;[17] nor did they choose to investigate the role of the National Endowment for Democracy in providing financial support to the movement.[18] Meanwhile they shamelessly ignored the millions of Hong Kong residents who didn't support the protests, who saw that "rioters and mobs were everywhere destroying public facilities, paralysing railway systems and so on but they were called 'Freedom Fighters' by Western countries."[19]

Conversely, what should be positive stories about China – for example in relation to poverty alleviation,[20] or its progress in the field of renewable energy,[21] or suppressing the Covid-19 pandemic[22] – are either ignored or magically transformed into anti-China stories. The announcement that China had succeeded in its goal of eliminating extreme poverty was "delivered with much bombast but few details", and the whole program was written off as part of a cunning strategy by Xi Jinping "to cement his position as the country's most powerful leader since Mao Zedong".[23] Literally millions of lives were saved as a result of China's dynamic Zero Covid strategy, and yet according to the *New York Times*, the CPC is simply trying to "use China's success in containing the virus to prove that its top-down governance model is superior to that of liberal democracies". While acknowledging that a policy of saving millions of lives unsurprisingly "still enjoys strong public support", this is put down to a familiar trope that Chinese people have "limited access to information and no tools to hold the authority accountable".[24]

Veteran political scientist Michael Parenti wrote in *Blackshirts and Reds* about the absurdity of Western propaganda against the socialist world during the Cold War, and how refraction through the lens of anti-communism could "transform any data about existing communist societies into hostile evidence." He notes:

> If the Soviets refused to negotiate a point, they were intransigent and belligerent; if they appeared willing to make concessions, this was but a skilful ploy to put us off our guard. By opposing arms limitations, they would have demonstrated their aggressive intent; but when in fact they supported most

> armament treaties, it was because they were mendacious and manipulative. If the churches in the USSR were empty, this demonstrated that religion was suppressed; but if the churches were full, this meant the people were rejecting the regimes atheistic ideology. If the workers went on strike (as happened on infrequent occasions), this was evidence of their alienation from the collectivist system; if they didn't go on strike, this was because they were intimidated and lacked freedom. A scarcity of consumer goods demonstrated the failure of the economic system; an improvement in consumer supplies meant only that the leaders were attempting to placate a restive population and so maintain a firmer hold over them.[25]

Parenti's observation certainly resonates with the contemporary media consensus against China. For such a media consensus to be coincidental would be a statistical impossibility. It represents precisely the current political agenda of the "privileged groups that dominate the domestic society and the state" (that is, the imperialist ruling classes); it aims precisely to manufacture consent for the New Cold War on China.

## Xinjiang

Nowhere is the propaganda model more visible than in relation to the mainstream media coverage of Xinjiang. The accusation that China is committing a genocide (or "cultural genocide") in Xinjiang has been repeated so frequently as to become almost an accepted truth in large parts of the West. Although the accusation is backed up with precious little evidence, the story has become a global media sensation and has led to the introduction of an escalating program of sanctions, plus a "diplomatic boycott" by various imperialist countries of the Beijing Winter Olympics in February 2022.[26] Furthermore, it has filtered into popular consciousness, fuelled by sophisticated social media campaigns. It has become the quintessential example of a *propaganda blitz*. As noted above, and consistent with Edwards and Cromwell's description, this propaganda blitz is represented across the corporate media's conservative-liberal spectrum, from *Fox News*[27] to the *New York Times*,[28] from the *Daily Mail*[29] to *The Guardian*.[30]

Herman and Chomsky's propaganda model explains how such a story picks up steam:

> For stories that are useful, the process will get under way with a series of government leaks, press conferences, white papers, etc... If the other major media like the story, they will follow it up with their own versions, and the matter quickly becomes newsworthy by familiarity. If the articles are written in an assured and convincing style, are subject to no criticisms or

> alternative interpretations in the mass media, and command support by authority figures, the propaganda themes quickly become established as true even without real evidence. This tends to close out dissenting views even more comprehensively, as they would now conflict with an already established popular belief. This in turn opens up further opportunities for still more inflated claims, as these can be made without fear of serious repercussions.[31]

The mass media is supplemented by much of the radical left in the imperialist heartlands. Popular progressive news outlet Democracy Now has parroted every lurid accusation against China in relation to Xinjiang.[32] Jacobin in 2021 gave a sympathetic interview to Sean R Roberts, author of *The War on the Uyghurs: China's Campaign Against Xinjiang's Muslims*, in which he claims that "what we see right now in the Uyghur region is a lot like the process of cultural genocide elsewhere in the world from a century ago, but benefitting from high-tech forms of repression that are available now in the twenty-first century".[33] Meanwhile Britain's *Socialist Worker* claims that "up to one million Uyghurs are locked up in internment camps."[34] Somewhat ironically, Noam Chomsky himself is not immune to the imperialist propaganda model, stating in a 2021 podcast episode that China's actions in Xinjiang are "terrible" and "highly repressive", and repeating the assertion (discussed at length below) that "there are a million people who have gone through reeducation camps."[35]

Meanwhile in the sphere of parliamentary politics, right and left have formed an unholy alliance in pursuit of the New Cold War on China. Besides right-wing fundamentalists such as Mike Pompeo, progressive Democratic Congresswoman Ilhan Omar has been hawkish regarding Xinjiang, calling on US businesses to study an Australian Strategic Policy Initiative (ASPI) report condemning China and ensure that their companies are not connected to Uyghur forced labour. Omar said:

> No American company should be profiting from the use of gulag labor, or from Uyghur prisoners who are transferred for work after their time in Xinjiang's concentration camps.[36]

## WHAT IS CHINA ACCUSED OF IN XINJIANG?

### Genocide

Of all the claims that are made in relation to China's treatment of Uyghur people, the most serious is that it is perpetrating a genocide. One of the last acts of Trump's State Department was, in January 2021, to declare that the Chinese government is "committing genocide and crimes against humanity through its wide-scale repression of Uyghurs and other predominantly Muslim ethnic minorities in its northwestern region of Xinjiang, including in its use of internment camps and forced sterilisation."[37] The Biden administration doubled down on this slander, claiming in its 2021 annual human rights report that "genocide and crimes against humanity occurred during the year against the predominantly Muslim Uyghurs and other ethnic and religious minority groups in Xinjiang", and that the components of this genocide included "the arbitrary imprisonment or other severe deprivation of physical liberty of more than one million civilians; forced sterilisation, coerced abortions, and more restrictive application of China's birth control policies; rape; torture of a large number of those arbitrarily detained; forced labor; and the imposition of draconian restrictions on freedom of religion or belief, freedom of expression, and freedom of movement."[38]

Canada's House of Commons quickly followed suit,[39] as did the French National Assembly.[40] The European Parliament adopted a somewhat less adventurist resolution claiming that Muslims in Xinjiang were at "serious risk of genocide."[41]

Genocide has a detailed definition under international law, which can be summarised as the purposeful destruction in whole or in part of a national, ethnic, racial or religious group.[42] It is rightly considered to be one of the gravest crimes against humanity. As such, it is not the sort of accusation that should be thrown around carelessly and without evidence. And yet imperialist ideologues routinely do exactly that. As Herman and Chomsky pointed out decades ago:

> genocide is an invidious word that officials apply readily to cases of victimisation in enemy states, but rarely if ever to similar or worse cases of victimisation by the United States itself or allied regimes.[43]

Prominent scholar and economist Jeffrey Sachs has written in relation to the Biden administration's accusations of genocide that "it has offered no proof, and unless it can, the State Department should withdraw the charge." Continuing, Sachs writes that the charge of genocide should never be made lightly. "Inappropriate use of the term may escalate geopolitical and military tensions and devalue the historical memory of genocides such as the Holocaust, thereby hindering the ability to prevent future genocides. It behoves the US government to make any charge of genocide responsibly, which it has failed to do here."[44]

What is the nature of the actual genocide charge? A 2021 report by a highly dubious Washington think-tank, the Newlines Institute for Strategy and Policy,[45] claims that the Chinese government has implemented "comprehensive state policy and practice" with "the intent to destroy the Uyghurs as a group." The report doesn't claim that Uyghurs are directly being killed, but that coercive birth control measures are being selectively applied such that the Uyghur population slowly dies off.

However, there is no credible data to support these claims. It is the case that the birth rate has been trending downwards in Xinjiang, but the same is true for every Chinese province. Meanwhile, the Uyghur population from 2010 to 2018 increased from 10.2 million to 12.7 million, an increase of 25 percent. During the same period, the Han Chinese population in Xinjiang increased by just 2 percent.[46] Reflecting on the reasons for the marginal downturn in Uyghur birthrate, Pakistani-Canadian peace activist Omar Latif noted that the causes are "the same as elsewhere;

> more women acquiring higher education and participating in the workforce; less necessity for parents to have more children to take care of them in old age; urbanisation; lessening of patriarchal controls over women; increased freedom for women to practice birth control.[47]

China's *one-child policy* was first implemented in 1978, at a time when China was relatively insecure about its ability to feed a large population (China has 18 percent of the global population but only around 12 percent of the world's arable land, along with chronic water scarcity).[48] The policy was in place until 2015, and largely serves to explain the long-term decline in the birth rate in China. However, national minorities – including Uyghurs – were exempt from the policy. Indeed the Uyghur population doubled during the period the one-child policy was in force. This pattern is replicated throughout China – according to the latest census data, the population of minority groups increased over the last decade by 10.26 percent (to 125 million), while that of Han Chinese grew by 4.93 percent (to 1.3 billion) – less than half the rate.

Another data point that tends to belie the claims of a genocide in Xinjiang is that average life expectancy in the region has increased from 30 years in 1949 to 75 years today.[49]

One question that the various anti-China think tanks have not addressed is: if there were a genocide taking place in Xinjiang – including the 'slow genocide' of discriminatory coercive birth control – would this not lead to a refugee crisis? There is certainly no evidence of such a crisis; no camps along the border with Pakistan or Kazakhstan, and so on. Repression, war, poverty and climate change have combined to produce numerous current refugee crises in Africa, Asia and the Middle East; it is highly implausible that a full-blown genocide in Western China would not lead to any such issue. A *Time* article in 2021 confirmed that, in spite of both the Trump and Biden administrations' outspoken criticisms of human rights abuses in Xinjiang, the US had not admitted a single Uyghur refugee in the preceding 12 months.[50] Given that, in the same time period, Biden offered a refuge to people "fleeing Hong Kong crackdown",[51] it's unimaginable that the US would not offer refugee status to thousands of Xinjiang Uyghurs fleeing persecution – if they existed.

Lamenting the fact that the Office of the High Commissioner for Human Rights 'Assessment of human rights concerns in the Xinjiang Uyghur Autonomous Region', issued in August 2022, fails to even mention the charge of genocide, Yale Law School academic Nicholas Bequelin lets slip that there simply is not a credible evidentiary basis for such a charge. "For the crime of genocide, you need to have several elements. One of the elements is intent. You need to be able to demonstrate, and to demonstrate convincingly, before a court, that the state had the intent of committing genocide. That's the first thing. The second is that you have a number of elements for the crime of genocide – which is that it has to be a systematic, widespread extermination, or attempted extermination, of a national, racial, religious, or ethnic group. There are elements that are present in the Chinese case, but it's not clear that the intent is to lead to the extermination of a particular ethnic group."[52]

The handful of reports on which the genocide charge is based do not provide anything like compelling evidence. What they put forward are some highly selective birth rate statistics, and the testimony of a small number of Uyghur exiles who claim to have been subjected to abuse. Working on the basis of 'innocent until proven guilty', China can by no means be considered as guilty of genocide.

An aside: at the time of writing, the total number of deaths caused by Covid-19 in Xinjiang is three.[53] It is very difficult to believe that state forces conducting a genocide against a given ethnic group would fail to take advantage of a pandemic in support of their project; indeed that the regional health authorities would go to significant lengths to prevent the people of this group dying from Covid-19.

## Cultural genocide

A somewhat more sophisticated accusation against the Chinese government is that is perpetrating a *cultural* genocide in Xinjiang – not wiping out the Uyghur population as such but the Uyghur *identity*, Uyghur *traditions*, Uyghur *beliefs*. Although cultural genocide is not defined under international law, it apparently refers to "the elimination of a group's identity, through measures such as forcibly transferring children away from their families, restricting the use of a national language, banning cultural activities, or destroying schools, religious institutions, or memory sites."[54]

While the accusation seems less extreme than the accusation of physical genocide, the claims of cultural genocide are nonetheless similarly lacking in evidentiary basis. For example, all schools in Xinjiang teach both Standard Chinese and one minority language, most often Uyghur.[55] Chinese banknotes have five languages on them: Chinese, Tibetan, Uyghur,

Mongolian and Zhuang.[56] Thousands of books, newspapers and magazines are printed in the Uyghur language. What's more, there are over 25,000 mosques in Xinjiang – three times the number there were in 1980, and one of the highest number of mosques per capita in the world (almost ten times as many as in the United States).[57]

Turkish scholar Adnan Akfirat observes that the Quran and numerous other key Islamic texts are readily available and have been translated into the Chinese, Uyghur, Kazakh and Kyrgyz languages. Further, "the Xinjiang Islamic Institute, headquartered in Urumqi, has eight branches in other cities such as Kashgar, Hotan and Ili, and there are ten theological schools in the region, including a Xinjiang Islamic School. These schools enrol 3,000 new students each year."[58] Akfirat states that Muslims in Xinjiang freely engage in their religious rituals, including prayer, fasting, pilgrimages, and celebrating Eid al-Fitr and Eid al-Adha.

These details have been confirmed by a steady stream of diplomats, officials and journalists that have visited Xinjiang in recent years. A diplomatic delegation in March 2021 included Pakistani Ambassador to China, Moin ul Haque, who explicitly rejected the accusations of religious persecution: "The notable and important thing is that there's freedom of religion in China and it's enshrined in the Constitution of China, which is a very important part… People in Xinjiang are enjoying their lives, their culture, their deep traditions, and most importantly, their religion."[59]

Fariz Mehdawi, Palestinian Ambassador to China, commented that there were a huge number of mosques and one could see there was respect for religious and ethnic traditions, saying: "You know, the number of mosques, if you have to calculate it all, it's something like 2,000 inhabitants for one mosque. This ratio we don't have it in our country. It's not available anywhere." It was put to Mehdawi that he could simply have been shown a Potemkin village. He replied: "Are we diplomats so naive that we could be manoeuvred to believe anything… Or are we part of a conspiracy, that we would justify something against what we had seen? I think this is not respectful… There is no conspiracy here, there is facts. And the fact of the matter is that China is rising and developing everywhere, including Xinjiang. Since some people are not happy about that, they would like to stop the rise of China by any means."[60]

Looking at different countries' voting records at the UN in relation to human rights in China, it's striking that the only Muslim-majority country that consistently votes in support of US-led slanders is NATO member Albania. During the 50th session of the Human Rights Council in 2022, members of the Organisation of Islamic Cooperation overwhelmingly co-sponsored the statement supporting China's position (by 37 to 1). This pattern is mirrored in Africa (33 to 2) and Asia (20 to 2).[61] It is very difficult to believe that the vast majority of Muslim-majority countries, and countries of the Global South, would stay silent in the face of a cultural genocide committed against Uyghur Muslims in China.

Given the lack of evidence for a cultural genocide; the data and reports concerning the protection of minority cultures in China; the large number of diplomatic missions to Xinjiang; and the near-consensus voice of Muslim-majority countries defending China against slander; the accusations of cultural genocide appear to be wholly insupportable.

## Concentration camps

The specific charge most frequently levelled against the authorities in Xinjiang is that they operate prison camps where Uyghur Muslims are locked up in huge numbers – the most oft-mentioned figure is one million, out of a population of 13 million.[62] The alleged purpose of these prison camps is to eradicate Uyghur Muslim culture and to brainwash people into supporting the government – to "breed vengeful feelings and erase Uyghur identity".[63]

The "million Uyghurs in concentration camps" story is a quintessential *propaganda blitz*. Through sheer repetition across the Western media, along with support from the US State Department, this startling headline has acquired the force of a widely-accepted truth. And yet the sources for this "news" are so spurious as to be laughable.

A 2018 *China File* article attempting to locate the source of this one million figure identifies four key pieces of research, by the German anthropologist Adrian Zenz; Washington DC-based non-profit Chinese Human Rights Defenders (CHRD); the Australian Strategic Policy Institute (ASPI); and Radio Free Asia (RFA) – a US government-funded outlet set up specifically to broadcast anti-communist propaganda in East Asia. A new player entered the game in 2021: the Newlines Institute, a think tank based at the Fairfax University of America, which issued the "first independent report" to authoritatively determine that the Chinese government has violated the UN convention on genocide. It is worthwhile considering whether these individuals and organisations most responsible for these high-profile accusations against China have any vested interests or ulterior motives.

Adrian Zenz was the first person to claim that a million Uyghurs were being held in concentration camps.[64] He is also something of a trailblazer in relation to allegations of forced labour and forced sterilisation. His relentless work slandering China has received an appreciative audience at *CNN*,[65] *The Guardian*,[66] *Democracy Now*,[67] and elsewhere. It is difficult to find a news report about China's alleged use of concentration camps that does not reference Zenz's work.

A hagiographic report in the *Wall Street Journal* highlights the outsized role of this one individual in the construction of a global anti-China slander machine: "Research by a born-again Christian anthropologist working alone from a cramped desk ... thrust China and the West into one of their biggest clashes over human rights in decades. Doggedly hunting down data in obscure corners of the Chinese internet, Adrian Zenz revealed a security buildup in China's remote Xinjiang region and illuminated the mass detention and policing of Turkic Muslims that followed. His research showed how China spent billions of dollars building internment camps and high-tech surveillance networks in Xinjiang, and recruited police officers to run them."[68]

Casually hinting at Zenz's ideological orientation, the article notes that "his faith pushes him forward" and that his previous intellectual activity includes co-authoring "a book re-examining biblical end-times."[69] He "feels very clearly led by God" to issue anti-China slanders. In other words, Zenz is not simply a politically-neutral data scientist with a passion for human rights. Rather he's a hardened anti-communist and Christian end-timer; he is employed as the Director in China Studies at the Victims of Communism Memorial Foundation,[70] an arch-conservative organisation set up by the United States Congress in 1993 in order to memorialise "the deaths of over 100,000,000 victims in an unprecedented imperial holocaust" such that "so evil a tyranny" as state socialism would never again be able to "terrorise the world."[71] In his book *Worthy to Escape: Why All Believers Will Not Be Raptured Before the Tribulation*, he urges the subjection of unruly children to "scriptural spanking" and describes homosexuality as "one of the four empires of the beast."[72]

Given Zenz's ideological affiliations and intellectual record, it would not be unreasonable to demand that his research be subjected to serious scrutiny. In reality, however, his evaluations regarding Xinjiang have been uncritically accepted and widely amplified by the Western media and political machine.

Another organisation lending its support to the accusation that "more than a million Uyghurs and members of other Turkic Muslim minorities have disappeared into a vast network of 're-education camps'" is the Australian Strategic Policy Institute (ASPI).[73] ASPI is a think-tank set up by the Australian government, and has become highly influential in terms of moulding the Australian public's attitude towards China. Its reports about Xinjiang are among the most-cited sources on the topic.

ASPI describes itself as "an independent, non-partisan think tank", but its core funding comes from the Australian government, with substantial contributions from the US Department of Defense and State Department (earmarked specifically for "Xinjiang human rights" work), as well as the UK Foreign, Commonwealth and Development Office, Amazon, Google, Facebook, Microsoft, BAE Systems, Lockheed Martin and others.[74] In summary, ASPI is knee-deep in the business of Cold War and the militarisation of the Pacific, and there is a clear conflict of interest when it comes to discussing human rights in China.

The most recent "non-partisan think tank" to amplify anti-China propaganda in relation to Xinjiang is the Newlines Institute, described by Jeffrey Sachs as "a project of a tiny Virginia-based university with 153 students, eight full-time faculty, and an apparently conservative policy agenda."[75] The Newlines report – "the first independent expert application of the 1948 Genocide Convention to the ongoing treatment of the Uyghurs in China"[76] – received extensive coverage in the Western media as the smoking gun proving China's culpability in relation to concentration camps, forced labour and cultural genocide. The report was put together by the institute's Uyghur Scholars Working Group, an illustrious group led by none other than Adrian Zenz. Canadian journalist Ajit Singh, in a detailed investigation for The Grayzone, points out that "the leadership of Newlines Institute includes former US State Department officials, US military advisors, intelligence professionals who previously worked for the 'shadow CIA' private spying firm, Stratfor, and a collection of interventionist ideologues." Further, the institute's founder and president is Ahmed Alwani, otherwise best known for having served on the advisory board for the US military's Africa Command.[77]

The BBC, *The Guardian*, the *New York Times*, the *Washington Post* and others all treated the Newlines report as if it represented the very pinnacle of academic rigour, without mentioning even in passing its connection with the US military-industrial complex.

It is abundantly clear that the popular narrative about Xinjiang prison camps rests on highly dubious sources. The evidence offered up by Zenz, ASPI and the like is a handful of individual testimonies along with a small selection of photographs and satellite pictures purporting to show prison camps. These pictures do appear to prove that some prisons exist, but this is not a terribly interesting or unusual phenomenon. China has some prisons, although its incarceration rate – 121 per 100,000 people – is less than 20 percent that of the US.[78]

Several commentators have pointed out that it is not easy to hide a million prisoners – approximately the population of Dallas. As Omar Latif comments: "Imagine the number of buildings and the infrastructure required to house and service that number of prisoners! With satellite cameras able to read a vehicle license plate, one would think the US would be able to show those prisons and prisoners in great detail."[79]

Perhaps the most iconic image purporting to show a Xinjiang prison camp is that of a group of men in a prison yard wearing blue boiler suits. This turns out to be a picture of a talk given at Luopu County Reform and Correction Centre, in April 2017.[80] The Luopu Centre is an ordinary prison, with ordinary criminals, but it has been "fallaciously used to prove, show, or insinuate either concentration camps or slave labor of Xinjiang people".[81]

## Deradicalisation

The Chinese authorities claim that what Western human rights groups are calling concentration camps are in fact vocational education centres designed to address the problem of religious extremism and violent separatism. They combine classes on sociology and ethics – focused on trying to undermine ideas of religious hatred – with classes providing marketable skills such that the attendees can find jobs and improve their standard of living. The basic idea is to improve people's life prospects so that they are less likely to be radicalised by fundamentalist sectarian groups.

The threat from such groups is real enough. The biggest among them is the East Turkestan Islamic Movement (ETIM), which up until October 2020 was classified by the US State Department as a terrorist group.[82] It has sent thousands of its militia to fight alongside Daesh and assorted al-Qaeda groups in Syria and.[83]

Between the mid 1990s and mid 2010s, there was a sequence of terrorist attacks in China carried out by Uyghur separatist outfits – in shopping centres, train stations and bus stations as well as Tiananmen Square, killing hundreds of civilians. This corresponds with an increase in terrorism across the Middle East and Central Asia, in no small measure related to the West's proxy wars against progressive or nationalist states in the region. Like any population, the Chinese people demand the right to safety and security; as such, terrorism is not a problem China's government can simply ignore.

The vocational centres were therefore set up as part of a holistic anti-terrorism campaign aimed at increasing educational attainment and economic prosperity, thereby addressing the disaffection that is known to breed radicalisation. Educational methods have been combined with a focus on improving living conditions: in the five years from 2014 to 2019, per capita disposable income increased by an average annual rate of 9.1 percent.[84]

China's approach to tackling terrorism is based on the measures advocated in the United Nations' *Plan of Action to Prevent Violent Extremism*, which "calls for a comprehensive approach encompassing not only essential security-based counter-terrorism measures but also systematic preventive steps to address the underlying conditions that drive individuals to radicalise and join violent extremist groups."[85] Thus China is actively attempting to operate within the framework of international law and best practice. This approach compares rather favourably with, for example, the US's operation of a torture camp for suspected terrorists, not to mention innocent victims snatched more or less at random, in Guantánamo Bay – itself an illegally-occupied area of Cuba.[86]

Without conducting extensive investigations on the ground, it is obviously not possible to verify the Chinese authorities' claims about how the vocational education centres are run. What we can say with certainty is that the accusations about genocide, cultural genocide, religious oppression and concentration camps are not backed by anything approximating sufficient proof. Meanwhile the most prominent accusers all, without exception, have a known axe to grind against China.

None of the foregoing is meant to deny that there are any problems in

Xinjiang; that Uyghur people are never mistreated or ethnically profiled by the police; or that there has never been any coercion involved in the deradicalisation program. But these problems – which are well-understood in China and which the government is actively addressing – are in no way unique to China. Certainly any discrimination against Uyghurs pales in comparison with, for example, the treatment of African-Americans and indigenous peoples in the United States, or the treatment of Dalits, Adivasis and numerous other minorities in India.

## Why Xinjiang?

The perverse propaganda campaign around Xinjiang serves multiple purposes. It is a component of the US-led New Cold War – a project of hybrid warfare designed to slow down China's rise, to maintain US hegemony and prevent the emergence of a multipolar world.[87] It also connects to a century-old pattern of vicious anti-communism that aims to disrupt the natural solidarity the working classes in the capitalist countries, and oppressed people generally, might otherwise feel towards the socialist world. Lastly, Xinjiang's geostrategic importance means that it has a special role in any overall strategy of weakening China. Bordering Russia, Mongolia, Kazakhstan, Kyrgyzstan, Tajikistan, Afghanistan and Pakistan, Xinjiang constitutes a key point along the major east-west land routes of the Belt and Road Initiative. It connects China to Central Asia and therefore also to the Persian Gulf, the Middle East, and Europe. Xinjiang is China's largest natural gas-producing region, is the centre of China's solar and wind power generation, and is crucially important for China's security.

British political scientist Jude Woodward noted that Xinjiang's location puts it at the heart of China's blossoming trade relationship with Central Asia – "part of the world where the confrontation between China's win-win geo-economics and the US's old style geopolitics are playing themselves out with the starkest contrast… China has proposed that Central Asia should be at the crossroads of a reimagined Eurasia connected by oil and gas pipelines, high speed trains and continuous carriageways, with stability underpinned by growth and fuelled by trade. China offers a vision of a world turned on its axis, placing not the 'middle kingdom' but the entire Asian continent at the centre of the next phase of human development."[88]

In order to disrupt this progress, the US has resorted to destabilisation and demonisation. The maximum goal is to lay the ground for a pseudo-independent Xinjiang which would in reality be a US client state and a powerful foothold for further aggression against China and other states in the region. The minimum, and far more likely, goal is to disrupt the value chains connecting China to the Eurasian land mass, thereby slowing down the Belt and Road Initiative and damaging China's trade relationships with Central Asia, the Middle East and Europe.

As an aside, the West's stoking of instability in Xinjiang and its imposition of sanctions expose the shallowness of its commitment to the fight against climate breakdown. In 2021, Xinjiang generated 2.48 trillion kilowatts of electricity from renewable sources (primarily solar and wind) – nearly 30 percent of China's total electricity consumption.[89] Around half of the world's supply of polysilicon, an essential component in solar panels, comes from Xinjiang.[90]

If the US and its allies were serious about pursuing carbon neutrality and preventing an ecological catastrophe, they would be working closely with China to develop supply chains and transmission capacity for renewable energy. China's investment in solar and wind power technology has already led to a dramatic reduction of prices around the world.[91] Instead, they are imposing blanket sanctions on China and attempting to cut Xinjiang out of clean energy supply chains.[92] This indicates rather clearly that the imperialist ruling classes are prioritising their anti-China propaganda war over preventing climate breakdown. It seems the slogan "better dead than red" lives on in the 21st century.

## Refuse consent

Malcolm X, the African-American civil rights leader and revolutionary, famously said that "if you're not careful, the newspapers will have you hating the people who are being oppressed, and loving the people who are doing the oppressing."[93]

China is rising. Its life expectancy has now overtaken that of the US.[94] Extreme poverty is a thing of the past, and people increasingly live well. China has established itself as a leading force in the fight against climate breakdown; in the fight to save humanity from pandemics; and in the movement towards a more democratic, multipolar system of international relations. It is "now the standard-bearer of the global socialist movement," in the words of Xi Jinping.[95]

The US and its allies are pursuing a New Cold War with the aim of weakening China, limiting its rise, and ultimately overturning the Chinese Revolution and ending the rule of the Communist Party. The barrage of anti-China propaganda provides the marketing for this New Cold War. The Western ruling classes want Chinese socialism to be associated with discrimination, authoritarianism and prison camps; not with ending poverty and saving the planet. Readers in the imperialist countries should consider whether they want to have their consent manufactured in this way; whether they share the foreign policy objectives of their ruling classes.

What would the likely repercussions be if the US and its allies were successful in their aims and the People's Republic of China suffered the same fate as the Soviet Union?

For one thing, the consequences in terms of the climate crisis would potentially be catastrophic. A capitalist government in China would have neither the will nor the resources to continue the projects of renewable energy, afforestation and conservation at the level they are currently being pursued. A pandemic on the scale of Covid-19 would be utterly devastating, resulting in several million – rather than tens of thousands of – Chinese deaths. Meanwhile malaria, cholera and other diseases could all be expected to make a comeback, given the perfect storm of poverty, overcrowding, rising temperatures and sea levels – 'Goldilocks conditions' for pathogens.

Poverty alleviation and common prosperity would be relegated to history. Hundreds of millions would be pushed into destitution by a ruling class that had no reason to prioritise their interests. Homelessness, violent crime and drug addiction would once again become commonplace, as they did in Russia following the Soviet collapse. Furthermore a capitalist China, desperate to earn the friendship and protection of the US, would likely end its international role promoting multipolarity and opposing imperialism.

We must resolutely oppose and expose anti-China slander, which aims to break the bonds of solidarity within the global working class and all those opposed to imperialism; which seeks to malign and undermine socialism; and which serves to perpetuate a moribund capitalist system that everyday generates more poverty, more misery, more oppression, more violence, more environmental destruction, and that increasingly threatens the very survival of humanity.

## NOTES

1 Roland Boer. *Socialism with Chinese Characteristics: A Guide for Foreigners*. Singapore: Springer, 2021, p11.
2 Chen Weihua 2021, *US should correct wrongs by ending propaganda war against China*, China Daily, accessed 27 August 2022, <https://www.chinadaily.com.cn/a/202110/15/WS6168b867a310cdd39bc6f0b4.html>.
3 Discussed in detail in Chapter 7.
4 Kwame Nkrumah. *Neo-Colonialism: The Last Stage of Imperialism*. Reprinted. London: Panaf, 2004.
5 David Edwards and David Cromwell. *Propaganda Blitz: How the Corporate Media Distort Reality*. London: Pluto Press, 2018, p1.
6 ibid, p8.
7 Owen Jones 2021, The right condemns China over its Uighur abuses. The left must do so too, The Guardian, accessed 27 August 2022, <https://www.theguardian.com/commentisfree/2021/jan/21/right-condemns-china-over-its-uighur-abuses-left-must-do>.
8 Carlos Martinez 2020, *Socialists should oppose the new cold war against China – a reply to Paul Mason*, Morning Star, accessed 27 August 2022, <https://morningstaronline.co.uk/article/socialists-should-oppose-new-cold-war-against-china-%E2%80%93-reply-paul-mason>.
9 Edward S. Herman and Noam Chomsky. *Manufacturing Consent: The Political Economy of the Mass Media*. London: Vintage Digital, 2010, p12
10 ibid, p78
11 ibid, p101
12 ibid, p111
13 ibid, p78
14 ibid, p490
15 *The Guardian view on Hong Kong's crackdown: an assault on political opposition*, The Guardian, accessed 28 August 2022, <https://www.theguardian.com/commentisfree/2021/jan/06/the-guardian-view-on-hong-kongs-crackdown-an-assault-on-political-opposition>.
16 See for example Kim Barker 2021, *In City After City, Police Mishandled Black Lives Matter Protests*, New York Times, accessed 28 August 2022, <https://www.nytimes.com/2021/03/20/us/protests-policing-george-floyd.html>.
17 Kenny Coyle 2020, *In Hong Kong, labour movement loyalties are divided*, Morning Star, accessed 19 September 2022, <https://morningstaronline.co.uk/article/kenny-coyle-based-interview-hk-trade-unionist-alice-mak>.
18 Tony Cheung and Chris Lau 2022, *Hongkongers with ties to US-backed group slammed by Beijing report could risk censure, analysts warn*, South China Morning Post, accessed 15 September 2022, <https://www.scmp.com/news/hong-kong/politics/article/3177383/hongkongers-ties-us-backed-group-slammed-beijing-report>.

19 Kenny Coyle 2022, *Hong Kong: truth is out*, Morning Star, accessed 28 August 2022, <https://morningstaronline.co.uk/article/f/hong-kong-truth-is-out>.
20 Discussed in Chapter 4.
21 Discussed in Chapter 6.
22 Carlos Martinez 2020, *Karl Marx in Wuhan: how Chinese socialism is defeating COVID-19*, Invent the Future, accessed 15 September 2022, <https://invent-the-future.org/2020/03/karl-marx-in-wuhan-how-chinese-socialism-is-defeating-covid-19/>.
23 Lily Kuo 2021, *China claims to have eliminated poverty, but the figures mask harsh challenges*, Washington Post, accessed 15 September 2022, <https://www.washingtonpost.com/world/asia_pacific/china-poverty-economy-growth/2021/02/25/9e92cb18-7722-11eb-9489-8f7dacd51e75_story.html>.
24 Li Yuan 2022, *China's 'Zero Covid' Mess Proves Autocracy Hurts Everyone*, New York Times, accessed 15 September 2022, <https://www.nytimes.com/2022/04/13/business/china-covid-zero-shanghai.html>.
25 Michael Parenti. *Blackshirts & Reds: Rational Fascism & the Overthrow of Communism*. San Francisco, Calif: City Lights Books, 1997, p43.
26 Ian Young 2022, *Canada and Britain join diplomatic boycott of Beijing Winter Olympics, amid human rights concerns*, South China Morning Post, accessed 20 September 2022, <https://www.scmp.com/news/china/diplomacy/article/3158979/canada-joins-diplomatic-boycott-beijing-winter-olympics-citing>.
27 Anders Hagstrom 2022, *Hacked Xinjiang files reveal China's Uyghur genocide details: 'Just kill them'*, Fox News, accessed 21 September 2022, <https://www.foxnews.com/world/china-xinjiang-uyghur-genocide-leak>.
28 Austin Ramzy 2019, *'Absolutely No Mercy': Leaked Files Expose How China Organized Mass Detentions of Muslims*, New York Times, accessed 21 September 2022, <https://www.nytimes.com/interactive/2019/11/16/world/asia/china-xinjiang-documents.html>.
29 Chris Pleasance 2022, *The truth about China's Uyghur camps Beijing is trying to hide: Hacked data reveals thousands of prisoners forced to undergo 're-education'… with a shoot-to-kill policy for anyone who tries to flee*, Daily Mail, accessed 21 September 2022, <https://www.dailymail.co.uk/news/article-10848301/Chinas-Uyghur-detention-camps-exposed-huge-leak-Xinjiang-police-data.html>.
30 Sarah Johnson 2021, *China's Uyghurs living in a 'dystopian hellscape', says Amnesty report*, The Guardian, accessed 21 September 2022, <https://www.theguardian.com/global-development/2021/jun/10/china-uyghur-xinjiang-dystopian-hellscape-says-amnesty-international-report>.
31 Herman and Chomsky, op cit, p122.

32 Danny Haiphong 2021, *Democracy Now amplifies State Department propaganda campaign against China behind progressive cover*, The Grayzone, accessed 21 September 2022, <https://thegrayzone.com/2021/02/22/democracy-nows-china-state-departments-cold-war/>.

33 Sean Roberts 2021, *Demanding an End to Uyghur Oppression*, Jacobin, accessed 21 September 2022, <https://jacobin.com/2021/04/uyghur-oppression-ccp-surveillance-reeducation-war-on-terror>.

34 Tomáš Tengely-Evans 2019, *Why does China persecute the Uyghur Muslims?*, Socialist Worker, accessed 21 September 2022, <https://socialistworker.co.uk/features/why-does-china-persecute-the-uyghur-muslims/>.

35 Yascha Mounk 2021, *Noam Chomsky on Identity Politics, Free Speech, and China*, The Good Fight podcast, accessed 24 September 2022, <https://www.persuasion.community/p/chomsky>.

36 Ilhan Omar 2020, *Rep. Omar Leads Letter to CEOs, including Apple, Amazon, and Google, Condemning the Use of Forced Uyghur Labor in China*, Ilhan Omar website, accessed 24 September 2022, <https://omar.house.gov/media/press-releases/rep-omar-leads-letter-ceos-including-apple-amazon-and-google-condemning-use>.

37 Edward Wong and Chris Buckley 2021, *U.S. Says China's Repression of Uighurs Is 'Genocide'*, New York Times, accessed 25 September 2022, <https://www.nytimes.com/2021/01/19/us/politics/trump-china-xinjiang.html>.

38 John Hudson 2021, *As tensions with China grow, Biden administration formalizes genocide declaration against Beijing*, Washington Post, accessed 25 September 2022, <https://www.washingtonpost.com/national-security/china-genocide-human-rights-report/2021/03/30/b2fa8312-9193-11eb-9af7-fd0822ae4398_story.html>.

39 *Canada's parliament declares China's treatment of Uighurs 'genocide'*, BBC News, accessed 25 September 2022, <https://www.bbc.co.uk/news/world-us-canada-56163220>.

40 *French lawmakers officially recognise China's treatment of Uyghurs as 'genocide'*, France24, accessed 25 September 2022, <https://www.france24.com/en/europe/20220120-french-lawmakers-officially-recognise-china-s-treatment-of-uyghurs-as-genocide>.

41 *Resolution on the human rights situation in Xinjiang, including the Xinjiang police files*, European Parliament, accessed 25 September 2022, <https://www.europarl.europa.eu/doceo/document/RC-9-2022-0310_EN.html>.

42 *Genocide*, United Nations Office on Genocide Prevention and the Responsibility to Protect, accessed 25 September 2022, <https://www.un.org/en/genocideprevention/genocide.shtml>.

43 Herman and Chomsky, op cit, p25

44 Jeffrey Sachs and William Schabas 2021, *The Xinjiang Genocide Allegations Are Unjustified*, Project Syndicate, accessed 25 September 2022, <https://www.project-syndicate.org/commentary/biden-should-withdraw-unjustified-xinjiang-genocide-allegation-by-jeffrey-d-sachs-and-william-schabas-2021-04>.

45 Chi Zao 2021, *Unsettling intentions and suspicious origins: D.C.-based Newlines Institute has more skeletons in its anti-China closet*, People's Daily, accessed 25 September 2022, <http://en.people.cn/n3/2021/0326/c90000-9832855.html>.

46 *Truth and fabrication on Xinjiang's population change, China Daily*, accessed 25 September 2022, <https://global.chinadaily.com.cn/a/202102/05/WS601cba78a31024ad0baa7830.html>.

47 Omar Latif 2021, *China, The West, And The Uighurs: A Special Report*, Canadian Peace Congress, accessed 25 September 2022, <https://www.canadianpeacecongress.ca/uncategorized/china-the-west-and-the-uighurs-a-special-report/>.

48 *Arable land (% of land area)*, World Bank, accessed 12 October 2022, <https://data.worldbank.org/indicator/AG.LND.ARBL.ZS>.

49 *Average life expectancy in Xinjiang grows to 74.7 years: white paper* (2021), Xinhua, accessed 2 October 2022, <http://www.xinhuanet.com/english/2021-07/14/c_1310060001.htm>.

50 Jasmine Aguilera 2021, *The U.S. Admitted Zero Uyghur Refugees Last Year. Here's Why, Time*, accessed 2 October 2022, <https://time.com/6111315/uyghur-refugees-china-biden/>.

51 Ben Fox 2021, *People fleeing Hong Kong crackdown get temporary US haven*, AP News, accessed 2 October 2022, <https://apnews.com/article/hong-kong-fd6eee4affe1edfbf74f5e635c8e6445>.

52 Isaac Chotiner 2022, *Why Hasn't the U.N. Accused China of Genocide in Xinjiang?*, The New Yorker, accessed 25 September 2022, <https://www.newyorker.com/news/q-and-a/why-hasnt-the-un-accused-china-of-genocide-in-xinjiang>.

53 *Number of novel coronavirus COVID-19 infection, death and recovery cases in Greater China as of June 7, 2022, by region*, Statista, accessed 2 October 2022, <https://www.statista.com/statistics/1090007/china-confirmed-and-suspected-wuhan-coronavirus-cases-region/>.

54 Kate Cronin-Furman 2018, *China Has Chosen Cultural Genocide in Xinjiang—For Now*, Foreign Policy, accessed 25 September 2022, <https://foreignpolicy.com/2018/09/19/china-has-chosen-cultural-genocide-in-xinjiang-for-now/>.

55 *Fact Check: Lies on Xinjiang-related issues versus the truth*, Global Times, accessed 26 September 2022, <https://www.globaltimes.cn/page/202102/1215149.shtml>.

56 *A Linguistic Look at China's Currency*, China Briefing, accessed 26 September 2022, <https://www.china-briefing.com/news/a-linguistic-

look-at-chinas-currency / >.

57 Md Enamul Hassan 2020, *Allegations of demolition of mosques in Xinjiang groundless*, People's Daily, accessed 26 September 2022, <http: / / en.people.cn / n3 / 2020 / 0821 / c98649-9737215.html>.

58 Adnan Akfirat 2021, *10 imperialist lies and Uygur truths (Part 2)*, CGTN, accessed 26 September 2022, <https: / / news.cgtn.com / news / 2021-02-25 / 10-imperialist-lies-and-Uygur-truths-Part-2--Y9bVWkDYME / index.html>.

59 *Pakistan fully supports China's position on Xinjiang: envoy*, Daily Times, accessed 26 September 2022, <https: / / dailytimes.com.pk / 743754 / pakistan-fully-supports-chinas-position-on-xinjiang-envoy / >.

60 *The Point: What do three ambassadors talk about Xinjiang with Liu Xin?*, YouTube, accessed 27 September 2022, <https: / / www.youtube.com / watch?v=ebeGipO6-gU>.

61 Casey Ho-yuk Wan 2022, *Bachelet's "Assessment of Human Rights Concerns in Xinjiang" Risks Discrediting the OHCHR and Politicizing the Human Rights Regime*, Friends of Socialist China, accessed 07 October 2022, <https: / / socialistchina.org / 2022 / 09 / 09 / bachelets-assessment-of-human-rights-concerns-in-xinjiang-risks-discrediting-the-ohchr-and-politicizing-the-human-rights-regime / >.

62 Lindsay Maizland 2022, *China's Repression of Uyghurs in Xinjiang*, Council on Foreign Relations, accessed 27 September 2022, <https: / / www.cfr.org / backgrounder / china-xinjiang-uyghurs-muslims-repression-genocide-human-rights>.

63 Chris Buckley 2018, *China Is Detaining Muslims in Vast Numbers. The Goal: 'Transformation.'*, New York Times, accessed 27 September 2022, <https: / / www.nytimes.com / 2018 / 09 / 08 / world / asia / china-uighur-muslim-detention-camp.html>.

64 Sébastian Seibt 2022, *Adrian Zenz, the academic behind the 'Xinjiang Police Files', on China's abuse of Uighurs*, France 24, accessed 28 September 2022, <https: / / www.france24.com / en / asia-pacific / 20220525-adrian-zenz-the-academic-behind-the-xinjiang-police-files-on-china-s-abuse-of-uighurs>.

65 *Dr. Adrian Zenz discusses leaked Xinjiang documents on CNN Newsroom*, YouTube, accessed 28 September 2022, <https: / / www.youtube.com / watch?v=25QhBJt3vCw>.

66 Patrick Wintour 2021, *Leaked papers link Xinjiang crackdown with China leadership*, The Guardian, accessed 28 September 2022, <https: / / www.theguardian.com / world / 2021 / nov / 29 / leaked-papers-link-xinjiang-crackdown-with-china-leadership>.

67 *Child Separation & Prison Camps: China's Campaign Against Uyghur Muslims Is 'Cultural Genocide'*, Democracy Now, accessed 28 September 2022, <https: / / www.democracynow.org / 2019 / 7 / 26 / china_xinjiang_uyghurs_internment_surveillance>.

68 Josh Chin 2019, *The German Data Diver Who Exposed China's Muslim Crackdown*, Wall Street Journal, accessed 28 September 2022, <https://www.wsj.com/articles/the-german-data-diver-who-exposed-chinas-muslim-crackdown-11558431005>.
69 Adrian Zenz and Marlon L. Sias. *Worthy to Escape: Why All Believers Will Not Be Raptured Before the Tribulation*. United States: Author Solutions, Incorporated, 2012.
70 *Adrian Zenz, Ph.D.*, Victims of Communism Memorial Foundation, accessed 2 October 2022, <https://victimsofcommunism.org/leader/adrian-zenz-phd/>.
71 Tarik Ata 2022, *Unveiling True Nature of Victims of Communism*, The International, accessed 02 October 2022, <https://www.internationalmagz.com/articles/unveiling-true-nature-of-victims-of-communism>.
72 Gareth Porter and Max Blumenthal 2021, *US State Department accusation of China 'genocide' relied on data abuse and baseless claims by far-right ideologue*, The Grayzone, accessed 12 October 2022, <https://thegrayzone.com/2021/02/18/us-media-reports-chinese-genocide-relied-on-fraudulent-far-right-researcher/>.
73 Vicky Xiuzhong Xu at al 2020, *Uyghurs for sale*, Australian Strategic Policy Institute, accessed 2 October 2022, <https://www.aspi.org.au/report/uyghurs-sale>.
74 *ASPI Funding*, Australian Strategic Policy Institute, accessed 02 October 2022, <https://www.aspi.org.au/about-aspi/funding>.
75 Jeffrey Sachs and William Schabas 2021, *The Xinjiang Genocide Allegations Are Unjustified*, Project Syndicate, accessed 25 September 2022, <https://www.project-syndicate.org/commentary/biden-should-withdraw-unjustified-xinjiang-genocide-allegation-by-jeffrey-d-sachs-and-william-schabas-2021-04>.
76 *The Uyghur Genocide: An Examination of China's Breaches of the 1948 Genocide Convention*, Newlines Institute for Strategy and Policy, accessed 2 October 2022, <https://newlinesinstitute.org/uyghurs/the-uyghur-genocide-an-examination-of-chinas-breaches-of-the-1948-genocide-convention/>.
77 Ajit Singh 2021, *'Independent' report claiming Uyghur genocide brought to you by sham university, neocon ideologues lobbying to 'punish' China*, The Grayzone, accessed 02 October 2022, <https://thegrayzone.com/2021/03/17/report-uyghur-genocide-sham-university-neocon-punish-china/>.
78 Emily Widra and Tiana Herring 2021, *States of Incarceration: The Global Context 2021*, Prison Policy Initiative, accessed 2 October 2022, <https://www.prisonpolicy.org/global/2021.html>.
79 Omar Latif 2021, *China, The West, And The Uighurs: A Special Report*, Canadian Peace Congress, accessed 25 September 2022, <https://www.

canadianpeacecongress.ca / uncategorized / china-the-west-and-the-uighurs-a-special-report / >.

80 Kate Woolford 2021, *Xinjiang: staying afloat in a wave of disinformation*, Challenge, accessed 2 October 2022, <https: / / challenge-magazine.org / 2021 / 04 / 13 / xinjiang-staying-afloat-in-a-wave-of-disinformation / >.

81 *Xinjiang: A Report and Resource Compilation*, Qiao Collective, accessed 2 October 2022, <https: / / www.qiaocollective.com / education / xinjiang>.

82 Joshua Lipes 2020, *US Drops ETIM From Terror List, Weakening China's Pretext For Xinjiang Crackdown*, Radio Free Asia, accessed 2 October 2022, <https: / / www.rfa.org / english / news / uyghur / etim-11052020155816.html>.

83 Amy Chew 2021, *Militant group ETIM, which has been targeted by China, remains active in Afghanistan, UN report says*, SCMP, accessed 2 October 2022, <https: / / www.scmp.com / week-asia / politics / article / 3143053 / militant-group-etim-which-has-been-targeted-china-remains-active>.

84 *Xinjiang's GDP grows 7.2 pct annually from 2014 to 2019*, Xinhua, accessed 2 October 2022, <http: / / www.xinhuanet.com / english / 2021-02 / 05 / c_139724061.htm>.

85 *Plan of Action to Prevent Violent Extremism*, United Nations Office of Counter-Terrorism, accessed 2 October 2022, <https: / / www.un.org / counterterrorism / plan-of-action-to-prevent-violent-extremism>.

86 Dean Weston 2004, *US occupation of Guantanamo Bay is illegal, says top lawyer*, Cuba Solidarity Campaign, accessed 4 October 2022, <https: / / cuba-solidarity.org.uk / cubasi / article / 32 / us-occupation-of-guantanamo-bay-is-illegal-says-top-lawyer>.

87 See Chapter 7.

88 Jude Woodward. *The US vs China: Asia's New Cold War? Geopolitical Economy.* Manchester: Manchester University Press, 2017, p281

89 *Xinjiang power generation from renewable energy integrates AI technologies to grasp real-time capacity*, Global Times, accessed 5 October 2022, <https: / / www.globaltimes.cn / page / 202202 / 1252283.shtml>.

90 Dan Murtaugh 2021, *Why It's So Hard for the Solar Industry to Quit Xinjiang*, Bloomberg, accessed 5 October 2022, <https: / / www.bloomberg.com / news / articles / 2021-02-10 / why-it-s-so-hard-for-the-solar-industry-to-quit-xinjiang>.

91 Dominic Chiu 2017, *The East Is Green: China's Global Leadership in Renewable Energy*, Center for International and Strategic Studies, accessed 5 October 2022, <https: / / www.csis.org / east-green-chinas-global-leadership-renewable-energy>.

92 Rebecca Angel 2021, *US bans target Chinese solar panel industry over Xinjiang forced labor concerns*, The Guardian, accessed 5 October 2022, <https: / / www.theguardian.com / world / 2021 / jun / 25 / us-bans-target-chinese-solar-panel-industry-over-xinjiang-forced-labor-concerns>.

93 *Malcolm X with Dick Gregory At the Audubon Ballroom (Dec. 13, 1964),* Malcolm X Files, accessed 6 October 2022, <http: / / malcolmxfiles. blogspot.com / 2013 / 07 / at-audubon-ballroom-dec-13-1964.html>.

94 Mary Hui 2022, *China's life expectancy is now higher than that of the US*, Quartz, accessed 6 October 2022, <https: / / qz.com / china-life-expectancy-exceeds-us-1849483265>.

95 William Zheng 2022, *Xi Jinping article gives insight into China's direction ahead of Communist Party congress*, SCMP, accessed 6 October 2022, <https: / / www.scmp.com / news / china / politics / article / 3192677 / xi-article-gives-insight-chinas-direction-ahead-party-congress>.

# 6

# China is building an ecological civilisation

> We must strike a balance between economic growth and environmental protection. We will be more conscientious in promoting green, circular, and low-carbon development. We will never again seek economic growth at the cost of the environment. (Xi Jinping)[1]

## The cost of development

Few events in human history have resonated throughout the world as profoundly as the Chinese Revolution. Standing in Tiananmen Square on 1 October 1949, pronouncing the birth of the People's Republic of China, Mao Zedong said "the Chinese people have stood up". In standing up, in building a modern socialist society and throwing off the shackles of feudalism, colonialism, backwardness, illiteracy and grinding poverty, China has blazed a trail for the entire Global South. Lifting hundreds of millions of people out of poverty has been described even by ardent capitalists as "the greatest leap to overcome poverty in history".[2]

In environmental terms, however, this progress has come at a cost. Just as economic development in Europe and the Americas was fuelled by the voracious burning of fossil fuels, China's development has been built to a significant degree on 'Old King Coal', the most polluting and emissions-intensive of the fossil fuels. Two decades ago, coal made up around 80 percent of China's energy mix. Environmental law expert Barbara Finamore notes that "coal, plentiful and cheap, was the energy source of choice, not just for power plants, but also for direct combustion by heavy industry and for heating and cooking in people's homes."[3]

China's use of coal was not based on ignorance or irresponsibility. Rather, it was a matter of development by any means necessary. The abundance of cheap fossil fuel energy enabled China to lift hundreds of millions out of poverty whilst simultaneously establishing itself as a global leader in science and technology, thereby building a foundation for the construction of a modern and sustainable socialist society. Schools, hospitals, roads, trains, factories and laboratories all need energy to build and operate. Chinese people now have energy in their homes, powering fridges, lights and washing machines – indispensable components of modern life.

Furthermore, China's ability to attract foreign investment and learn from US, European and Japanese technology was in no small measure based on turning itself into a manufacturing hub to which the advanced capitalist countries exported their production processes. Martin Jacques observes that "40 percent of China's energy goes into producing exports for Western markets, in other words, the source [of China's greenhouse gas emissions] is multinationals rather than Chinese firms. The West has, in effect, exported part of its own greenhouse emissions to China."[4] The developed countries have been able to "socialise and export the costs of environmental destruction",[5] reducing domestic pollution and emissions whilst maintaining unsustainable levels of consumption.

The choice facing China in the last decades of the 20th century was between economic development with environmental degradation, or underdevelopment with environmental conservation. Western environmentalists can't reasonably complain about the Chinese people opting for the former. Development is recognised by the UN as a human right.[6] Advanced countries fuelled their own industrial revolutions with coal and oil; they bear responsibility for the bulk of currently existing atmospheric greenhouse gases (the US and Europe have contributed to just over half the cumulative carbon dioxide emissions since 1850, whilst constituting around 15 percent of the global population).[7] It would be hypocritical in the extreme for these countries to tell poor countries that they don't have the right to develop; to feed, clothe, house and educate people. If advanced countries want developing countries to leapfrog fossil fuel-based development, the primary responsibility is on them to provide the technology and the finance – which principle of "common but differentiated responsibilities" is a cornerstone of international environmental law.[8]

## Changing priorities

Nonetheless, there is no getting away from the fact that China now faces a looming ecological crisis. It overtook the US as the biggest overall emitter of carbon dioxide in 2007[9] (although its per capita emissions are around half those of the US, Canada and Australia).[10] Martin Jacques writes that, as a result of China having "torn from the eighteenth century to the twenty-first century in little more than three decades", it has worked up "a huge ecological deficit of two centuries accumulated in just a few decades."[11]

Even without the last few decades of rapid industrialisation, China is particularly vulnerable to the effects of climate change. According to the World Food Programme, China is one of the most disaster-prone countries in the world, with up to 200 million people exposed to the effects of droughts and floods.[12] Already hundreds of thousands have to be evacuated every summer in response to flooding in the Pearl River Delta.[13] High levels of air pollution in the major cities are a major health issue for the population. US environmentalist and China specialist Judith Shapiro observes:

> China is poorly endowed with farmable land and its water resources are unevenly distributed both geographically and seasonally. It has nearly a quarter of the world's population but only five percent of its water resources and seven percent of its arable land... China's per capita water resources are already among the lowest in the world, at just one-fourth of the world average.[14]

Environmental issues have become a top priority for China. Over the last decade in particular, the Chinese political leadership has focussed its attentions on transitioning to a green model of development in order both to contribute to the global fight against climate breakdown and immediately improve the wellbeing of the Chinese people. Barbara Finamore notes that the CPC leadership has accelerated efforts to "transform its economic structure from one reliant on fossil fuel-driven heavy industry and manufacturing to one based on services, innovation, clean energy, and environmental sustainability."[15] Chinese policy-makers have started to de-emphasise GDP growth and to encourage green development, whereby "living standards continue to rise, but in a way that is much less energy and carbon intensive."[16] The goal is to construct "an energy and resource efficient, environmentally friendly structure of industries, pattern of growth, and mode of consumption."[17] In her popular 2013 book *The Entrepreneurial State*, economist Mariana Mazzucato notes approvingly that China more than any other country is prioritising clean technologies "as part of a strategic vision and long-term commitment to economic growth."[18]

In the first volume of *The Governance of China*, published in 2014, President Xi Jinping put forward a comprehensive outline of China's commitments in relation to the environment:

> China will respect and protect nature, and accommodate itself to nature's needs. It will remain committed to the basic state policy of conserving resources and protecting the environment. It will promote green, circular and low-carbon development,

> and promote ecological progress in every aspect of its effort to achieve economic, political, cultural and social progress. China will also develop a resource-efficient and environmentally friendly geographical layout, industrial structure, mode of production and way of life, and leave to our future generations a working and living environment of blue skies, green fields and clean water.[19]

The leadership's increasing focus on environmental issues reflects a growing concern among the public, especially now that China, while still a developing country, is no longer poor. GDP growth has become less of a priority for hundreds of millions of Chinese. "In terms of social conditions and public opinions, with the gradual improvement of people's lives, there is a fundamental change of social mentality from 'satisfying basic needs' to 'pursuing environmental protection', from 'seeking survival' to 'seeking ecology.'"[20]

## Taking action

> The world has never before seen a climate programme on this scale... China has stepped up its climate leadership dramatically in recent years, and is now increasingly seen as filling the leadership void left by the US. (Fred Krupp, Environmental Defence Fund president)[21]

In order to avert climate breakdown, humans need to find ways to meet their needs without releasing greenhouse gases into the atmosphere and without causing permanent damage to the ecosystem. There are numerous components to this, the most urgent of which is to decarbonise our energy systems such that we can power our lives from non-fossil sources.

China has been aggressively pursuing decarbonisation for over a decade. In his address to the UN General Assembly in 2020, Xi Jinping announced two major goals agreed by the Chinese government: to peak carbon dioxide emissions before 2030 and to achieve carbon neutrality before 2060.[22] He stated bluntly that:

> humankind can no longer afford to ignore the repeated warnings of nature and go down the beaten path of extracting resources without investing in conservation, pursuing development at the expense of protection, and exploiting resources without restoration.[23]

China has reiterated its goals on carbon peaking and neutrality many times, has formulated a detailed action plan around them, and has incorporated them into law.[24] At the World Economic Forum in January 2022, Xi stated that the realisation of carbon neutrality is an "intrinsic requirement of China's own high-quality development and a solemn pledge to the international community."[25]

China's goals are of historic significance. Columbia University professor Adam Tooze enthused that, with Xi Jinping's 2020 announcement:

> China's leader may have redefined the future prospects for humanity… As the impact of his remarks sank in, climate modellers crunched the numbers and concluded that, if fully implemented, China's new commitment will by itself lower the projected temperature increase by 0.2-0.3 deg C. It is the largest favourable shock that their models have ever produced.[26]

According to a recent study published in *Science*, these targets are "largely consistent" with the goal established in the Paris Agreement (2015) of limiting overall average global warming to 1.5 degrees centigrade above the pre-industrial era.[27] Meanwhile, credible analysis indicates that China's emissions will likely peak several years earlier than 2030.[28] And, unlike the major capitalist countries, China has a very strong record when it comes to meeting its international commitments. Even the *New York Times* had to reluctantly admit that "Beijing has met or has come close to meeting every major energy and environmental target it has set."[29]

## Cutting out coal

Not all fossil fuels are created equal. Carbon dioxide emissions per unit of energy generated are twice as high for coal as for natural gas, and the air pollution impact is an order of magnitude higher. As such, reigning in coal use is a major ongoing project for China, a country where, as recently as 2007, over 80 percent of generated electricity came from coal sources.[30]

In the 15-year period from 2007 to 2022, coal's share of the power mix was reduced from 81 percent to 56 percent,[31] putting it in the same range as Australia – a country which could and should have begun its low-carbon transition decades ago, and which has a per capita coal production figure eight times higher than China.[32] Various commentators have pointed out that China continues to build new coal-fired power plants; however, these are almost invariably modern, cleaner and more efficient replacements for existing plants.

In 2017, China's National Energy Administration cancelled plans to build more than 100 coal-fired power plants, in order to divert power generation efforts into the renewable sector. This will eliminate 120 gigawatts of future coal-fired capacity.[33] Beijing closed its last coal-fired plant in 2017.[34] One particularly symbolic project is a giant floating solar farm – the largest in the world – on top of a former coal mine in Anhui.[35] Datong, China's "coal capital" is seeking to put its coal reserves to better use: producing hydrogen for use in emissions-free hydrogen-powered vehicles and electricity storage.[36]

Foreign Ministry Spokesperson Zhao Lijian reported in July 2022 that:

> By the end of last month, the share of coal-fired power in China's installed power capacity dropped to a historic low of under 50 percent; total emissions of the coal-fired power industries reduced by nearly 90 percent over a decade; coal consumption by power generation units has been slashed, saving over 700 million tonnes of raw coal over the past decade.[37]

The drop in coal consumption has already had a noticeable impact in the big cities. The *New York Times* observed that, in the period from 2014 to 2018, Chinese cities cut concentrations of atmospheric fine particulates by an average of 34 percent.[38] Beijing in the 1990s was among the most polluted cities in the world, but due to a decade-long 'war on pollution', its air quality index has improved by 50 percent.[39] In 2019, Beijing dropped out of the list of the 200 most-polluted cities.[40] Writing in 2012, Martin Jacques talks about China having 16 of the world's 20 worst-polluted cities.[41] A decade later, only two Chinese cities are on the list.[42]

Although it will take China many more years to completely phase out coal, it has already announced that it will not finance any new coal-fired power plants abroad. Meanwhile, US-based analysts KJ Noh and Michael Wong note that the bulk of China's coal plants are now "advanced supercritical or ultra-supercritical plants, which means they are much more efficient and cleaner than many of the industrial-era legacy plants of the US".[43]

## Investing in renewables

While reducing its use of coal, China is rapidly becoming the first "renewable energy superpower",[44] accounting for 46 percent of new solar and wind power generating capacity in 2021.[45] International energy analyst Tim Buckley observes that China is the world leader in "wind and solar installation, in wind and solar manufacturing, in electric vehicle production, in batteries, in hydro, in nuclear, in ground heat pumps, in grid transmission and distribution, and in green hydrogen." In summary, "they literally lead the world in every zero-emissions technology today."[46]

China is responsible for around a third of global renewable energy investment, and 28 percent of its electricity is already generated from renewable sources (compared to 20 percent for the US).[47] Out of 12.7 million jobs in the renewables industry worldwide, 42 percent (over five million) are in China.[48] The Chinese government has set itself the target of getting renewable energy sources (including solar, wind, nuclear and hydropower) to 33 percent of its total energy mix by 2025.[49] Non-fossil energy sources are set to supply 50% of China's electric power generation by 2030.[50]

China has been the world's largest producer of solar panels since 2009, and it now accounts for over 80 percent of global solar panel production.[51] China's investment in solar power research and development has been so extensive as to push down prices worldwide to a level where solar is increasingly competitive with fossil fuels. An International Energy Agency report notes: "Chinese industrial policies focusing on solar PV as a strategic sector and on growing domestic demand have enabled economies of scale and supported continuous innovation throughout the supply chain. These policies have contributed to a cost decline of more than 80 percent, helping solar PV to become the most affordable electricity generation technology in many parts of the world."[52] In general, China's sustained investment in renewable energy has meant a global reduction in costs – an important contribution to global decarbonisation.

The People's Republic has also been pushing forward in wind power, with data indicating that "China now operates almost half of the world's installed offshore wind, with 26 gigawatts of a total of 54 gigawatts worldwide" – a statistic that prompted Elizabeth Sawin, co-director of US climate think-tank Climate Interactive to remark: "While the US can't quite agree to build back better, China just builds better".[53]

China's progress on renewables has been such that, in November 2022, the Nobel Sustainability Trust Foundation issued a letter or recommendation, publicly commending China's carbon-neutral leadership:

> China's renewable energy installed capacity accounts for one-third of the world's. More than 50% of the world's wind power equipment and more than 85% of the world's photovoltaic equipment components come from China. The cumulative investment in renewable energy has reached 380 billion US dollars, ranking first in the world.[54]

China's renewable energy capacity as of 2021 was 1,020 GW – three times more than the second country on the list (the US).[55] This is expected to reach around 1,500 GW by 2030.[56] Five of the ten biggest solar parks in the world are in China.[57] "Every hour, China now erects another wind turbine, and installs enough solar panels to cover a soccer field."[58]

Construction has begun on a series of hybrid wind and solar-power bases in the north-western part of the county, "which by 2030 will contain about as much renewable capacity as currently in all of Europe."[59] Alongside these bases is the construction of ultra-high voltage transmission lines to transport the energy to the densely populated southern and eastern zones.[60]

One of the most complex challenges facing widespread adoption of renewables is transmission of variable power from point of production to point of use. Environmental expert Mike Berners-Lee notes that "China is investing in huge transmission lines to move electricity from one end of its country to the other. There are losses on the way but it is an increasingly doable exercise."[61] Chinese scientists have recently developed the world's first prototype of a superconducting hybrid power line. The full-scale version will transmit energy from one side of the country to the other with zero resistance.[62]

China is also innovating on "green hydrogen" production – converting solar or wind energy into hydrogen via electrolysis. Hydrogen can be used directly as a battery fuel, and also has a potentially highly significant role in transmission, as it can be sent from point of production to point of use in existing gas pipelines. At the time of writing (2023), construction of the world's largest green hydrogen factory is underway in Kuqa, Xinjiang.[63]

## Nuclear power

China is also leading research into nuclear power, including fourth-generation reactors, the first of which was connected to the grid in December 2021.[64] Fourth-generation reactors promise to be significantly safer and to produce far less radioactive waste than earlier nuclear technology.[65]

In 2021, China surpassed France in nuclear energy generation to become the second-highest nuclear producer, behind the US.[66] As part of its commitment to reaching carbon neutrality, China has "plans to generate an eye-popping amount of nuclear energy, quickly and at relatively low cost," with a view to building over 150 new reactors in the next 15 years, "more than the rest of the world has built in the past 35."[67]

Nuclear energy is of course highly controversial, especially in the wake of the 2011 Fukushima disaster.[68] The question of whether nuclear power has a significant long-term role to play in meeting human energy needs is beyond the scope of this book. However, premature phasing out of nuclear power (as has happened in Germany and other countries) before it can be immediately replaced with solar or wind energy seems decidedly shortsighted. As David Wallace-Wells points out in *The Uninhabitable Earth*:

> Already, more than 10,000 people die from air pollution daily. That is considerably more each day than the total number of people who have ever been affected by the meltdowns of nuclear reactors.[69]

Nuclear power currently makes an important contribution to the energy mix in many countries, and in the words of Mike Berners-Lee, "anyone taking a firm anti-nuclear stance needs to have a coherent plan for the low carbon future without it."[70] Nuclear power is the main source of electricity in France and, "as a result, France has about half the carbon emissions per head of the OECD as a whole."[71]

Nuclear power will likely continue to be one of the important non-fossil fuel energy sources for the medium-term future, and China's investment to make it safer, cheaper and less contaminating is therefore a valuable contribution to the overall project of decarbonising the world's energy systems.

China is among the world leaders in the effort to generate energy through nuclear fusion,[72] which has the potential to someday generate unlimited, safe, emissions-free and radioactive waste-free power.[73] There is a long-running joke that viable nuclear fusion reactors are "always 30 years away",[74] but Chinese scientists – working in collaboration with their counterparts in Russia, the US and elsewhere – have made promising progress in recent years.[75]

## Energy efficiency

While it is less headline-grabbing than replacing fossil fuels with renewable energy, it's widely understood that improving energy efficiency is one of the most crucial steps towards reducing the quantities of greenhouses gases we are placing in the atmosphere. Neil Hirst, former Director of the International Energy Agency, opines that "the biggest part [of a transition to a zero-carbon economy] is to improve the energy efficiency of all the main areas of energy use, power generation, heating of buildings, transport, and industry."[76] For developing countries in particular, *carbon intensity* – carbon dioxide emissions per unit of gross domestic product – is a valuable metric, since it encapsulates two indispensable and sometimes contradictory goals: improvement of living standards, and reduced impact on the natural environment. China pledged at the 2009 United Nations Climate Change Conference in Copenhagen that it would reduce its carbon intensity by two-thirds by 2030, and is on track to achieve this goal ahead of time. It has already succeeded in halving its carbon emissions per unit of GDP since 2005,[77] and by almost 75 percent since 1990.[78]

According to the *International Energy Efficiency Scorecard*, which ranks 25 of the world's largest energy users on 36 efficiency metrics, China is in 9th position for energy efficiency – one place ahead of the US, and the highest ranking of any developing country.[79] Such progress has been achieved, in Barbara Finamore's words, "thanks to strong government commitment, ambitious targets, and effective policies for energy conservation and emission reduction."[80]

## Low-carbon transport

Globally, transport is responsible for around one-fifth of carbon dioxide emissions.[81] Along with the emissions from industry (around 20 percent) and agriculture (around 10 percent), these are among the most difficult emissions to get rid of, because so many of the vehicles in existence are reliant on burning hydrocarbons in an internal combustion engine.

China is the only country so far to have made really meaningful progress in terms of decarbonising transport. The *14th Five Year Plan for a Modern and Comprehensive Transportation System (2021-2025)*, published in January 2022, sets the goal of 72 percent of China's urban public buses being electric by 2025. As of 2021, the figure is 59 percent, up from 16 percent in 2016.[82] A number of major Chinese cities, including Shenzhen, Tianjin and Guangzhou have already achieved 100 percent bus fleet electrification.[83] Around 98 percent of the world's electric buses are in China.[84]

Investment regulations are being introduced that will effectively phase out fossil fuel-based cars in the next few years.[85] More electric cars are sold per year in China than in the rest of the world put together.

> The Chinese government has spent nearly $60 billion in the last decade to create an industry that builds electric cars, while also reducing the number of licenses available for gasoline-powered cars to increase demand for electric cars. And Beijing plans to spend just as much over the next decade.[86]

To go with all the electric cars, there is also a network of 1.15 million electric vehicle charging stations – 65 percent of the global total.[87]

High-speed rail (HSR) is another important tool for decarbonising transport. Here again, China is well out in front, with more high-speed rail miles than the rest of the world combined.[88] As of 2022, China has 37,900 kilometres of HSR, and over 75 percent of China's cities with a population of 500,000 or more have a high-speed rail link.[89] Compare this with the US, which has a grand total of 80 km of HSR.[90]

HSR has reduced the journey time between Beijing and Xi'an (similar to the distance between London and Berlin) to 4.5 hours, down from 11 hours on a regular train.[91] As a result, inter-city transport in China increasingly takes place on rails rather than in the air. From a climate point of view, this is good news: rail produces far lower emissions and, since HSR is electrically powered, its path to becoming emissions-free follows that of the electricity grid.

## Reforestation

Left to their own devices, trees absorb atmospheric carbon dioxide, thereby mitigating the greenhouse effect. One of the reasons for the climate crisis humanity now faces is that we've cut down so many trees in order to make way for us to live and to grow our food. Reforestation and afforestation could have a profoundly positive impact in our fight against climate catastrophe. Scientists recently estimated that a vast reforestation programme "has the potential to cut the atmospheric carbon pool by about 25 percent".[92]

Xi Jinping has often emphasised the importance of forest development:

> Forests are the mainstay and an important resource for the land ecosystem. They are also an important ecological safeguard for the survival and development of mankind. It is hard to imagine what would happen to the earth and human beings without forests.[93]

China is carrying out the largest forestation project in the world,[94] planting forests "the size of Ireland" in a single year[95] and doubling forest coverage from 12 percent in 1980 to 23 percent in 2020 (sadly the global trend is in the opposite direction).[96] The government's target is to continue increasing coverage until it reaches at least 26 percent, by 2035.[97] Meanwhile, hundreds of national parks have been developed and a third of the country's land has been placed behind an "ecological protection red line."[98]

It should be noted that there has been some valid criticism of the "rush to reforest" in China and several other countries, on the basis of poor tree selection and other factors. "With a little more knowledge and long-term thinking, the rewards would have been even greater, with greater sandstorm prevention, carbon storage and habitat."[99] Such criticisms are being actively addressed in current reforestation and afforestation projects, for example the *Millennium show forest*, which, "unlike a general urban afforestation project, follows the principles of natural forest succession to construct a close-to-natural urban forest composed of mixed-aged, multi-layered (canopy, mid-level, and understory), mixed species forests."[100]

## Towards a Green GDP

Gross Domestic Product (GDP), which measures the market value of all goods and services produced in a specific time period, is a global standard for measuring national economic performance. With large parts of its economy geared towards manufacturing consumer goods for the global market, Chinese policy has since the 1980s made GDP growth one of its top priorities. This was in the context of the CPC leadership having defined the principal contradiction in Chinese society as being between people's ever-growing material and cultural needs and China's relatively backward social productive forces. A strong orientation towards GDP growth represented a development-at-all-costs strategy, one that can only be said to have been phenomenally successful.

At the 19th Congress of the CPC in 2017, Xi Jinping announced that the party's definition of the principal contradiction facing Chinese society had changed; that it was now between unbalanced and inadequate development and the people's ever-growing needs for a better life.

> While China's overall productive forces have significantly improved and in many areas our production capacity leads the world, our problem is that our development is unbalanced and

> inadequate. This has become the main constraining factor in meeting the people's increasing needs for a better life.[101]

Addressing unbalanced development means shifting emphasis from *quantity* of growth to *quality* of growth: pursuing high-quality development – "a change from seeking growth to seeking better growth." Such growth is "innovative, coordinated, green, open and inclusive", and seeks to find "development opportunities while preserving Nature, and achieve win-win in both ecological conservation and high-quality development."[102] It incorporates a "new vision of green development and a way of life and work that is green, low-carbon, circular and sustainable."[103] Such a vision shifts the development goal "from maximising growth to maximising net welfare," in the words of the influential Chinese economist Hu Angang.[104]

Hu Angang proposes a 'Green GDP' that comprises nominal GDP, green investment measures (environmental protection, renewable energy usage, energy saving measures), investment in human capital (education, health, research), alongside a subtractive component for greenhouse gas emissions, pollution, forest depletion, mineral depletion and losses from natural disasters. Such a model encourages moderate consumption, low emissions, and the preservation of ecological capital as a fundamental economic goal. Its basic aim is "the accumulation of green wealth and improved human welfare to achieve harmony between humanity and nature."[105]

The concept of a Green GDP is implicitly recognised in China's updated economic strategy and its de-emphasising of traditional GDP as the central measure of economic performance. What's more, a number of major Chinese cities are experimenting with implementations of Green GDP or a variant of it. Shenzhen is the first city in the world to have adopted an accounting system based on gross ecosystem product (GEP) – "the total value of final ecosystem goods and services supplied to human well-being in a region annually… measured in terms of biophysical value and monetary value."[106] Finamore observes that, since 2013, GDP growth has been deprioritised as a measure for evaluating the performance of regional officials. The evaluation criteria now "also focus on the quality and sustainability of economic development, including progress in reducing emissions."[107]

## The West attempts to shift responsibility onto China

As early as 2015, China was being recognised by the UN's leading climate expert for its "undisputed leadership".[108] Unfortunately, as part of the West's escalating campaign of hostilities against China – and in order to deflect from their own shameful lack of progress in environmental protection – the US and its allies have been conducting a coordinated campaign to shift responsibility for the climate crisis on to China. For example, US President Joe Biden claimed on the eve of the COP26 Summit in 2021 that China "basically didn't show up in terms of any commitments to deal with climate change."[109] He further stated that meaningful progress on climate change negotiations is "going to require us to continue to focus on what China's not doing."[110]

The "it's all China's fault" narrative rests on two key themes: first, that China has for the last few years been the world's largest emitter (in absolute terms) of greenhouse gases; second, that China has committed to achieving carbon neutrality by 2060, whereas the US and Britain have said they will bring all greenhouse gas emissions to net zero by 2050. Such a narrative is flawed in several ways:

First, China is the world's most populous country, with a population of 1.4 billion. Measured on a per capita basis, China's emissions are very ordinary – around the same level as Austria and Ireland.[111] The per capita emissions figure for the US and Australia is almost twice as high.

Second, the comparison of current annual emissions distorts the overall picture. Greenhouse gases don't suddenly disappear from the atmosphere; carbon dioxide hangs around for hundreds of years. In terms of cumulative emissions – the quantity of excess greenhouse gases in the atmosphere right now – the US is responsible for 25 percent, although it contains just four percent of the world's population. As agrarian sociologist Max Ajl puts it, "North Atlantic capitalism enclosed the atmosphere as a dump for its waste eons ago."[112] China, with 18 percent of the world's population, is responsible for 13 percent of cumulative emissions.[113] Over the course of two hundred years, Europe, North America and Japan have become modern industrialised countries, burning enormous quantities of assorted fossil fuels and creating an environmental crisis. Now it seems they want to both shift the blame onto others and pull up the ladder of development.

Third, the reason China's emissions have gone up in recent decades while the West's emissions have gone down has nothing to do with people in the rich countries compromising on their lifestyles, and very little to do with governments making impressive progress on decarbonisation. Rather, it's that the advanced capitalist countries have exported their emissions to the developing world. Chinese emissions are not to any significant degree caused by luxury consumption – average household energy consumption in the US and Canada is nine times higher than in China.[114] Canadian ecosocialist Ian Angus writes that, while more greenhouse gas is now produced in China than in any other country, a great deal of those emissions are "generated to produce goods that are destined for the Global North. Rich countries have outsourced a significant part of their environmental destruction to the Global South."[115]

Fourth, and related, is the fact that China is a developing country. The leading capitalist countries of Europe, North America and Japan reached peak greenhouse gas emissions in the 1980s, after nearly two centuries of industrialisation. If they succeed in achieving net zero emissions by 2050, their journey from peak carbon to net zero will have taken six or seven decades. Before the founding of the People's Republic in 1949, China's economy was based overwhelmingly on small-scale agriculture. There was very little industry, very little transport infrastructure; only a tiny fraction of the population had access to modern energy. Since then, China's use of fossil fuels has steadily increased as it has industrialised and modernised. If it meets its targets of reaching peak emissions by 2030 and zero carbon by 2060, both achievements will have taken less than half the time they took in the major capitalist countries.

Furthermore, while China makes world-leading progress in transitioning away from fossil fuels, the major capitalist countries are failing dismally. The US passed the Inflation Reduction Act in August 2022, including climate commitments that Joe Biden considers to be a landmark success of his presidency to date.[116] This set of climate commitments is the most important so far from the US; unfortunately, that's not saying very much. Certainly it's nowhere near the type of unprecedented action the world needs. Even if the US meets its targets under the Inflation Reduction Act, by 2027 it will still be generating significantly less renewable energy than China will generate in 2022.

Meanwhile the US is driving NATO's proxy war against Russia, which is nothing short of disastrous in environmental terms. In order to punish Russia, to consolidate the Western military-economic-ideological alliance, and to generate profits for the US's domestic fossil fuel industry, the Biden administration has been heavily promoting sanctions on Russian gas and pushing Europe towards reducing its reliance on Russian energy long term. Among the results of this are: a major increase in US exports of fracked shale gas to Europe;[117] the reactivation of coal plants in Germany and elsewhere;[118] along with ramped-up oil and gas extraction in the North Sea.[119] All of these are significantly more damaging in environmental terms than Russian natural gas.

At the UN climate summit in Copenhagen in 2009, rich nations pledged to channel 100 billion US dollars a year to less wealthy nations in order to help them adapt to climate change and transition to emissions-free energy systems. Even though "compared with the investment required to avoid dangerous levels of climate change, the $100-billion pledge is minuscule",[120] the rich nations have not kept their promise. The US spends upwards of 800 billion dollars a year on its military,[121] but seems to be almost entirely unresponsive to the demands of the Global South for climate justice.

The persistent attempts by imperialist politicians and media to blame China for the climate crisis are pure propaganda. In fact, even leading US politicians have occasionally recognised China's progress. Back in December 2019, setting out his vision for the US to accelerate its decarbonisation, John Kerry (currently US Special Presidential Envoy for Climate) observed in an article for the *New York Times* that "China is becoming an energy superpower" and that "China has surpassed us for the lead in renewable energy technology."[122] In August 2022, he acknowledged that China had "generally speaking, outperformed its commitments" in relation to environmental issues. "They had said they will do X, Y and Z and they have done more… China is the largest producer of renewables in the world. They happen to also be the largest deployer of renewables in the world."[123]

Sadly, the US has not responded to China's progress by stepping up cooperation for the benefit of humanity. Instead, it has imposed sanctions on Chinese-manufactured solar power materials, based on disgraceful slander about "slave labour" in Xinjiang.[124] Discussing a previous round of tariffs launched by the Trump administration against China's solar panel industry, Barbara Finamore commented:

> The damage this policy will cause vastly outweighs any potential benefits. Higher-priced panels will significantly reduce the pace of new solar energy installations, increase climate change emissions, and lead to significant job losses nationwide.[125]

It's all too clear that there is a bipartisan consensus in the US that waging a Cold War against China is more important than either boosting the domestic economy or saving the planet.

## Global leadership

> China will make a green contribution to the 21st century, and this will be China's greatest contribution to human development. (Hu Angang)[126]

The fruits of Chinese investment in green energy are being reaped beyond the borders of the People's Republic, with Chinese companies supplying renewable energy infrastructure around the world. Charlie Campbell writes in *Time* that "China is better placed than the US to instil green energy practices in the developing world" and that the Belt and Road Initiative "provides an opportunity to export green technology across Central Asia and Africa."[127]

Chinese financing for renewable power generation overseas increased more than fourfold between 2015 and 2019, and now accounts for the large majority of Chinese-financed overseas power generation capacity. Ma Xinyue of Boston University's Global Development Policy Center opines that "by combining rapid phase-out of coal finance across the world and facilitating the world's energy and economic transition, China has the opportunity to assume international climate leadership during an absolutely critical time."[128]

Chinese policy banks such as Eximbank and the China Development

Bank are leading the finance of significant projects throughout the developing world, including the enormous Quaid-e-Azam Solar Power Park in Pakistan.[129] Latin America's largest solar plant, Cauchari Solar Park in Argentina, was built with Chinese investments and technological assistance.

> The world's highest altitude facility provided power to 160,000 families and turned into a poverty alleviation and social welfare effort when it hired local residents after providing technical training, and was projected to generate $400 million in net profits for the province, widening fiscal space for establishing new schools.[130]

China is actively supporting Cuba's bid to generate 24 percent of its electricity from renewable sources by 2030, and Cuba has joined the China-initiated Belt and Road Energy Partnership.[131]

China is also involved in a number of green energy projects in Africa, including the construction of Zambia's largest hydropower plant, the Kafue Gorge Lower Hydropower Station.[132] Nigerian journalist Otiato Opali writes:

> From the Sakai photovoltaic power station in the Central African Republic and the Garissa solar plant in Kenya, to the Aysha wind power project in Ethiopia and the Kafue Gorge hydroelectric station in Zambia, China has implemented hundreds of clean energy, green development projects in Africa, supporting the continent's efforts to tackle climate change."[133]

Addressing the UN General Assembly in September 2021, Xi Jinping announced that China will not build any new coal-fired power plants overseas, and would increase its support for developing countries to pursue green and low-carbon development.[134] The announcement didn't come out of the blue – Christoph Nedopil, a development economist at Fudan University in Shanghai, notes that "China's government institutions were working with Chinese and international partners to evaluate a possible coal exit for a number of years."[135] It's worth noting in passing that, contrary to media-fuelled myth, China has never been the principal backer of overseas coal power. China makes up 13 percent of investment in such projects; the rest comes mostly from Japan, the US and Britain.[136]

China's ministries of commerce and of ecology and environment have issued a comprehensive set of guidelines for greening foreign investment. These constitute "the most comprehensive document by any country regulator to guide environmental management of overseas projects by either public or private companies."[137] This document sends a very strong signal to both state-owned and private companies that, going forward, outbound foreign investment should always consider environmental impact as a top priority. In a presumably inadvertent admission of the strengths of socialist governance, *China Dialogue* notes that "such policy signals are more important to Chinese businesses, especially state-owned ones, which are more driven by top-down signals from government and state leaders, as compared to many western businesses, which are more influenced by bottom-up signals, such as financial markets, shareholders or civil society."[138]

Aside from its investment activities, China also offers an example for others to follow in terms of charting a course towards sustainability. In Hu Angang's words, China's model can "provide southern countries with a new path leading to ecological civilisation and development – the green development path."[139]

## Conclusion: socialism is the key

> More than in most countries, if a policy idea is seen as a good thing, the Chinese can bring it about. (Mike Berners-Lee)[140]

> While China has made moves to implement its radical conception of ecological civilisation, which is built into state planning and regulation, the notion of a Green New Deal has taken concrete form nowhere in the West. (John Bellamy Foster)[141]

Scientists have understood the issues surrounding climate change for a long time. The UN Framework Convention on Climate Change, with its objective of "stabilising greenhouse gas concentrations in the atmosphere at a level that would prevent dangerous anthropogenic interference with the climate system", was adopted in 1992 and ratified by 154 countries. And yet precious little progress has been made at a global level. Indeed, more than half of all carbon dioxide emissions in the industrial era have been generated in the three decades since then.[142]

Economic anthropologist Jason Hickel writes: "The past half-century is littered with milestones of inaction. A scientific consensus on anthropogenic climate change first began to form in the mid-1970s… The UN Framework Convention on Climate Change (UNFCCC) was adopted in 1992 to set non-binding limits on greenhouse gas emissions. International climate summits – the UN Conference of Parties – have been held annually since 1995 to negotiate plans for emissions reductions. The UN framework has been extended three times, with the Kyoto Protocol in 1997, the Copenhagen Accord in 2009, and the Paris Agreement in 2015. And yet global CO2 emissions continue to rise year after year, while ecosystems unravel at a deadly pace."[143]

This lack of progress seems inexcusable. Humanity has done almost nothing in the face of a global existential crisis, and the reason is simply that the dominant economic system in the world is capitalism. As Ian Angus bluntly states:

> When protecting humanity and planet might reduce profits, corporations will always put profits first... Capital's only measure of success is accumulation. How much more profit was made in this quarter than in the previous quarter? How much more today than yesterday? It doesn't matter if the sales include products that are directly harmful to both humans and nature.[144]

When a society is organised primarily around the pursuit of private profit, rather than addressing the long-term needs of humanity, the question of saving the planet will never be an urgent priority for the ruling class.

Fred Magdoff and John Bellamy Foster describe the absurd situation in the US where "three out of four oil and gas lobbyists in Washington in 2010 formerly worked for the federal government", the result of which is that even such limited environmental regulations as exist don't get properly enforced.

> Given the power exercised by business interests over the economy, state, media, and even theoretically independent nonprofit organisations, it is extremely difficult to effect fundamental changes opposed by corporations. It therefore makes it next to impossible to have a rational and ecologically sound energy policy, health care system, agricultural and food system, industrial policy, trade policy, and educational system.[145]

The balance of power in capitalist countries is such that even relatively progressive governments find it very difficult to prioritise long-term needs of the population over short-term interests of capital. Meanwhile, "everywhere in China today, and at all levels, there are enormous efforts being made to restore the environment."[146] The fundamental reason is that China is "a socialist country of people's democratic dictatorship under the leadership of the working class based on an alliance of workers and farmers; all power of the state in China belongs to the people."[147]

China's economic development proceeds according to state plans, not market anarchy. As a result, the interests of private profit are subordinate to the needs of society.

Dierdre Griswold writes:

> China's economic planners have the power to make decisions that cost a lot of money, but will benefit the people – and the world – over the long run. They're not driven by profits and each quarter's bottom line. In countries where the super-rich run and control everything, you get a well-financed campaign of lies by the polluting corporations to turn public opinion against science and the environmental movement. But not in China.[148]

China can direct investment and resources towards green development precisely because of the socialist basis of its economy. China's enormous investments in renewable energy, energy efficiency, electric vehicles, afforestation and 'circular' waste management have largely been made by state banks, and its projects carried out largely by state-owned enterprises, according to strategic guidelines laid out by the government.

One example is how the Chinese government manages unemployment resulting from coal power plants being shut down. Barbara Finamore notes that the state "set aside a $15 billion fund to relocate and retrain laid-off workers, and has encouraged firms and local governments to help find new jobs for them, including in the services sector, which is growing rapidly."[149] Hundreds of thousands of workers in polluting industries have been able to re-skill and get jobs working in the clean energy sector. It's a planned economy that makes this possible.

Mariana Mazzucato has written that "what is separating China from its international peers is its courage to commit to renewable energy and innovation in the short and long run."[150] She makes this point in order to encourage Western governments to be more courageous in their pursuit of a green agenda – a noble motivation. But of course it's primarily a question not of courage but of political power. As Hu Angang points out, "the capitalist development model has a fundamental and irreconcilable contradiction between infinite capital expansion and limited natural resources".[151]

China still faces an intimidating array of obstacles on its path to realising an ecological civilisation. Judith Shapiro notes that there's a growing middle income group – currently estimated to be nearing half a billion people – which aspires to "own automobiles, live in spacious homes and apartments with comfortable and fashionable furnishings, eat higher up the food chain by switching from grain to meat-centred diets, and increase household energy use by using more appliances, heat, and air conditioning."[152] Local officials struggle with conflicting goals of economic growth and environmental protection, tending through habit to privilege the former over the latter. Furthermore, China is still a developing country and millions of its people still live in relative poverty. Their immediate needs include using significantly more energy than they currently do, and meanwhile China is still "sitting on a mountain of cheap coal."

However, China is more focused on this issue than any other country and its progress is already formidable and its commitment unquestionable. In his work report to the 20th National Congress of the CPC in October 2022, Xi Jinping said:

> Humanity and nature make up a community of life. If we extract from nature without limit or inflict damage on it, we are bound to face its retaliation. China is committed to sustainable development and to the principles of prioritising resource conservation and environmental protection and letting nature restore itself. We will protect nature and the environment as we do our own lives. We will continue to pursue a model of sound development featuring improved production, higher living standards, and healthy ecosystems to ensure the sustainable development of the Chinese nation.[153]

Those in the major capitalist countries should take inspiration from China's example of addressing the ecological crisis, and feed this inspiration into a powerful mass movement capable of effecting the meaningful change that humanity desperately needs. Just as progress made on social welfare in the European socialist countries in the mid-20th century created tremendous pressure on the capitalist ruling classes to grant concessions to the working class (in the form of universal education, social housing and healthcare systems), so can China's environmental strategy in the 21st century create pressure on the capitalist ruling classes to stop destroying the planet and commit to climate justice.

Mao Zedong said in 1956 that, by the beginning of the 21st century, China would have become "a powerful socialist industrial country" and that "she ought to have made a greater contribution to humanity."[154] Over the last decade in particular, China has emerged as the undisputed leader in the fight against climate breakdown, and the results of this leadership are reverberating globally. It would be difficult to overstate the profound significance of this for our species and planet.

## NOTES

1 Xi Jinping. *The Governance of China*. Beijing: Foreign Languages Press, 2014, p231

2 *World Bank Group President Says China Offers Lessons in Helping the World Overcome Poverty*, World Bank, accessed 20 February 2023, <https: / / www.worldbank.org / en / news / press-release / 2010 / 09 / 15 / world-bank-group-president-says-china-offers-lessons-helping-world-overcome-poverty>.

3 Barbara Finamore. *Will China Save the Planet?* Environmental Futures. Cambridge, UK ; Medford, MA, USA: Polity, 2018, p18

4 Martin Jacques. *When China Rules the World: The End of the Western World and the Birth of a New Global Order. 2. ed*. New York, NY: Penguin Books, 2012, p180

5 John Bachtell 2018, *China builds an 'Ecological Civilization' while the world burns*, People's World, accessed 21 February 2023, <https: / / www.peoplesworld.org / article / china-builds-an-ecological-civilization-while-the-world-burns / >.

6 *Declaration on the Right to Development* (1986), Office of the High Commissioner for Human Rights, accessed 21 February 2023, <https: / / www.ohchr.org / en / instruments-mechanisms / instruments / declaration-right-development>.

7 Hannah Ritchie 2019, *Who has contributed most to global CO2 emissions?*, Our World in Data, accessed 21 February 2023, <https: / / ourworldindata.org / contributed-most-global-co2>.

8 Zhang Yanzhu and Zhang Chao 2022, *Thirty years with common but differentiated responsibility, why do we need it ever more today?*, Blavatnik School of Government / University of Oxford, accessed 21 February 2023, <https: / / www.bsg.ox.ac.uk / blog / thirty-years-common-differentiated-responsibility-why-do-we-need-it-ever-more-today>.

9 John Vidal and David Adam 2007, *China overtakes US as world's biggest CO2 emitter*, The Guardian, accessed 21 February 2023, <https: / / www.theguardian.com / environment / 2007 / jun / 19 / china.usnews>.

10 *CO2 emissions (metric tons per capita)*, World Bank, accessed 21 February 2023, <https: / / data.worldbank.org / indicator / EN.ATM.CO2E.PC>.

11 Jacques, *op cit*, p179

12 *China*, World Food Program, accessed 21 February 2023, <https: / / www.wfp.org / countries / china>.

13 *China activates emergency response to support flood-hit Guangdong* (2018), China Daily, accessed 21 February 2023, <http: / / www.chinadaily.com.cn / a / 201809 / 02 / WS5b8bde96a310add14f38919f.html>.

14 Judith Shapiro. *China's Environmental Challenges*. Second edition. Malden, MA: Polity Press, 2016, p65

15 Finamore, *op cit*, p28

16 Hirst, *op cit*, p74

17 Wang Zhihe et al 2014, *The Ecological Civilization Debate in China*, Monthly Review, accessed 21 February 2023, <https: / / monthlyreview.org / 2014 / 11 / 01 / the-ecological-civilization-debate-in-china / >.

18 Mariana Mazzucato. *The Entrepreneurial State: Debunking Public vs Private Sector Myths*. London: Penguin Books, 2018, p181

19 Xi Jinping, *op cit*, p231

20 Zhang Yunfei and Li Na, *Usher in a New Era of Socialist Ecological Progress*, Renmin University of China Press, 2017

21 *Top polluter China unveils nationwide carbon market* (2017), Business Standard, accessed 21 February 2023, <https: / / www.business-standard.com / article / pti-stories / top-polluter-china-unveils-nationwide-carbon-market-117121901350_1.html>.

22 Matt McGrath 2020, *Climate change: China aims for 'carbon neutrality by 2060'*, BBC News, accessed 21 February 2023, <https: / / www.bbc.co.uk / news / science-environment-54256826>.

23 *Full text: Statement by Xi Jinping at General Debate of 75th UNGA*, China Daily, accessed 21 February 2023, <https: / / www.chinadaily.com.cn / a / 202009 / 23 / WS5f6a640ba31024ad0ba7b1e7.html>.

24 *Action Plan for Carbon Dioxide Peaking Before 2030*, Department of Resource Conservation and Environmental Protection, accessed 21 February 2023, <https: / / en.ndrc.gov.cn / policies / 202110 / t20211027_1301020.html>.

25 *Xi Jinping Attends the 2022 World Economic Forum Virtual Session and Delivers a Speech*, Ministry of Foreign Affairs of the People's Republic of China, accessed 21 February 2023, <https: / / www.fmprc.gov.cn / eng / zxxx_662805 / 202201 / t20220118_10629754.html>.

26 Adam Tooze 2020, *Did Xi Just Save the World?*, Foreign Policy, accessed 21 February 2023, <https: / / foreignpolicy.com / 2020 / 09 / 25 / xi-china-climate-change-saved-the-world%e2%80%a8 / >.

27 You Xiaoying 2021, *China's 2060 climate pledge is 'largely consistent' with 1.5C goal, study finds*, Carbon Brief, accessed 21 February 2023, <https: / / www.carbonbrief.org / chinas-2060-climate-pledge-is-largely-consistent-with-1-5c-goal-study-finds / >.

28 Liu Swithin 2022, *Guest post: Why China is set to significantly overachieve its 2030 climate goals*, Carbon Brief, accessed 21 February 2023, <https: / / www.carbonbrief.org / guest-post-why-china-is-set-to-significantly-overachieve-its-2030-climate-goals / >.

29 Angel Hsu 2021, *Don't Be So Quick to Doubt China's Climate Change Dedication*, New York Times, accessed 21 February 2023, <https: / / www.nytimes.com / 2021 / 11 / 07 / opinion / cop26-china-climate.

html>.

30 *Electricity production from coal sources (% of total) – China*, World Bank, accessed 21 February 2023, <https://data.worldbank.org/indicator/EG.ELC.COAL.ZS?locations=CN>.

31 *China to cut coal use share below 56% in 2021*, Reuters, accessed 21 February 2023, <https://www.reuters.com/world/china/china-cut-coal-use-share-below-56-2021-2021-04-22/>.

32 *Coal production per capita, 2021*, Our World In Data, accessed 21 February 2023, <https://ourworldindata.org/grapher/coal-prod-per-capita>.

33 Michael Forsythe 2017, *China Cancels 103 Coal Plants, Mindful of Smog and Wasted Capacity*, New York Times, accessed 21 February 2023, <https://www.nytimes.com/2017/01/18/world/asia/china-coal-power-plants-pollution.html>.

34 Stephen Chen 2017, *Beijing shuts down its last coal-fired power plant as part of bid to clear air*, South China Morning Post, accessed 21 February 2023, <https://www.scmp.com/news/china/society/article/2080270/beijing-shuts-down-its-last-coal-fired-power-plant-part-bid-clear>.

35 Leanna Garfield 2018, *China's latest energy megaproject shows that coal really is on the way out*, Business Insider, accessed 21 February 2023, <https://www.businessinsider.com/china-floating-solar-farm-coal-mine-renewable-energy-2018-1?r=UK>.

36 *China's coal capital transforming into hydrogen hub*, China Daily, accessed 21 February 2023, <http://www.chinadaily.com.cn/a/201908/25/WS5d6239d5a310cf3e35567b9b.html>.

37 *Foreign Ministry Spokesperson Zhao Lijian's Regular Press Conference on July 28, 2022*, Ministry of Foreign Affairs of the People's Republic of China, accessed 21 February 2023, <https://www.fmprc.gov.cn/mfa_eng/xwfw_665399/s2510_665401/2511_665403/202207/t20220728_10729508.html>.

38 Michael Greenstone 2018, *Four Years After Declaring War on Pollution, China Is Winning*, New York Times, accessed 21 February 2023, <https://www.nytimes.com/2018/03/12/upshot/china-pollution-environment-longer-lives.html>.

39 *Pollution in Beijing is Down by Half Since the Last Olympics, Adding Four Years onto Lives* (2022), Air Quality Life Index (University of Chicago), accessed 21 February 2023, <https://aqli.epic.uchicago.edu/news/pollution-in-beijing-is-down-by-half-since-the-last-olympics-adding-four-years-onto-lives/>.

40 *Beijing set to exit list of world's top 200 most-polluted cities: data*, Reuters, accessed 21 February 2023, <https://www.reuters.com/article/us-china-pollution-beijing/beijing-set-to-exit-list-of-worlds-top-200-most-polluted-cities-data-idUSKCN1VX05Z>.

41 Jacques, *op cit*, p179
42 *These are 20 most polluted cities in the world; Rajasthan city tops the list* (2022), Hindustan Times, accessed 21 February 2023, <https://www.hindustantimes.com/environment/these-are-20-most-polluted-cities-in-the-world-rajasthan-city-tops-the-list-101647954069826.html>.
43 KJ Noh and Michael Wong 2021, *China offers solutions to climate change*, Asia Times, accessed 21 February 2023, <https://asiatimes.com/2021/11/china-offers-solutions-to-climate-change/>.
44 Dominic Dudley 2019, *China Is Set To Become The World's Renewable Energy Superpower, According To New Report*, Forbes, accessed 21 February 2023, <https://www.forbes.com/sites/dominicdudley/2019/01/11/china-renewable-energy-superpower/?sh=d00df01745a2>.
45 Douglas Broom 2022, *These 4 charts show the state of renewable energy in 2022*, World Economic Forum, accessed 21 February 2023, <https://www.weforum.org/agenda/2022/06/state-of-renewable-energy-2022/>.
46 Nick O'Malley 2022, *What if China saved the world and nobody noticed?*, Sydney Morning Herald, accessed 21 February 2023, <https://www.smh.com.au/environment/climate-change/what-if-china-saved-the-world-and-nobody-noticed-20220818-p5bavz.html>.
47 Lili Pike et al 2022, *China is beating the U.S. in clean energy. Can America catch up? The race in five charts.*, Grid, accessed 21 February 2023, <https://www.grid.news/story/global/2022/08/17/china-is-beating-the-us-in-clean-energy-can-america-catch-up-the-race-in-five-charts/>.
48 *Global renewable energy jobs hit 12.7 mln, with China accounting for 42 pct: report* (2022), Xinhua, accessed 21 February 2023, <https://english.news.cn/20220922/45a980ba9b5241699694b1f29d1f951e/c.html>.
49 *China says a third of electricity will come from renewables by 2025*, Reuters, accessed 21 February 2023, <https://www.reuters.com/business/sustainable-business/china-says-third-electricity-will-come-renewables-by-2025-2022-06-01/>.
50 Dong Wenjuan and Qi Ye 2018, *Utility of renewable energy in China's low-carbon transition*, Brookings, accessed 21 February 2023, <https://www.brookings.edu/2018/05/18/utility-of-renewable-energy-in-chinas-low-carbon-transition/>.
51 *China currently dominates global solar PV supply chains*, International Energy Agency, accessed 21 February 2023, <https://www.iea.org/reports/solar-pv-global-supply-chains/executive-summary>.
52 *ibid*
53 David Vetter 2022, *China Built More Offshore Wind In 2021 Than Every*

*Other Country Built In 5 Years*, Forbes, accessed 21 February 2023, <https://www.forbes.com/sites/davidrvetter/2022/01/26/china-built-more-offshore-wind-in-2021-than-every-other-country-built-in-5-years/>.

54 Uwe Parpart 2022, *Nobel recognition for China's carbon-neutral leadership*, Asia Times, accessed 21 February 2023, <https://asiatimes.com/2022/11/nobel-recognition-for-chinas-carbon-neutral-leadership/>.

55 *Leading countries in installed renewable energy capacity worldwide in 2021*, Statista, accessed 21 February 2023, <https://www.statista.com/statistics/267233/renewable-energy-capacity-worldwide-by-country/>.

56 Simon Göss 2022, *China should comfortably meet its 2030 Renewables target. But its emissions?*, Energy Post, accessed 21 February 2023, <https://energypost.eu/china-should-comfortably-meet-its-2030-renewables-target-but-its-emissions/>.

57 Philip Wolfe 2021, *The world's largest solar parks*, PV Magazine, accessed 21 February 2023, <https://www.pv-magazine.com/2021/09/23/the-worlds-largest-solar-parks/>.

58 Finamore, *op cit*, p69

59 Tom Hancock 2022, *These Are the Megaprojects in China's $1 Trillion Infrastructure Plan*, Bloomberg, accessed 21 February 2023, <https://www.bloomberg.com/news/features/2022-08-25/how-china-will-spend-1-trillion-on-infrastructure-to-boost-economy>.

60 *China's State Grid to invest $22 bln in ultra high voltage power lines -report* (2022), Reuters, accessed 21 February 2023, <https://www.reuters.com/business/energy/chinas-state-grid-invest-22-bln-ultra-high-voltage-power-lines-report-2022-08-03/>.

61 Mike Berners-Lee. *There Is No Plan(et) B: A Handbook for the Make or Break Years*. Cambridge ; New York, NY: Cambridge University Press, 2019, p73

62 Stephen Chen 2019, *China develops superconducting hybrid power line that could span the country*, South China Morning Post, accessed 21 February 2023, <https://www.scmp.com/news/china/science/article/3024737/china-develops-superconducting-hybrid-power-line-could-span>.

63 Zhang Tong 2022, *China building world's largest 'green hydrogen' factory*, South China Morning Post, accessed 21 February 2023, <https://www.scmp.com/news/china/science/article/3188751/china-building-worlds-largest-green-hydrogen-factory>.

64 Sonal Patel 2022, *China Starts Up First Fourth-Generation Nuclear Reactor*, Power, accessed 21 February 2023, <https://www.powermag.com/china-starts-up-first-fourth-generation-nuclear-reactor/>.

65 Alice Shen 2019, *How China hopes to play a leading role in developing next-generation nuclear reactors*, South China Morning Post, accessed 21 February 2023, <https: / / www.scmp.com / news / china / science / article / 2181396 / how-china-hopes-play-leading-role-developing-next-generation>.

66 Echo Xie 2021, *China powers up fourth-generation nuclear reactor in steady zero-carbon push*, South China Morning Post, accessed 21 February 2023, <https: / / www.scmp.com / news / china / science / article / 3160448 / china-powers-fourth-generation-nuclear-reactor-steady-zero>.

67 Dan Murtaugh and Krystal Chia 2021, *China's Climate Goals Hinge on a $440 Billion Nuclear Buildout*, Bloomberg, accessed 21 February 2023, <https: / / www.bloomberg.com / news / features / 2021-11-02 / china-climate-goals-hinge-on-440-billion-nuclear-power-plan-to-rival-u-s>.

68 *Fukushima disaster: What happened at the nuclear plant?*, BBC News, accessed 21 February 2023, <https: / / www.bbc.co.uk / news / world-asia-56252695>.

69 David Wallace-Wells. *The Uninhabitable Earth: A Story of the Future.* London: Allen Lane, 2019, p101

70 Berners-Lee, *op cit*, p77

71 Hirst, *op cit*, p132

72 Ben Turner 2022, *China's $1 trillion 'artificial sun' fusion reactor just got five times hotter than the sun*, Live Science, accessed 21 February 2023, <https: / / www.livescience.com / chinas-1-trillion-artificial-sun-fusion-reactor-just-got-five-times-hotter-than-the-sun>.

73 Alasdair Lane 2022, *Nuclear fusion has been a pipe dream for decades, but it might actually be on the cusp of commercial viability*, Fortune, accessed 21 February 2023, <https: / / fortune.com / 2022 / 11 / 14 / nuclear-fusion-has-been-a-pipe-dream-for-decades-but-it-might-actually-be-on-the-cusp-of-commercial-viability / >.

74 Nathaniel Scharping 2016, *Why Nuclear Fusion Is Always 30 Years Away*, Discover, accessed 21 February 2023, <https: / / www.discovermagazine.com / technology / why-nuclear-fusion-is-always-30-years-away>.

75 Holly Chik 2022, *Chinese scientists hail 'important step' towards nuclear fusion from 'artificial sun'*, South China Morning Post, accessed 21 February 2023, <https: / / www.scmp.com / news / china / science / article / 3196825 / chinese-scientists-hail-important-step-towards-nuclear-fusion-artificial-sun>.

76 Hirst, *op cit*, p112

77 *China cuts carbon emissions per unit of GDP by half from 2005*, China Daily, accessed 21 February 2023, <https: / / www.chinadaily.com.cn / a / 202206 / 16 / WS62aa12e5a310fd2b29e62ee1.html>.

78 *CO2 emissions (kg per PPP $ of GDP) – China*, World Bank, accessed 21

February 2023, <https://data.worldbank.org/indicator/EN.ATM.CO2E.PP.GD?locations=CN>.
79 *International Energy Efficiency Scorecard* (2022), American Council for an Energy-Efficient Economy, accessed 21 February 2023, <https://www.aceee.org/international-scorecard>.
80 Finamore, *op cit*, p112
81 Hannah Ritchie 2020, *Cars, planes, trains: where do CO2 emissions from transport come from?*, Our World in Data, accessed 21 February 2023, <https://ourworldindata.org/co2-emissions-from-transport>.
82 *Share of pure electric city busses and trolley busses in China's cities from 2016 to 2021*, Statista, accessed 21 February 2023, <https://www.statista.com/statistics/1331786/share-of-pure-electric-city-busses-and-trolleybusses-in-china/>.
83 Chenzi Yiyang and Vincent Fremery 2022, *E-bus Development in China: From Fleet Electrification to Refined Management*, Transition China, accessed 21 February 2023, <https://transition-china.org/mobilityposts/e-bus-development-in-china-from-fleet-electrification-to-refined-management/>.
84 Katharina Buchholz 2021, *What's really driving the trend in e-vehicles? Your local electrical bus*, World Economic Forum, accessed 21 February 2023, <https://www.weforum.org/agenda/2021/03/municipal-buses-lead-electrification-effort>.
85 Echo Huang 2018, *China's making it super hard to build car factories that don't make electric vehicles*, Quartz, accessed 21 February 2023, <https://qz.com/1500793/chinas-banning-new-factories-that-only-make-fossil-fuel-cars>.
86 Akshat Rathi 2019, *Five things to know about China's electric-car boom*, Quartz, accessed 21 February 2023, <https://qz.com/1517557/five-things-to-know-about-chinas-electric-car-boom >.
87 David Sickels 2022, *China has 65% of public EV charging stations worldwide*, The Buzz, accessed 21 February 2023, <https://www.thebuzzevnews.com/china-public-ev-charging-stations/>.
88 Lili Pike 2019, *How green is China's high-speed rail?*, China Dialogue, accessed 21 February 2023, <https://chinadialogue.net/en/energy/11174-how-green-is-china-s-high-speed-rail/>.
89 Ben Jones 2022, *Past, present and future: The evolution of China's incredible high-speed rail network*, CNN, accessed 21 February 2023, <https://edition.cnn.com/travel/article/china-high-speed-rail-cmd/index.html>.
90 *High-speed rail in the United States*, Wikipedia, accessed 21 February 2023, <https://en.wikipedia.org/wiki/High-speed_rail_in_the_United_States>.
91 Harrison Jacobs 2019, *Alexandria Ocasio-Cortez included high-speed rail in her Green New Deal. After riding China's superfast bullet train*

*that could go from New York to Chicago in 4.5 hours, it's clear how far behind the US really is,* Business Insider, accessed 21 February 2023, <https: / / www.businessinsider.com / china-bullet-train-speed-map-photos-tour-2018-5>.

92 Jane Braxton Little 2021, *Lessons from the rush to reforest,* China Dialogue, accessed 21 February 2023, <https: / / chinadialogue.net / en / nature / lessons-from-the-rush-to-reforest / >.

93 Xi Jinping 2014, *op cit,* p229

94 *China's 40-Year, Billion-Tree Project Is a Lesson for the World* (2020), Bloomberg, accessed 21 February 2023, <https: / / www.bloomberg.com / news / articles / 2020-09-14 / china-s-40-year-billion-tree-project-is-a-lesson-for-the-world>.

95 Jamie Fullerton 2018, *China to plant forest the size of Ireland in bid to become world leader in conservation,* The Telegraph, accessed 21 February 2023, <https: / / www.telegraph.co.uk / news / 2018 / 01 / 05 / china-plant-forest-size-ireland-bid-become-world-leader-conservation / >.

96 *Forest area (% of land area) – China,* World Bank, accessed 21 February 2023, <https: / / data.worldbank.org / indicator / AG.LND.FRST.ZS?locations=CN>.

97 *Why is a quarter of world's new forest area coming from China?,* People's Daily, accessed 21 February 2023, <http: / / en.people.cn / n3 / 2022 / 1003 / c90000-10154575.html>.

98 *One-third of China's land protected under ecological 'red line' scheme* (2022), Reuters, accessed 21 February 2023, <https: / / www.reuters.com / world / china / one-third-chinas-land-protected-under-ecological-red-line-scheme-2022-09-19 / >.

99 Braxton Little, *op cit,* <https: / / chinadialogue.net / en / nature / lessons-from-the-rush-to-reforest / >.

100 Li Hui-Ping et al. *New Approaches in Urban Forestry to Minimize Invasive Species Impacts: The Case of Xiongan New Area in China.* Insects. 2020 May 12;11(5):300. doi: 10.3390 / insects11050300. PMID: 32408656; PMCID: PMC7290593.

101 *Principal contradiction facing Chinese society has evolved in new era: Xi* (2017), Xinhua, accessed 21 February 2023, <http: / / www.xinhuanet.com / english / 2017-10 / 18 / c_136688132.htm>.

102 *Xi Jinping on China's high-quality development* (2021), Xinhua, accessed 21 February 2023, <http: / / www.xinhuanet.com / english / 2021-08 / 02 / c_1310102511.htm>.

103 *Full text of President Xi's speech at opening of Belt and Road forum,* Xinhua, accessed 21 February 2023, <http: / / www.xinhuanet.com / english / 2017-05 / 14 / c_136282982.htm>.

104 Hu Angang. *China: Innovative Green Development.* Second Edition. Singapore: Springer Verlag, 2017, p42

105 *ibid*, p27

106 He Huifeng 2021, *China's tech hub Shenzhen moves ahead with GDP alternative that measures value of ecosystem goods and services*, South China Morning Post, accessed 21 February 2023, <https: / / www.scmp.com / economy / china-economy / article / 3126757 / chinas-tech-hub-shenzhen-moves-ahead-gdp-alternative-measures>.

107 Finamore, *op cit*, p24

108 Suzanne Goldenberg 2015, *US 'playing catch-up to China' in clean energy efforts, UN climate chief says*, The Guardian, accessed 21 February 2023, <https: / / www.theguardian.com / environment / 2015 / nov / 03 / us-china-clean-energy-economy-climate-change>.

109 Marc Santora et al 2021, *Who's attending (Biden and Modi), and who isn't (Putin and Xi)*, New York Times, accessed 21 February 2023, <https: / / www.nytimes.com / 2021 / 11 / 01 / world / europe / cop26-global-leaders-attending.html>.

110 David Herszenhorn 2021, *Biden says Russia, China 'didn't show up' on climate change commitments*, Politico, accessed 21 February 2023, <https: / / www.politico.eu / article / biden-says-russia-china-didnt-show-up-on-climate-change-commitments / >.

111 *CO2 emissions (metric tons per capita)*, World Bank, accessed 21 February 2023, <https: / / data.worldbank.org / indicator / EN.ATM.CO2E.PC?most_recent_value_desc=true>.

112 Max Ajl. *A People's Green New Deal*. London: Pluto Press, 2021, p31

113 Hannah Ritchie 2019, *Who has contributed most to global CO2 emissions?*, Our World In Data, accessed 21 February 2023, <https: / / ourworldindata.org / contributed-most-global-co2>.

114 Lindsay Wilson 2021, *Average Household Electricity Consumption – 2022*, Shrink That Footprint, accessed 21 February 2023, <https: / / shrinkthatfootprint.com / average-household-electricity-consumption / >.

115 Ian Angus. *Facing the Anthropocene: Fossil Capitalism and the Crisis of the Earth System*. New York: Monthly Review Press, 2016, p165

116 *The Inflation Reduction Act*, White House, accessed 21 February 2023, <https: / / www.whitehouse.gov / briefing-room / statements-releases / 2022 / 08 / 15 / by-the-numbers-the-inflation-reduction-act / >.

117 Jarrett Renshaw and Scott Disavino 2022, *Analysis: U.S. LNG exports to Europe on track to surpass Biden promise*, Reuters, accessed 21 February 2023, <https: / / www.reuters.com / business / energy / us-lng-exports-europe-track-surpass-biden-promise-2022-07-26 / >.

118 Kate Connolly 2022, *Germany to reactivate coal power plants as Russia curbs gas flow*, The Guardian, accessed 21 February 2023, <https: / / www.theguardian.com / world / 2022 / jul / 08 / germany-reactivate-coal-power-plants-russia-curbs-gas-flow>.

119 Alex Lawson 2022, *UK offers new North Sea oil and gas licences despite climate concerns,* The Guardian, accessed 21 February 2023, <https: / / www.theguardian.com / business / 2022 / oct / 07 / uk-offers-new-north-sea-oil-and-gas-licences-despite-climate-concerns>.

120 Jocelyn Timperley 2021, *The broken $100-billion promise of climate finance – and how to fix it,* Nature, accessed 21 February 2023, <https: / / www.nature.com / articles / d41586-021-02846-3>.

121 Mike Stone 2022, *U.S. Congress moves to boost Biden's record defense budget,* Reuters, accessed 21 February 2023, <https: / / www.reuters.com / world / us / us-congress-moves-boost-bidens-record-defense-budget-2022-06-22 / >.

122 John Kerry and Ro Khanna 2019, *Don't Let China Win the Green Race,* New York Times, accessed 21 February 2023, <https: / / www.nytimes.com / 2019 / 12 / 09 / opinion / china-renewable-energy.html>.

123 Eleni Varvitsioti and Aime Williams 2022, *Climate envoy John Kerry seeks restart to US emissions talks with China,* Financial Times, accessed 21 February 2023, <https: / / www.ft.com / content / a1007c8b-4b9d-4ba1-8587-6cee53ed43fa>.

124 Nichola Groom 2022, *U.S. blocks more than 1,000 solar shipments over Chinese slave labor concerns,* Reuters, accessed 21 February 2023, <https: / / www.reuters.com / world / china / exclusive-us-blocks-more-than-1000-solar-shipments-over-chinese-slave-labor-2022-11-11 / >.

125 Finamore, *op cit,* p75

126 Hu Angang, *op cit,* p201

127 Charlie Campbell 2017, *Why an Unlikely Hero Like China Could End Up Leading the World in the Fight Against Climate Change,* Time, accessed 21 February 2023, <https: / / time.com / 4800747 / china-climate-change-paris-agreement-trump / >.

128 Ma Xinyue 2021, *China's shifting overseas energy footprint,* China Dialogue, accessed 21 February 2023, <https: / / chinadialogue.net / en / energy / chinas-shifting-overseas-energy-footprint / >.

129 Zofeen T Ebrahim 2015, *China helps Pakistan build world's largest solar farm,* China Dialogue, accessed 21 February 2023, <https: / / chinadialogue.net / en / energy / 8160-china-helps-pakistan-build-world-s-largest-solar-farm / >.

130 Azhar Azam 2022, *China-Argentina cooperation set to grow and prosper,* China Daily, accessed 21 February 2023, <https: / / global.chinadaily.com.cn / a / 202203 / 15 / WS622fed1fa310cdd39bc8c993.html>.

131 Chris Devonshire-Ellis 2022, *Unlocking US Sanctions: China Signs Construction & Energy Deals With Cuba,* Silk Road Briefing, accessed 21 February 2023, <https: / / www.silkroadbriefing.com / news / 2022 / 01 / 03 / unlocking-us-sanctions-china-signs-construction-energy-deals-with-cuba / >.

132 *Construction of Chinese-built hydropower plant in Zambia nears*

*completion* (2022), Xinhua, accessed 21 February 2023, <https://english.news.cn/20220722/4ffbe59cea84447a84b018d2b49d6f3f/c.html>.

133 Otiato Opali 2022, *China's clean energy investments growing rapidly in Africa,* China Daily, accessed 21 February 2023, <https://www.chinadaily.com.cn/a/202208/30/WS630d6e5da310fd2b29e74f5e.html>.

134 Shi Yi 2021, *China to stop building new coal power projects overseas,* China Dialogue, accessed 21 February 2023, <https://chinadialogue.net/en/energy/china-to-stop-building-new-coal-power-projects-overseas/>.

135 Dennis Normile 2021, *Environmentalists hail China's vow to stop building coal-fired power plants abroad,* Science, accessed 21 February 2023, <https://www.science.org/content/article/environmentalists-hail-china-s-vow-stop-building-coal-fired-power-plants-abroad>.

136 *ibid*

137 Christoph Nedopil et al 2022, *Understanding China's latest guidelines for greening the Belt and Road,* China Dialogue, accessed 21 February 2023, <https://chinadialogue.net/en/business/understanding-chinas-latest-guidelines-for-greening-the-belt-and-road/>.

138 *ibid*

139 Hu Angang, *op cit,* p10

140 Berners-Lee, *op cit,* p213

141 John Bellamy Foster 2022, *Ecological Civilization, Ecological Revolution,* Monthly Review, accessed 21 February 2023, <https://monthlyreview.org/2022/10/01/ecological-civilization-ecological-revolution/>.

142 *More than half of all CO2 emissions since 1751 emitted in the last 30 years,* Institute for European Environmental Policy, accessed 21 February 2023, <https://ieep.eu/news/more-than-half-of-all-co2-emissions-since-1751-emitted-in-the-last-30-years>.

143 Jason Hickel. *Less is More: How Degrowth Will Save the World*. United Kingdom: Random House, 2020, p20

144 Angus, *op cit,* p114

145 Fred Magdoff and John Bellamy Foster. *What Every Environmentalist Needs to Know About Capitalism*. United States: Monthly Review Press, 2011, p90

146 John Bellamy Foster, *op cit.*

147 Xi Jinpiing 2022, *Full text of the report to the 20th National Congress of the Communist Party of China,* Xinhua, accessed 21 February 2023, <https://english.news.cn/20221025/8eb6f5239f984f01a2bc45b5b5db0c51/c.html>.

148 Dierdre Griswold 2017, *China takes another big step away from CO2,* Workers World, accessed 21 February 2023, <https://www.workers.

org/2017/01/29359/>.
149 Finamore, *op cit*, p46
150 Mazzucato, *op cit*, p230
151 Hu Angang, *op cit*, p5
152 Shapiro, *op cit*, p193
153 Xi Jinping 2022, *Full text of the report to the 20th National Congress of the Communist Party of China*, Xinhua, accessed 21 February 2023, <https://english.news.cn/20221025/8eb6f5239f984f01a2bc45b5b5db0c51/c.html>.
154 Mao Zedong 1956, *In Commemoration of Dr Sun Yat-Sen*, Marxist Internet Archive, accessed 21 February 2023, <https://www.marxists.org/reference/archive/mao/selected-works/volume-5/mswv5_55.htm>.

# 7

# Oppose the New Cold War on China

Since the launch of Obama's 'Pivot to Asia' in 2012, the US has prioritised China containment over all other foreign policy commitments. This includes steadily increasing its presence in the South China Sea and encouraging China's neighbours in their various territorial claims. Obama also initiated an expansion of US military, diplomatic and economic cooperation with other countries in the region. The overarching strategic goal of the proposed Trans-Pacific Partnership (TPP) was to isolate China and to draw East and Southeast Asia back into the US economic – and ideological – orbit.

The Trump administration, while dropping the TPP due to its domestic unpopularity, escalated the Pivot in other respects: launching a trade war in January 2018, imposing a ban on Huawei, attempting to ban TikTok and WeChat, spreading conspiracy theories about the origins of Covid-19, ordering the kidnapping of Huawei CFO Meng Wanzhou, and turning 'decoupling' into a buzzword. Anti-China propaganda became – and has remained – pervasive in the West.

Alongside the economic and information warfare, there has been a rising militarisation of the Pacific and a deepening of a China encirclement strategy that goes back to the arrival of the US Navy's Seventh Fleet in the Taiwan Strait in 1950, just a few months after the establishment of the People's Republic. Recent years have witnessed ever more frequent US naval operations in the South China Sea; increased weapons sales to Taiwan; the undermining of the One China policy; the encouraging of Japan's re-armament; the deployment of the Terminal High Altitude Area Defence (THAAD) anti-ballistic missile defence system in South Korea and

Guam; the establishment of a US marine base in northern Australia; and the bulking up of the Indo-Pacific Command.

## Wars hot and cold, new and old

The term 'Cold War' was originally coined by US financier Bernard Baruch in 1947 to describe the increasingly tense post-war relationship between the capitalist world and the socialist world. "Let us not be deceived; we are today in the midst of a Cold War. Our enemies are to be found abroad and at home. Let us never forget this: Our unrest is the heart of their success."[1] The term "came to signal an American concept of warfare against the Soviet Union: aggressive containment without a state of war."[2]

Historians in the West typically regard the Cold War as an elaborate ideological struggle between two superpowers with comparable motivations – a *clash of civilisations* in which the capitalists and communists slugged it out for supremacy. Such an interpretation ignores the fundamental class struggle dynamics at play.

The Soviets hoped to avoid a return to hostilities following the shared Allied victory in World War II; as such they consistently proposed a system of *peaceful coexistence* in which they – and other countries – would enjoy the right to build the society of their own choosing, without the constant threat of war. Vladimir Shubin, former head of the Africa section of the international department of the Communist Party of the Soviet Union, writes:

> The 'Cold War' was not part of our political vocabulary; in fact the term was used in a strictly negative sense… For us the global struggle was not a battle between the two 'superpowers' assisted by their 'satellites' and 'proxies', but a united fight of the world's progressive forces against imperialism.[3]

"A man is judged by the company he keeps", goes the saying. During the Cold War period, the Soviet Union's allies included the people of Vietnam fighting against imperialist domination; the people of Korea fighting against imperialist domination; the people of South Africa, Angola, Mozambique, Namibia, Guinea Bissau, Algeria and elsewhere, fighting against colonialism and apartheid; the people of Cuba, Grenada, Chile, Nicaragua and elsewhere, fighting for the right to construct socialist societies.

The US and its allies fought a very different kind of Cold War: a global hybrid war against socialism and non-alignment. A secret report written for, and circulated by, President Truman in 1950 bluntly asserted that "every consideration of devotion to our fundamental values and to our national security demands that we seek to achieve them by the strategy of the cold war"; and that the purpose of such a strategy was "to foster a world environment in which the American system can survive and flourish."[4]

The essence of the Cold War was thus a protracted struggle by the US and its allies to protect the long-term viability of the imperialist world system – and, by corollary, weaken the global socialist and anti-imperialist movement. And this war was not always very cold. In Korea, in Vietnam, Laos, Cambodia, Angola, Mozambique, Indonesia, Chile, Argentina, Brazil and elsewhere, the Cold War wrought death and destruction on a horrifying scale.

## A new enemy in a new century

The US won the Cold War by default when the Soviet Union ceased to exist on 31 December 1991. The USSR's dissolution was not accompanied by the promised peace dividend. Rather, the removal of the Soviet Union as a bulwark against imperialist hegemony meant the launch of a new era of NATO expansionism and war; an untrammelled and invigorated US-led militarism, which has thought nothing of destroying Iraq, Yugoslavia, Afghanistan, Libya and Syria.

Martin Jacques writes that the Soviet collapse "greatly enhanced America's pre-eminent position, eliminating its main adversary and resulting in the countries of the former Soviet bloc opening their markets and turning in many cases to the US for aid and support. Never before, not even in the heyday of the British Empire, had a nation's power enjoyed such a wide reach." The US's global position "seemed unassailable, and at the turn of the millennium terms like 'hyperpower' and 'unipolarity' were coined to describe what appeared to be a new and unique form of power."[5]

Along with expanding the US's sphere of economic and political influence into the former socialist countries, strategists developed a new obsession: maintaining the new single-superpower status quo and forestalling the rise of any potential geopolitical challenger. These aims are captured in rather stark terms in the *Wolfowitz Doctrine*, the Defense Planning Guidance for 1994–99 led by then-Deputy Secretary for Defense Paul Wolfowitz:

> Our first objective is to prevent the re-emergence of a new rival, either on the territory of the former Soviet Union or elsewhere, that poses a threat on the order of that posed formerly by the Soviet Union… Our strategy must now refocus on precluding the emergence of any potential future global competitor.[6]

The adoption of the *Pivot to Asia* reflects a consensus in US ruling circles that the "future global competitor" in question is China. This in turn reflects China's emergence as the principal driver of global economic growth and the corresponding rise in its influence. China containment is now blossoming into a multifaceted hybrid war – "a combination of unconventional and conventional means using a range of state and non-state actors that run across the spectrum of social and political life."[7]

The picture Jude Woodward paints of the original Cold War bears a chilling resemblance to the current state of US-China relations:

> The USSR was variously surrounded by a tightening iron noose of US military alliances, forward bases, border interventions, cruise missiles and naval exercises. Economically it was shut out of international trade organisations, subjected to bans and boycotts and excluded from collaboration on scientific and technological developments. It was diplomatically isolated, excluded from the G7 group of major economies and awarded an international pariah status. It was designated as uniquely undemocratic. Any opponents of this 'Cold War' and accompanying nuclear arms race were stigmatised as disloyal apologists, closet 'reds' or spies and subjected to McCarthyite witch-hunts.[8]

The techniques of the original Cold War have been updated and adapted for a new enemy in a new century, but the political essence is the same. The US and its allies still seek to maintain the overall stability and long-term viability of the imperialist world system. This system is under threat from China, which is coalescing forces throughout the world in support of a new, multipolar world order; by definition a negation of the US hegemonist project for military and economic control of the planet.

Thus, much like the original Cold War, the New Cold War is a sustained conflict, initiated and led by the US, between the forces of imperialism, hegemony and unipolarity on the one hand, and the forces of socialism, sovereignty and multipolarity on the other.

## Why now?

Much is made of the 'China threat', which forms the basis of a new McCarthyism in the West. This threat is real enough, albeit not in the sense that it's used by bourgeois politicians and journalists. China does not seek to rule the world, nor does it seek to "undermine democracy worldwide".[9] It is however increasingly challenging the established imperialist world order – economically, strategically and ideologically.

To the extent that China's extraordinary growth was driven by low-cost, low-margin, low-tech, large-scale manufacturing within US-led supply chains – and to the extent that the abundant supply of cheap, competent, diligent and well-educated Chinese labour has made a considerable number of Americans very rich – the US cautiously tolerated China's emergence from generalised poverty. From the early 1970s, the two countries were able to build a mutually beneficial relationship, albeit one rife with complexities, contradictions and the ever-present possibility of confrontation.

But China's long-term strategy was not aimed at permanently playing a subservient role in a globalised economy dominated by the US. As Yang

Weimin, a senior economist in the Chinese government, said in 2018 discussing the nascent trade war: "You can't let China only make t-shirts while the US does high-tech. That is unreasonable."[10]

China's economic structure gives the CPC government various powerful levers for directing production. In particular, the publicly-owned banks, the dominance of state-owned enterprises in the 'commanding heights' of industry, and the enforcement of a strict set of regulations on private business have allowed the country to steadily rise up the value chain and construct an advanced economy. "China is the only authentically emergent country", wrote Samir Amin.[11] Chinese scientific research is increasingly world-class. China is the biggest trading partner of most countries in the world, and has become a major source of investment in other countries, especially developing countries. It's leading the way in the battle against climate breakdown – the sort of thing the West expects to dominate, that feeds into a pervasive (albeit largely subconscious) assumption that the predominantly white nations of Western Europe and North America are fundamentally more civilised and enlightened than the rest of the world.

If China's progress were occurring within a framework of US-led imperialism; if US finance capital were able to exercise meaningful control over the process, it would be less of a problem. Japan, Germany, South Korea have all become significant players in the global economy in the post-war era, but since their rise has occurred within the boundaries of the imperialist world system, it hasn't provoked any strategic crisis in Washington (although there have of course been contradictions and rivalries, most notably in relation to Japan). These countries largely play by the US's rules, and are to a greater or lesser degree militarily and politically beholden to the US.

As a non-white country; a country that consistently aligns itself and identifies with the Global South; a country with a Communist Party-led government; a country that rejects the neoliberal consensus; a country where the capitalist class does not dictate policy; China represents a substantial threat in the battle of ideas. Furthermore, particularly over the last decade, China has become proactive in global politics, promoting a multipolar model of international relations.

China's unprecedented increase in economic strength and geopolitical influence has provoked a renewed resolve in the US ruling class to 'contain' China; to apply the methods of Cold War against it in order to limit its rise and to secure a *New American Century*.

## Trump to Biden – plus ça change

Barack Obama was explicit that the purpose of his 'pivot' was to preserve US hegemony: "We have to make sure America writes the rules of the global economy… Because if we don't write the rules for trade around the world – guess what – China will."[12] Nonetheless, Obama's overall anti-

China strategy was accompanied by some level of sensible cooperation with Beijing, particularly around environmental issues – the Paris Climate Agreement came about in no small part due to the coordination between the US and China.

The Trump administration maintained Obama's overall anti-China stance but dropped the sophistication and cooperation. Trump came to power with a promise to stop China 'raping' the US economy. Key members of his top team included such fanatical China hawks as Mike Pompeo, John Bolton, Stephen Bannon, Robert Lighthizer and Peter Navarro. Their approach was characterised by threats, bluster, blackmail, demagoguery and racism.

Trump insisted that China – aided and abetted by previous US governments – was the cause of all the US's economic problems. China's trade imbalance with the US was "the greatest theft ever perpetrated by anyone or any country in the history of the world".[13] The decline of US manufacturing was attributed to Chinese currency undervaluation rather than to the ruthlessness and decrepitude of neoliberal capitalism. (Singaporean academic and former diplomat Kishore Mahbubani noted wryly that, rather than blaming China for everything, living standards in the US might improve "if America stopped fighting unnecessary foreign wars and used its resources to improve the well-being of its people."[14])

The Trump team initiated a trade war, imposing increasingly heavy tariffs on Chinese imports. Essentially they wanted China to agree to buy hundreds of billions' worth of US produce that it didn't need; end state subsidies to key industries; allow US companies unrestricted access to Chinese markets while accepting tariffs on Chinese exports; and stop negotiating technology transfer deals with US companies. Alongside this attempt at a new round of unequal treaties, they moved to protect the US domination of hi-tech industry, imposing a ban on Huawei and seeking to ban popular Chinese mobile apps TikTok and WeChat.

Trump and Pompeo generated mass hostility towards China by engaging in flagrant racism, most notably blaming the coronavirus pandemic on China and referring to it as 'kung flu' or 'the China virus'. Meanwhile the White House revived the Quadrilateral Security Dialogue (the Quad), a strategic alliance of the US, Japan, Australia and India, widely understood to be an instrument of China containment. Mike Pompeo confirmed that the objective for the Quad was to become an "Asian NATO".[15]

With Joe Biden's victory in the presidential elections, many hoped for an easing of tensions between the US and China. Such hopes have been dashed. The New Cold War has become an invariant of a declining US capitalism determined to hold on to global hegemony via whatever means it can muster. Hostility towards China is a consensus, bipartisan position in the US. Biden has made his view abundantly clear, stating in one of his first speeches as president that "China has an overall goal to become the leading country in the world, the wealthiest country in the world and the most powerful country in the world; that's not going to happen on my watch."[16]

There are of course some tactical differences between Trump and Biden when it comes to Pacific strategy. Trump tended towards a unilateralist position, demanding that allies in Japan and Europe fall in line behind the US. Biden is attempting to construct an ostensibly more consensual alliance among traditional US partners, albeit within the framework of "restored American leadership" – a strategy that is very clearly manifested in the proxy war NATO is waging against Russia.

One of the Biden team's first acts was to try and undermine the EU-China investment deal.[17] Having failed to prevent the deal being signed, the US coordinated with the EU, Canada and UK to impose a set of sanctions on China over its alleged human rights abuses in Xinjiang, with Secretary of State Antony Blinken talking up "our ongoing commitment to working multilaterally to advance respect for human rights".[18] When China then imposed reciprocal sanctions, the EU decided (at the State Department's urging) that it would 'freeze' the deal.[19]

There is little sign that the trade war will be dialled down, in spite of the fact that it has manifestly failed in its stated aim of restoring US manufacturing greatness – a failure Biden himself noted on the campaign trail.[20] Biden has repeated Trump's talking points about China's "coercive and unfair" trade practices[21] and its "abuses of the international system."[22]

## Sanctions and semiconductors

The Biden administration has launched a 'chip war' against China, imposing wide-ranging and unprecedented restrictions on the export of semiconductors, which are core to the functioning of electronic devices. Advances in semiconductors are driving – and will continue to drive – transformative change in a wide range of industries, from energy to medicine to space research. The Belfer Center report estimates that China is on course to become "a top-tier player in the semiconductor industry by 2030."[23] Preventing (or at least slowing) such a development is a key priority for the US.

The CHIPS and Science Act, signed into law by Biden in August 2022, is "the next stage in a series of measures to weaken China's tech capabilities and global influence"; to "crush China's tech advancement", in the words of British economist Michael Roberts.[24] Martin Wolf opined in the *Financial Times* that this chip war is "far more threatening to Beijing than anything Donald Trump did. The aim is clearly to slow China's economic development. That is an act of economic warfare… It will have huge geopolitical consequences."[25]

This issue goes beyond economics. If China outpaces the US in technological innovation, it will shift the entire global balance of forces; it will significantly weaken the ability of the imperialist powers to impose their will on the rest of the world; and it will showcase the fundamental validity of socialism as a means of propelling human progress. As Deng Xiaoping famously commented in 1984, "the superiority of the socialist system is demonstrated, in the final analysis, by faster and greater development of the productive forces than under the capitalist system."[26]

Indeed, developments in technology in the coming decades form a crucial component of the material basis for the progression to a more advanced socialism. British researcher Keith Lamb writes:

> China's goal of building a modern socialist country by 2049 is predicated on mastering semiconductor technology which is the linchpin of the modern age, making innovations such as self-driving electric vehicles, fully-automated AI production systems, and supercomputers possible.[27]

Such are the reasons for the wave of sanctions connected to the semiconductor industry. The US wants to restrict China's ability to import semiconductors and, more importantly, to prevent China achieving self-sufficiency in semiconductor production. Blacklisting SMIC, China's biggest manufacturer of computer chips, in December 2020, means that it is no longer able to source supplies from US companies. Chinese chip designers have been cut off from access to leading-edge chip design tools.[28] Meanwhile Huawei has been prevented from importing chips, impacting its production of high-end smartphones.[29] The US has been able to enforce many of these sanctions on an international scale, by virtue of its 'long-arm jurisdiction' – sanctioning non-US chipmakers that use US-made components. One notable absurdity here is that Taiwan, a region of China, complies with the US sanctions regime, and therefore Taiwan Semiconductor Manufacturing Company (TSMC) – the world's most valuable semiconductor company – has been forced to stop its exports to the companies on the US Entity List, including Huawei.[30]

Another area in which the Biden administration is ramping up Cold War hostility is by imposing sanctions on Chinese-manufactured solar energy materials. China is by far the world's largest producer of solar energy, with an installed capacity of 254 GW – more than three times that of the US, and growing fast.[31] China also produces the bulk of the global supply of polysilicon (a key material in the production of solar panels). Johannes Bernreuter, author of the Polysilicon Market Outlook 2024, predicts that "China's share in the global solar-grade polysilicon output will approach 90 percent in the coming years."[32]

Unable to compete on price or productivity, the US has resorted to imposing sanctions on large parts of China's solar panel industry – ostensibly on the basis of evidence-free and comprehensively debunked claims of the manufacturers using Uyghur forced labour (discussed in Chapter 5: *Manufacturing consent for the containment and encirclement of China*). This is profoundly irresponsible and short-sighted behaviour. Chinese investment in solar technology over the course of the last 10-15 years has pushed the entire industry forward, and has brought prices down to a level where solar power is more cost-effective than fossil fuel alternatives in many parts of the world. This is an important contribution to the global struggle to prevent climate breakdown. The Western powers should be working closely with China and other countries on developing and deploying clean energy, rather than imposing sanctions with a view to gaining some fleeting economic advantage.

## Containment and encirclement

There is also a basic continuity between the Trump and Biden administrations at the military level of the New Cold War, with Biden heavily promoting the 'Quad' alliance[33] and, according to the Chinese Ministry of Defence, significantly increasing the US military presence and surveillance in the Pacific.[34]

In 2021, the US, Britain and Australia surprised and shocked the world with the announcement of a new trilateral security pact, AUKUS. Under this agreement, writes Jenny Clegg:

> the US and UK are to equip Australia with nuclear-powered submarines, not only violating the nuclear Non-Proliferation Treaty but also subverting the nuclear weapons free zones of South East Asia and the South Pacific.[35]

Since then, it has been announced that the AUKUS countries will cooperate on the development of hypersonic weapons.[36] AUKUS enhances military cooperation between these three colonial and neocolonial powers in the Pacific region, and is obviously part of a broader strategy of China containment and encirclement. In early 2023, the US secured access to four additional military bases in the Philippines – "a key bit of real estate which would offer a front seat to monitor the Chinese in the South China Sea and around Taiwan", according to the BBC.[37]

China's most senior diplomat, Wang Yi, summed up this creeping militarisation:

> From strengthening the Five Eyes to peddling the Quad, from piecing together AUKUS to tightening bilateral military alliances, the US is staging a five-four-three-two formation in the Asia-Pacific, [the purpose of which is] to establish an Indo-Pacific version of NATO ... and maintain the US-led system of hegemony.[38]

Biden and his associates have directed significant efforts towards undermining the One China policy, supporting separatists in Taiwan and attempting to stoke hostility across the Taiwan Strait. General Mark Milley, chairman of the US Joint Chiefs of Staff, has pledged that the US would "support Taiwan militarily" if China attempted to use force to bring about national reunification.[39] Biden has stated multiple times – in clear contravention of the US's commitments and with no basis in international law – that the US would intervene militarily on Taiwan's behalf.[40]

In December 2022, the US introduced the Taiwan Enhanced Resilience Act, providing for 10 billion dollars' direct military aid to Taiwan – the first time such aid has been given on this scale.[41] The 2022 National Defense Authorization Act, which signed off on a military budget of close to a trillion dollars, provides an alarmingly clear indication that Washington is preparing for war against China, with Taiwan as the trigger. "Taiwan is by far the most referenced geographic area in the bill, with 438 mentions, more than Russia, with 237, and Ukraine, with 159."[42]

Closely connected with these efforts to bolster the military strength of Taiwanese separatists is the US's strong support for Japan's remilitarisation. In December 2022, the Japanese government approved three new strategic documents which constitute a serious shift away from Japan's post-war peace constitution (which renounced war and forbade the establishment of a standing military.[43] US Secretary of Defense Lloyd Austin enthused that these documents "reflect Japan's staunch commitment to upholding the international rules-based order and a free and open Indo-Pacific." He added that "we support Japan's decision to acquire new capabilities that strengthen regional deterrence, including counterstrike capabilities."[44] As the US's most reliable regional ally, Japan plays a key role in the US's evolving project of China encirclement.

## The ghost of Senator McCarthy

Gerald Horne described the McCarthyite Red Scare of the 1940s and 50s as being the "handmaiden of the Cold War."[45] Similarly, Cold War historian Ellen Schrecker points out the inextricable link between US foreign policy and McCarthyism:

> Opposition to the Cold War had been so thoroughly identified with communism that it was no longer possible to challenge the basic assumptions of American foreign policy without incurring suspicions of disloyalty.[46]

As such, the ferocious anti-communism of the era was a domestic reflection of US imperialism's planet-wide war against the socialist countries and the Global South. WEB Du Bois noted in 1952 that the US ruling class wanted to prevent ordinary people "from daring to think or talk against the determination of big business to reduce Asia to colonial subserviency to American industry; to re-weld the chains of Africa; to consolidate United States control of the Caribbean and South America; and above all to crush socialism in the Soviet Union and China."[47]

In the early 21st century, we are witnessing a startlingly similar phenomenon. With China being both a communist-led state and a nation of non-white people, the modern shade of McCarthyism combines anti-communist 'red scare' with anti-Asian 'yellow peril', fomenting a social panic that draws on multiple layers of 20th century propaganda.

During the Trump era, China was accused in *Newsweek* of attempting to "transform our prized academic institutions into a system that is submissive to the objectives of China's totalitarian dictatorship."[48] China was apparently "cultivating relationships with county school boards and local politicians", with Chinese groups "practising their nefarious actions in the shadows" and, worst of all, "groups loyal to communist China are operating out in the open."[49]

The FBI opened up extensive investigations into Chinese scientists, for example hounding cancer researcher Juan Tang for her alleged links to the Chinese military.[50] The National Institutes of Health fired dozens of scientists for receiving funding from Chinese institutions,[51] and over a thousand Chinese researchers have had their visas revoked.[52] In the realm of entertainment, US Attorney General William Barr has accused companies including Disney and Apple of "enabling the government in Beijing to amass influence and wealth at the expense of the US and Western democratic values."[53]

Biden and his team have at least dialled down the racist rhetoric a few notches. However, anti-China fear-mongering has continued to gain pace via relentless propaganda, as well as investigation into Chinese academics, and the shutting down of Confucius Institutes. US-based professor of East Asian history Ken Hammond writes:

> The US government has been pursuing several efforts to further restrict any flow of information about China not under its control. The Confucius Institutes which had brought opportunities for Chinese language study to tens of thousands of young people across the country have almost all been forced to close by pressure on their host universities from the Department of Defense and the State Department. The Department of Justice has been launching high-profile investigations of both Chinese scholars working at American research universities and of other American scholars and scientists who have research contacts or connections with Chinese academic institutions. Many of these cases fall apart before they reach the courts, but they generate scare headlines and serve to intimidate the broader academic community.[54]

Tragically – but predictably – this McCarthyite propaganda has led to an alarming rise in incidents of anti-Asian hate crimes, including the horrific Atlanta spa massacre in 2021.[55]

## No winners

A crucial difference between the original Cold War and the current one is that the US is very unlikely to 'win' the New Cold War. Compared to the Soviet Union in the 1980s, China is much stronger economically, much more integrated into the global economy, has much stronger political leadership, and has learned several crucial lessons from the Soviet collapse (see Chapter 3: *Will China suffer the same fate as the Soviet Union?*).

Soviet GDP never exceeded 40 percent of US GDP, but China will surpass the US in absolute GDP terms in the coming few years. Its deep integration into global value chains, and the fact that it is the largest trading partner of the majority of the world's countries, mean that stability in China is crucial for the global economy.

The Regional Comprehensive Economic Partnership (RCEP), signed in November 2020, puts China at the centre of the largest trade bloc in history, comprising 30 percent of the world's population (it includes Australia, Brunei, Cambodia, China, Indonesia, Japan, Laos, Malaysia, Myanmar, New Zealand, the Philippines, Singapore, South Korea, Thailand, and Vietnam).[56] China is not at meaningful risk of becoming isolated.

Decoupling from China would be highly detrimental to the US economy, as it would mean losing access to a Chinese market of 1.4 billion people and increasing the production cost of a vast array of commodities. Tariffs on Chinese goods have a direct and immediate impact on US businesses that rely on these products (most are intermediate goods, used in the production process for consumer goods). Even *Foreign Affairs* magazine, published by the Council on Foreign Relations, has described the trade war as "unwinnable", noting that "tariffs have hit US consumers harder than their Chinese counterparts."[57]

The US will also likely be unsuccessful in its attempt to deny China access to markets and components it needs to further upgrade its economy. As Peter Frankopan has observed: "If, as seems likely, necessity is the mother of invention, then it may well prove that attempts to strangle technological developments by starving other states of components and knowledge will only serve to accelerate them."[58]

The outlook for the New Cold Warriors is not promising. China is not internationally isolated, is not suffering economic stagnation, and is not facing a crisis of legitimacy. The Chinese government enjoys enormous popularity at home, the result of ever-improving living standards at all levels of society. Wages are rising, social welfare is improving. According to an extensive study conducted by the Kennedy School of Government at Harvard University, 93 percent of Chinese people are satisfied with their central government.[59]

So the New Cold War is doomed to failure – but it can do plenty of damage along the way. Cold War tensions can easily develop into violent confrontation. As noted above, millions of people in Africa, Asia, Latin America and the Caribbean experienced the Cold War as being decidedly hot. And history indicates that the US and its allies are not above using military means in order to maintain their 'sphere of influence' intact.

Meanwhile climate change presents an unprecedented global threat. If humanity is to avoid triggering any of the several planetary tipping points, it will have to address its environmental challenges with the utmost coordination and cooperation. Mahbubani puts it pithily: "If climate change makes the planet progressively uninhabitable, both American and Chinese citizens will be fellow passengers on a sinking ship."[60]

Much the same logic applies to the major public health threats faced by humanity: pandemics and antimicrobial resistance. At an economic and cultural level, the New Cold War means a reduced global division of labour, reduced productivity, reduced learning, reduced cross-pollination of knowledge and ideas. In terms of geopolitics, it threatens to slow down and complicate the process of creating a more multipolar and democratic system of international relations. Militarily, it increases tensions and the risk of war, including nuclear war. In summary, this New Cold War poses enormous danger to humanity.

## Unite to oppose the US-led New Cold War on China

The original Cold War was waged by the US and its allies not just against the Soviet Union but against the forces of socialism and national sovereignty worldwide. It was a protracted and multifaceted struggle to ensure the preservation of an imperialist status quo. The same is true of the New Cold War. It's being waged by the US and its allies not just against China but the entire Global South, against the very notion of multipolarity, against the possibility of a democratic system of international relations and the end of hegemony.

China is a strong and consistent supporter of multipolarity – an international order in which there are multiple centres of power, creating an equilibrium that increases the costs of war and conflict, and promotes peaceful cooperation and integration (discussed in detail in Chapter 2: *Neither Washington Nor Beijing?*).

Multipolarity provides a path for the defeat of modern imperialism; it involves weakening the forces of polarisation of wealth and power; it deprives the imperialist bloc of its power to determine the fate of the rest of the world through military action, sanctions and destabilisation. Because it enhances the sovereignty of the non-imperialist countries, it also by corollary helps to create appropriate conditions for those countries to pursue socialist experiments. Thus Samir Amin: "Multipolarity will provide the framework for the possible and necessary overcoming of capitalism."[61]

Or as Xi Jinping put it in Moscow in 2013:

> All countries, irrespective of size, strength and wealth, are equal. The right of the people to independently choose their development paths should be respected, interference in the internal affairs of other countries opposed, and international fairness and justice maintained. Only the wearer of the shoes knows if they fit or not. Only the people can best tell if the development path they have chosen for their country suits or not.[62]

A multipolar, multilateral world order based on the principles of the UN Charter is precisely what the US ruling class is trying to avoid. This is the most powerful driver of the New Cold War. The imperialist powers – particularly the US, but generally supported by Canada, Western Europe, Australia and Japan – seek to maintain a status quo which provides maximum benefit to the US (with some crumbs to its allies) at the expense of the rest of the world.

All those that oppose imperialism must resolutely and consistently oppose the US-led New Cold War in all its manifold forms.

## NOTES

1 Andrew Glass 2010, *Bernard Baruch coins term 'Cold War,' April 16, 1947*, Politico, accessed 22 February 2023, <https://www.politico.com/story/2010/04/bernard-baruch-coins-term-cold-war-april-16-1947-035862>.

2 Odd Arne Westad. *The Global Cold War: Third World Interventions and the Making of Our Times*. Cambridge ; New York: Cambridge University Press, 2007, p3

3 Vladimir Shubin. *The Hot 'Cold War': The USSR in Southern Africa*. London : Scottsville, South Africa: Pluto Press ; University of KwaZulu-Natal Press, 2008, p3

4 *A Report to the President Pursuant to the President's Directive of January 31, 1950*, Office of the Historian, accessed 22 February 2023, <https://history.state.gov/historicaldocuments/frus1950v01/d85>

5 Martin Jacques. *When China Rules the World: The End of the Western World and the Birth of a New Global Order*. 2. ed. New York, NY: Penguin Books, 2012, p1

6 *Excerpts From Pentagon's Plan: 'Prevent the Re-Emergence of a New Rival'* (1992), New York Times, accessed 22 February 2023, <https://www.nytimes.com/1992/03/08/world/excerpts-from-pentagon-s-plan-prevent-the-re-emergence-of-a-new-rival.html>.

7 Vijay Prashad. *Washington Bullets*. New York: Monthly Review Press, 2020, p118

8 Jude Woodward. *The US vs China: Asia's New Cold War?* Geopolitical Economy. Manchester: Manchester University Press, 2017, p31

9 Josh Rogin 2019, *Opinion: China's efforts to undermine democracy are expanding worldwide*, Washington Post, accessed 22 February 2023, <https://www.washingtonpost.com/opinions/2019/06/27/chinas-efforts-undermine-democracy-are-expanding-worldwide/>.

10 Bob Davis and Lingling Wei. *Superpower Showdown: How the Battle between Trump and Xi Threatens a New Cold War*. First edition. New York: Harper Business, 2020, p241

11 Samir Amin 2013, *China 2013*, Monthly Review, accessed 22 February 2023, <https://monthlyreview.org/2013/03/01/china-2013/>.

12 Barack Obama 2015, *Remarks by the President on Trade*, The Obama White House, accessed 22 February 2023, <https://obamawhitehouse.archives.gov/the-press-office/2015/05/08/remarks-president-trade>.

13 Cited in Peter Frankopan. *The New Silk Roads: The Present and Future of the World*. London, England: Bloomsbury Publishing, 2018, p112

14 Kishore Mahbubani. *Has China Won? The Chinese Challenge to American Primacy*. First edition. New York: PublicAffairs, 2020, p263

15 Guy Taylor 2020, *Mike Pompeo confronts 'Asian NATO' hurdles in Asian allies meeting*, Washington Times, accessed 22 February 2023, <https://www.washingtontimes.com/news/2020/oct/5/mike-pompeo-

confronts-asian-nato-hurdles-asian-all/>.
16 David Charter and Alistair Dawber 2021, *I'll save world from an over-mighty China, vows Joe Biden*, The Times, accessed 22 February 2023, <https://www.thetimes.co.uk/article/ill-save-world-from-an-over-mighty-china-vows-biden-q0trblhcp>.
17 Demetri Sevastopulo 2020, *Biden team voices concern over EU-China investment deal*, Financial Times, accessed 22 February 2023, <https://www.ft.com/content/2f0212ab-7e69-4de0-8870-89dd0d414306>.
18 Michael Peel 2021, *China retaliates after US, EU and UK impose sanctions*, Financial Times, accessed 22 February 2023, <https://www.ft.com/content/27871663-cebc-433c-b9bf-4ef28a55d73e>.
19 Vincent Ni 2021, *EU parliament 'freezes' China trade deal over sanctions*, The Guardian, accessed 22 February 2023, <https://www.theguardian.com/world/2021/may/20/eu-parliament-freezes-china-trade-deal-over-sanctions>.
20 Jacob Pramuk 2020, *Biden slams Trump's trade war even as he calls to 'get tough' on China*, CNBC, accessed 22 February 2023, <https://www.cnbc.com/2019/07/11/joe-biden-slams-trump-china-trade-war-in-foreign-policy-speech.html>.
21 Demetri Sevastopulo 2021, *Joe Biden holds first call with Xi Jinping since taking office*, Financial Times, accessed 22 February 2023, <https://www.ft.com/content/d637fa79-0002-41ee-97ab-08bb5c472562>.
22 Demetri Sevastopulo 2021, *Antony Blinken blasts China in first phone call*, Financial Times, accessed 22 February 2023, <https://www.ft.com/content/f2e8f0d6-db17-42af-886f-901f751b4a9f>.
23 Matt Haldane 2022, *US-China chip war is overheating*, South China Morning Post, accessed 25 February 2023, <https://www.scmp.com/economy/article/3189695/us-china-chip-war-overheating>.
24 Michael Roberts 2022, *Chips: the new arms race*, The Next Recession, accessed 25 February 2023, <https://thenextrecession.wordpress.com/2022/12/11/chips-the-new-arms-race/>.
25 Martin Wolf 2022, *Geopolitics is the biggest threat to globalisation*, Financial Times, accessed 25 February 2023, <https://www.ft.com/content/8954a5f8-8f03-4044-8401-f1efefe9791b>.
26 Deng Xiaoping 1984, *Building a Socialism with a Specifically Chinese Character*, China.org.cn, accessed 25 February 2023, <http://www.china.org.cn/english/features/dengxiaoping/103371.htm>.
27 Keith Lamb 2021, *U.S. seeks to engage in tech war by strangling China's semiconductor industry*, CGTN, accessed 25 February 2023, <https://news.cgtn.com/news/2021-11-23/U-S-to-wage-a-tech-war-by-strangling-China-s-semiconductor-industry-15q13B7M1uE/index.html>.
28 Jordan Schneider 2021, *Will China Hit Back on Chips?*, ChinaTalk, accessed 25 February 2023, <https://chinatalk.substack.com/p/will-

china-hit-back-on-chips>.
29 Ina Fried 2019, *Huawei's smartphone effort takes a giant hit*, Axios, accessed 25 February 2023, <https://www.axios.com/huaweis-smartphone-effort-takes-a-giant-hit-03390bfc-bb30-4465-b177-2dc17d9469f1.html>.
30 Coco Feng and Che Pan 2021, *US-China tech war: supercomputer sanctions on China begin to bite as Taiwan's TSMC said to suspend chip orders*, South China Morning Post, accessed 25 February 2023, <https://www.scmp.com/tech/tech-war/article/3129362/us-china-tech-war-supercomputer-sanctions-china-begin-bite-taiwans>.
31 *Installed solar energy capacity*, Our World In Data, accessed 25 February 2023, <https://ourworldindata.org/grapher/installed-solar-pv-capacity?country=CHN~IND~USA~Europe>.
32 Kelly Pickerel 2021, *No avoiding it now: Soon the Top 4 polysilicon manufacturers will be based in China*, Solar Power World, accessed 25 February 2023, <https://www.solarpowerworldonline.com/2021/05/no-avoiding-it-now-soon-the-top-4-polysilicon-manufacturers-will-be-based-in-china/>.
33 Debasish Roy Chowdhury 2021, *Quad is Key to Biden's Strategy in Asia, But the Four-Way Alliance Is Ambiguous and Contradictory*, Time, accessed 22 February 2023, <https://time.com/5947674/quad-biden-china/>.
34 *China says US increasing military activity directed at it* (2021), Associated Press, accessed 22 February 2023, <https://apnews.com/article/china-government-and-politics-a49e31397090530e947af7e1590064dd>.
35 Jenny Clegg 2022, *NATO and AUKUS: the makings of an Asian NATO*, Friends of Socialist China, accessed 22 February 2023, <https://socialistchina.org/2022/04/27/nato-and-aukus-the-makings-of-an-asian-nato/>.
36 Dan Sabbagh and Daniel Hurst 2022, *Aukus pact extended to development of hypersonic weapons*, The Guardian, accessed 22 February 2023, <https://www.theguardian.com/politics/2022/apr/05/aukus-pact-extended-to-development-of-hypersonic-weapons>.
37 Rupert Wingfield-Hayes 2023, *US secures deal on Philippines bases to complete arc around China*, Journal, accessed 22 February 2023, <https://www.bbc.co.uk/news/world-asia-64479712>.
38 *State Councilor and Foreign Minister Wang Yi Meets the Press* (2022), Ministry of Foreign Affairs of the People's Republic of China, accessed 23 February 2023, <https://www.fmprc.gov.cn/eng/zxxx_662805/202203/t20220308_10649559.html>.
39 Amber Wang 2022, *Top US general vows military support for Taiwan, warns Beijing against conflict*, South China Morning Post, accessed 24 February 2023, <https://www.scmp.com/news/china/diplomacy/article/3199125/top-us-general-vows-military-support-taiwan-warns-beijing-against-conflict>.

40 Justin McCurry and Vincent Ni 2022, *US would defend Taiwan if attacked by China, says Joe Biden*, The Guardian, accessed 24 February 2023, <https://www.theguardian.com/world/2022/may/23/us-would-defend-taiwan-if-attacked-by-china-says-joe-biden>.

41 Bochen Han 2022, *Pentagon bill includes up to US$10 billion in grants and loans to Taiwan for arms sales*, South China Morning Post, accessed 24 February 2023, <https://www.scmp.com/news/china/military/article/3202466/pentagon-bill-includes-us10-billion-grants-and-loans-taiwan-arms-sales>.

42 Andre Damon 2022, *Record US military budget prepares for "future conflict with China"*, World Socialist Website, accessed 24 February 2023, <https://www.wsws.org/en/articles/2022/12/10/earp-d10.html>.

43 Watanabe Tsuneo 2023, *What's New in Japan's Three Strategic Documents*, Center for Strategic and International Studies, accessed 25 February 2023, <https://www.csis.org/analysis/whats-new-japans-three-strategic-documents>.

44 *Secretary of Defense Austin Statement on Japan's Release of its New Strategy Documents (National Security Strategy, National Defense Strategy, and Defense Buildup Program)* (2022), US Department of Defense, accessed 25 February 2023, <https://www.defense.gov/News/Releases/Release/Article/3248224/secretary-of-defense-austin-statement-on-japans-release-of-its-new-strategy-doc/>.

45 Gerald Horne. *Paul Robeson: The Artist as Revolutionary*. Revolutionary Lives. London: Pluto Press, 2016, p100

46 Ellen Schrecker. *The Age of McCarthyism: A Brief History with Documents*. 2nd ed. The Bedford Series in History and Culture. Boston: Bedford/St. Martin's, 2002, p93

47 W. E. B. Du Bois. *In Battle for Peace: The Story of My 83rd Birthday*. Oxford University Press, 2014, p104

48 Newt Gingrich and Claire Christensen 2020, *Infiltration: Communist China's Campaign to Reshape U.S. Education*, Newsweek, accessed 25 February 2020, <https://www.newsweek.com/infiltration-communist-chinas-campaign-reshape-us-education-opinion-1531432>.

49 Nick Givas 2020, *Pompeo warns governors of Chinese infiltration into US: 'It's happening in your state'*, Fox News, accessed 25 February 2023, <https://www.foxnews.com/politics/pompeo-warns-governors-of-china-infiltration>.

50 Nidhi Subbaraman 2020, *US investigations of Chinese scientists expand focus to military ties*, Science, accessed 25 February 2023, <https://www.nature.com/articles/d41586-020-02515-x>.

51 Jeffrey Mervis 2020, *Fifty-four scientists have lost their jobs as a result of NIH probe into foreign ties*, Science Magazine, accessed 9 April 2023 <https://www.science.org/content/article/fifty-four-scientists-have-lost-their-jobs-result-nih-probe-foreign-ties>

52 *Over 1,000 Chinese researchers leave US amid tech theft crackdown* (2020), South China Morning Post accessed 9 April 2023 < https://www.scmp.com/news/world/united-states-canada/article/3112323/over-1000-chinese-researchers-leave-us-amid-tech>

53 Chris Strohm 2020, *Barr Says Disney, Apple and Other Firms Are Now Pawns of China*, Bloomberg, accessed 9 April 2023, <https://www.scmp.com/news/world/united-states-canada/article/3112323/over-1000-chinese-researchers-leave-us-amid-tech>.

54 Ken Hammond 2023, *Demonizing China's COVID policies is fearmongering*, Global Times, accessed 25 February 2023, <https://www.globaltimes.cn/page/202301/1283712.shtml>.

55 Annika Constantino 2021, *Atlanta spa shooter who targeted Asian women pleads guilty to four of eight murders*, CNBC, accessed 25 February 2023, <https://www.cnbc.com/2021/07/27/atlanta-spa-shooter-who-targeted-asian-women-pleads-guilty-to-four-counts-of-murder.html>.

56 *RCEP: Asia-Pacific countries form world's largest trading bloc* (2020), BBC News, accessed 25 February 2023, <https://www.bbc.co.uk/news/world-asia-54949260>.

57 Weijian Shan 2019, *The Unwinnable Trade War*, Foreign Affairs, accessed 25 February 2023, <https://www.foreignaffairs.com/articles/asia/2019-10-08/unwinnable-trade-war>.

58 Frankopan, *op cit*, p176

59 Alex Lo 2020, *Beijing enjoys greater legitimacy than any Western state*, South China Morning Post, accessed 25 February 2023, <https://www.scmp.com/comment/opinion/article/3093825/beijing-enjoys-greater-legitimacy-any-western-state>.

60 Mahbubani. *op cit*, p265

61 Samir Amin. *Beyond US Hegemony? Assessing the Prospects for a Multipolar World*. New York: World Book Pub. ; Sird ; UKZN Press ; Zed Books ; Distributed in the USA exclusively by Palgrave Macmillan, 2006, p149

62 Xi Jinping 2013, *Follow the Trend of the Times and Promote Peace and Development in the World*, Ministry of Foreign Affairs of the People's Republic of China, accessed 25 February 2023, <https://www.fmprc.gov.cn/mfa_eng/wjdt_665385/zyjh_665391/t1033246.shtml>.

Urumqi: mosque

# Appendix

# The universalisation of 'liberal democracy'

Carlos Martinez and Danny Haiphong

*The following article, co-authored by Danny Haiphong and Carlos Martinez, was published in the academic journal* International Critical Thought *in 2022.*[1]

THE word democracy is connected to a large and diverse body of meaning. In the broadest sense, it simply refers to the exercise of power – directly or indirectly – by the people. However, in the leading capitalist countries, its meaning is much more specific: it has become synonymous with the system of 'liberal democracy', characterised by a multi-party parliament, universal suffrage, the separation of powers, and a strong emphasis on the protection of private property.

This narrow definition is widely considered in the West as a universal and absolute truth. Indeed, in the dominant Western narrative, adherence to the principles of liberal democracy constitutes the fundamental dividing line in global politics. On one side there is a group of 'democracies' (including the US, Canada, Australia, New Zealand, most of Europe, Japan, India and South Korea) and on the other side a group of 'non-democracies' or 'authoritarian regimes' (including the People's Republic of China, the Democratic People's Republic of Korea, Vietnam, Laos, Cuba, Iran, Russia, Venezuela, and most of the countries of Asia, Africa and Latin America).

The obvious weakness of this definition is that it makes no reference to social class. It presents democracy as a purely procedural phenomenon and masks the underlying political and economic structure. In contrast, Mao Zedong considered that the particulars of governance in any given society reflect nothing more than "the form in which one social class or another chooses to arrange its apparatus of political power to oppose its enemies and protect itself".[2] The important question therefore, wholly obscured in Western discourse, is which social class dominates political power? Which class is the ruling class?

There is a conspicuous intersection of liberal democracies and developed capitalist countries. That is to say, those states that conform to the precepts of liberal democracy also operate an economic system based on the private ownership of the means of production, distribution and exchange; a society whose basic contradiction is "between the social character of production and the private character of ownership";[3] a society where the accumulation of vast wealth by a small group of capitalists has as its parallel the "accumulation of misery, the torment of labour, slavery, ignorance, brutalisation and moral degradation"[4] among the lowest layers of society.

Clearly the correlation between liberal democracy and capitalism cannot be coincidental; indeed it reflects a truth described by Vladimir Lenin over a century ago, that "a democratic republic is the best possible political shell for capitalism".[5] The purpose of any state – democratic or otherwise – is to uphold an economic status quo; a particular form of class rule. Liberal democracy should therefore be considered as a euphemism for capitalist democracy, the democratic limits of which are strictly defined by the need to reinforce capitalist production relations.

The economic core of capitalism is a division of society into, on the one hand, those that own and deploy capital and, on the other, those that must earn a living by selling their labour power. The essential role of the capitalist state is to preserve this relationship: the exploitation of the majority by the minority. In ordinary times, this takes place quite naturally as a result of tradition, culture, routine; but in case of less ordinary times, a capitalist state always has recourse to a police force, secret services and an army – "special bodies of armed men", to use Frederick Engels' expression.

Liberal democracy allows people to vote for one or other capitalist party, but it does not allow for substantive changes to the economic system. In the face of a conflict of interests between the ruling class and the working classes, the capitalist state invariably comes down on the side of the ruling class. As such, it is incapable of meeting the basic needs of the majority. Ending poverty, ending unemployment, divesting from the military-industrial complex, ending wars of aggression, suppressing Covid-19, providing good quality housing, taking meaningful steps to decarbonise the economy: all these should be possible in an advanced modern society, and all reflect the needs and demands of ordinary people; yet capitalist states consistently fail to deliver them.

Engels made a profound observation on the limits of capitalist democracy, discussing the issue of homelessness. He pointed out that, since "there are already enough buildings for dwellings in the big towns to relieve immediately the real housing shortage through a rational utilisation of these buildings", a government representing the public interest would simply expropriate the empty buildings and transfer them "to homeless workers or to workers presently living in excessively overcrowded apartments". Indeed in 2017, in the wake of the tragic Grenfell Tower fire in London, progressive politician Jeremy Corbyn (then leader of the Labour Party) proposed exactly that: that the government seize empty property and transfer it to those rendered homeless by the fire.

Corbyn's suggestion was not, needless to say, taken up. Engels made his observations on the housing question in 1872, but even today in 2021, capitalist states are unable to solve this problem, because expropriating unoccupied buildings runs counter to the interests of the capitalist class. The US, Britain and Australia are wealthy countries, but New York, London and Sydney are suffering an epidemic of homelessness. Meanwhile in China, the housing problem has basically been solved. The reason China can place such a strong emphasis on poverty alleviation, or pandemic suppression, or ecological conservation, is that it is a socialist democracy, responsive to the needs of the vast majority of the population.

Within a capitalist democracy, it is possible for the working classes to win certain concessions and improve their situation. The immovable red line, however, is the position of the capitalist class as ruling class. Lenin wrote:

> Freedom is always hemmed in by the narrow limits set by capitalist exploitation, and consequently always remains, in reality, a democracy for the minority, only for the propertied classes, only for the rich. Freedom in capitalist society always remains about the same as it was in the ancient Greek republics: freedom for the slaveowners. Owing to the conditions of capitalist exploitation the modern wage slaves are so crushed by want and poverty that 'they cannot be bothered with democracy', 'they cannot be bothered with politics'; in the ordinary peaceful course of events the majority of the population is debarred from participation in public and political life.[6]

Occasionally there is some disruption to this 'ordinary peaceful course of events' and the true nature of the capitalist state is exposed. The treatment of the US communist movement and the radical organisations of oppressed minorities in the late 1960s and early 1970s provides an instructive example. When groups such as the Black Panther Party started to organise and educate significant numbers of people from working class and oppressed communities; when they openly and effectively questioned the superiority of capitalism; when they roundly denounced US imperialism and promoted solidarity with the people of China, Vietnam, Korea, Cuba, Algeria and Palestine; their experience of democracy become demonstrably less 'liberal'. Their leaders were assassinated or kidnapped; their offices were destroyed; the FBI conducted an elaborate campaign of infiltration, disinformation and destabilisation; the judiciary arranged numerous frame-ups. A plethora of measures – overt and covert, legal and illegal – was used by the 'liberal democratic' state to put an end to their project.

Such examples lay bare the truth that the state under capitalism is always an instrument of capitalist class rule. Bourgeois democracy is certainly far preferable to fascism, which is capitalist class rule enforced through naked violence; but it is capitalist class rule nonetheless.

In his Gettysburg Address, Abraham Lincoln famously called for "government of the people, by the people, for the people".[7] A hundred and fifty years later, economist Joseph Stiglitz described the US democratic system as being "of one percent, by one percent, for one percent".[8] This captures the fundamentally plutocratic nature of the prevailing system in the capitalist democracies. In spite of this, the West's dominance in the realms of media and academia has been leveraged to universalise capitalist democracy, "to conceal from the people the bourgeois character of modern democracy; to portray it as democracy in general or 'pure democracy'".[9]

It is crucial that progressive humanity challenges this universalisation. As the Cuban revolutionary Che Guevara once remarked, "we should not allow the word 'democracy' to be utilised to represent the dictatorship of the exploiting classes".[10]

## The people's democratic dictatorship and China's emerging socialist democracy

Having put an end to foreign occupation, defeated the reactionary nationalist forces in the Civil War and established the People's Republic, New China had to develop a model of governance appropriate to its conditions. This model could hardly follow the Western model, installing the capitalist class as ruling class. With a relatively small and weak bourgeoisie, such a system would inevitably give way to neocolonial domination by the advanced capitalist countries – as was the fate of the 1911 Revolution which had finally overthrown dynastic rule but which failed to unite the country, expel the occupying forces, dismantle feudalism, or meaningfully improve the living conditions of most Chinese people.

Mao Zedong wrote in 1949, just three months before the proclamation of the PRC:

> There are bourgeois republics in foreign lands, but China cannot have a bourgeois republic because she is a country suffering under imperialist oppression. The only way is through a people's republic led by the working class.

Such a republic would need to "unite the working class, the peasantry, the urban petty bourgeoisie and the national bourgeoisie" in the formation of a domestic united front under the leadership of the working class. This would pave the way for a "people's democratic dictatorship based on the alliance of workers and peasants".[11]

To those raised on a diet of Western democratic theory, the idea of a "democratic dictatorship" sounds absurd. Mao however, a rigorous Marxist-Leninist, well understood the relationship between democracy and dictatorship; that the two always coexist within a society based on class division. Whereas a capitalist democracy is a manifestation of the dictatorship of the bourgeoisie, socialist democracy means the dictatorship of the working class.

This much was commonly understood among Marxists at the time. Mao's great theoretical innovation on the question of the socialist state was to clarify and expand the scope of its democracy to include non-proletarian forces – the peasantry above all, the urban petty bourgeoisie and the national bourgeoisie. All these classes had an interest in the modernisation of China, its unity, its sovereignty, its emergence; moreover, all could accept and appreciate the need for the leadership of the Communist Party and the support of the socialist camp. As such, in the people's democratic dictatorship, the vast masses of the people were to enjoy democratic rights and representation.

What about dictatorship? This was to be imposed on the landlord class and that section of the capitalist class that was ready to do the bidding of US-led imperialism (essentially, the remnants of the defeated Guomindang). These classes were to be deprived of the right to political participation and representation.

Mao and his comrades assessed that, given the readiness of external forces led by the US to intervene on the side of counter-revolutionary elements within China, the political suppression of the pro-feudal and pro-imperialist forces was indispensable in order to protect the revolution. Without that suppression, a coalition of domestic and foreign reactionary forces would overthrow people's democracy, "and disaster will befall the revolutionary people".[12]

US intellectual Michael Parenti gives a brief summary of the need for the 'dictatorship' component of socialist democracy:

> For a people's revolution to survive, it must seize state power and use it to (a) break the stranglehold exercised by the owning class over the society's institutions and resources, and (b) withstand the reactionary counterattack that is sure to come.[13]

The great Cuban revolutionary leader Fidel Castro put it even more succinctly: "Within the revolution, everything; against the revolution, nothing".[14]

Thus the system of governance established from 1949 was a people's democratic dictatorship. This continues to be enshrined in China's constitution, and is the basis for the numerous mechanisms of government that operate in China today. While Chinese socialism has continued to evolve, each generation of the CPC leadership has been clear about upholding the basic structure of socialist democracy. Indeed, "adherence to the people's democratic dictatorship" was one of the Four Cardinal Principles defined by Deng Xiaoping at the beginning of the Reform and Opening Up period as being prerequisites for China's successful socialist modernisation.[15]

Recently, in order to expand the discussion both inside and outside China about the nature of China's democratic system, the CPC leadership has theorized whole-process people's democracy. Addressing a central conference on work related to people's congresses, Xi Jinping made a powerful observation about the limitations of liberal democracy:

> If the people are awakened only at voting time and dormant afterward; if the people hear big slogans during elections but have no say after; if the people are favoured during canvassing but are left out after elections, this is not true democracy.[16]

This echoes Marx's comment that, in a capitalist democracy, "the oppressed are allowed once every few years to decide which particular representatives of the oppressing class shall represent and repress them in parliament".[17]

In China's whole-process people's democracy, by contrast, democratic rights are available at all levels of society and at all times. Ongoing participation in governance is strongly encouraged. The legislative system is based on electoral representation and operates at the national level (the National People's Congress, NPC, the highest organ of state power) as well as at provincial, city, county and village levels. Parallel to the congress system is an elaborate system of consultative democracy, the Chinese People's Political Consultative Conferences.

Roland Boer describes the process by which legislation can be passed at the NPC:

> By the time a piece of legislation comes up for a vote, it has undergone an extremely long and arduous process of deliberation and consultation. Multiple meetings take place, feedback is sought, and differences in opinion are aired without holding back. Indeed, contrary arguments are encouraged and expected, with debate, revision, and further debate until a consensus is reached. Only then can the legislation arrive at the NPC for a vote.[18]

Near-term economic and social objectives are consolidated into five-year national development plans. These plans are not simply the work of the politburo; they represent "the crystallization of tens of thousands of rounds of discussions and consultations at all levels of the Chinese state and society," a "real democratic decision-making process".[19]

China's system of socialist democracy is very much a work in progress; it continues to evolve and improve. However, its content is already far more meaningfully democratic than its Western counterpart in terms of the engagement of ordinary people in running society.

## How the working class in the West experiences democracy

Democracy in the West is an expression of class interests and not merely an idea worthy of achievement. The experience of Western democracy for the working class is therefore characterised by a stark gap between rhetoric and reality. Workers are taught from a very young age that if they elect the correct representative into government, then their needs and interests will be met. Civic engagement in the form of voting is heralded as the highest expression of 'civilisation'.

This rhetoric renders Western democracy 'exceptional' and conceals the fundamental contradictions of the capitalist mode of development. These contradictions give Western democracy its particular form. Western societies are governed by capitalist states which have relied upon centuries of colonialism to enrich a particular class, the capitalist class. The formation of the United States' democracy, for example, has its roots in the profitable enslavement and conquest of African and Indigenous peoples.[20] Slavery and colonialism required political and social exclusion to reproduce this peculiar form of class exploitation.

To this day, the US political system is mired in a number of problems related to race and class inequality. Voter suppression laws prevent the working class, especially African American workers, from participating in the process of democracy. The United States still uses the Electoral College to determine the presidency despite the fact that the process is rooted in the historic struggle of slave owners to exert disproportionate influence and deny African slaves the right to vote.[21] However, even when participation is possible, the working class is without a mechanism for addressing their material problems.

The United States provides the starkest example of how the structure of the capitalist state serves the interests of the wealthy. Democracy in the United States is defined by a choice between two political parties, the Democratic Party and the Republican Party, that compete for what Karl Marx described as the right to repress the interests of the working class.[22] The choice, however, is a narrow one. Each political party appeals to different voting blocs. The Democratic Party's most active support base among the population resides in the urban, northern, and coastal areas of the United States while the Republican Party derives much of its support from the Southern and rural regions of the country.

Despite significant rhetorical differences, efforts to achieve bipartisanship are viewed as essential to the upkeep of democracy. Disagreement or what US experts call 'gridlock' is denounced as an impediment to political progress. Such a characterisation of the US's version of Western democracy obfuscates the fact that the Democratic and Republican Party both subscribe to a policy agenda that serves the same class interests. Democratic and Republican representatives in Congress overwhelmingly support increasing a military budget that is already larger than the next eleven countries combined at $750 billion.[23] Furthermore, representatives of both parties have supported the reduction of social welfare programs, the expansion of police and prison budgets, tax reductions, bailout measures, and a host of other policies which have caused a decline in living standards for workers and a worsening of race relations.[24]

That the US's two main political parties share a common policy agenda is unsurprising when the donors for each party are taken into consideration. Fortune 500 companies provide enormous sums to US political candidates to ensure their interests are met.[25] Wall Street banks and private military contractors tend to donate to Democrats and Republicans on a non-partisan basis but have scaled up their support for Democratic Party presidential candidates such as Joe Biden.[26] Boeing CEO Dave Calhoun told the US media that the world's second-largest military contractor in the world did not need to make a definitive choice between Joe Biden and Donald Trump because both signalled strong support for the defence industry.[27] Joe Biden would go on to nominate former Raytheon board member Lloyd Austin as his Secretary of Defense shortly after his victory in the 2020 presidential selection.

The gap between the rhetoric and reality of 'democracy' in the West has produced devastating consequences over the course of the Covid-19 global pandemic. Both political parties politicised Covid-19 instead of coming together to implement a policy agenda that protected human life. Then-President Donald Trump blamed China for the pandemic while the Democratic Party blamed Republicans for non-compliance with Covid-19 protocols. Neither political party was willing to support consistent public health measures necessary to curb viral transmission. Nearly 800,000 people in the United States have died from Covid-19 as a result, a disproportionate number of whom come from the poorest sections of the working class in the African American and Hispanic communities.[28]

The US's disastrous response to Covid-19 reflects the inherent contradictions of so-called Western democracy. Western democracy speaks of being by, for, and of the people in theory but not in practice. As Albert Szymanski notes:

> the capitalist state must act to maximise and guarantee profits and ensure the process of capitalist accumulation, regardless of whether representatives of the capitalist class or a proletarian party are occupying governmental positions. To act otherwise would result in a general economic collapse because of withdrawal of cooperation by the capitalist class.[29]

Historically, any democratic reforms implemented within the capitalist state have come as a result of popular organisation against the underpinnings of that state. African-Americans chartered a course of democratic reconstruction after more than a century of resistance against chattel bondage. The decades-long fight against Jim Crow segregation and racial violence led to the passage of the Voting Rights Act of 1965 and other protections against race-based discrimination. Labour organisation was also key in opening space for democratic rights. In 1934 alone, 1.5 million workers went on strike and won legal recognition for the right to form a union.

Still, in each case of successful reform, the state maintained its overall character as an instrument of oppression of the working class by the capitalist class. Western democracy and its particular variant in the United States can thus be better described as a dictatorship of the capitalist class. In the current period, neither the Democratic Party nor its Republican opposition support a living wage, student debt relief, or substantial investments in public infrastructure or climate policy. Workers cannot vote themselves out of poverty because no such choice exists within the two-party system. Furthermore, the working class cannot vote against policies such as high military budgets which only serve to enrich corporate executives and divert resources away from the needs of ordinary people. The working class is therefore denied the agency to transform its material conditions within a political process that is dictated by the exploiter class.

## 'Liberal democracy' as an instrument of hegemony

Because capital accumulation and hegemony are key features of Western imperialism, the rise of socialist democracy has been historically treated by the West as a threat to the so-called virtues of "liberal democracy." The Cold War, for example, was supported by the most powerful business interests in the West. During the Cold War, the United States and its Western allies adopted a hostile policy toward socialist and anti-colonial movements around the world. Korea, China, the Soviet Union, Cuba and dozens of other nations were subject to countless acts of aggression, including direct military intervention.

The effort to keep socialism at bay also extended into the domestic political sphere. Former Senator Joseph McCarthy represented the face of an anti-communist crusade that led to the imprisonment, exile, and harassment of activists, journalists, and prominent members of society who were accused of working with "the Reds".[30] The fall of the Soviet Union shifted the focus of the West onto another perceived threat: terrorism. Following the September 11th 2001 terrorist attacks in the United States, Western governments argued that outside forces were plotting to undermine "liberal democracy". Former US President George W. Bush articulated this sentiment clearly in his declaration of the War on Terror:

> Americans are asking 'Why do they [terrorists] hate us?' They hate what they see right here in this chamber: a democratically elected government. Their leaders are self-appointed. They hate our freedoms: our freedom of religion, our freedom of speech, our freedom to vote and assemble and disagree with each other.[31]

The War on Terror was thus framed as a war to defend democracy. What the War on Terror actually provided was a convenient narrative that united the US and its Western allies around common military ventures such as the occupation of Afghanistan and the invasion of Iraq. Western governments also invested enormous resources in the construction of a surveillance apparatus that infringed on the privacy of all citizens. Far from the expansion of so-called "democracy," the War on Terror fuelled political instability in the West and destroyed entire societies at the expense of hundreds of thousands of lives.

Major corporations in the defence and oil industries have been the true winners of the War on Terror. US defence contractors accumulated more than half of the $14 trillion spent on the two-decade invasion of Afghanistan alone.[32] Oil and fossil fuel corporations have also enjoyed massive profits in their bid to supply military operations with fuel. Former US Federal Reserve Chair Alan Greenspan expressed sadness "that it is politically inconvenient to acknowledge what everyone knows: the Iraq war is largely about oil".[33] The intimate relationship between oil profits and the War on Terror has rapidly made the US military one of the largest polluters on the planet.[34]

In both the Cold War and the War on Terror, Western "liberal democracy" represents an ideological expression of hegemony. The concepts of freedom and democracy are reduced in reality to the "freedom" of Western corporations and governments to "democratically" dominate world affairs. This pattern has taken on a new form in the current period. The threat of terrorism has been supplanted by what the United States calls "strategic competition" with Russia and China.[35] China and its model of socialist democracy has been under particular assault from the US and its allies.

Experts and activists have referred to the escalating assault on China as a "New Cold War" or a "hybrid war". Policies of the New Cold War include sanctions on China's tech sector, an increase in US and Western military presence in the South China Sea, and political interference in China's internal affairs regarding Hong Kong and Taiwan. Ideology is an equally important feature of the New Cold War. The United States and its Western allies routinely portray China as an "authoritarian" regime and an egregious violator of human rights in an effort to contrast China's political system with the so-called democratic values of the "rules-based international order".[36]

However, democracy is clearly not the primary concern of the New Cold War given the actual record of the West's massive human rights violations around the world. Democracy is an instrument of hegemony in a period of decline in the West. Capitalist economies in the West have experienced several decades of economic contraction that has been complemented with harsh cyclical crises. The United States' share of the global economy in GDP terms has decreased by fifty percent since 1960.[37] Economists predict that China will become the largest economy in the world in GDP terms by 2028 while others have observed that China has already become the largest overall economy in the world in Purchasing Power Parity (PPP) terms.[38]

Anxieties over China's economic rise were made clear in March 2021 when US President Joe Biden explained his belief that China has

> an overall goal to become the leading country in the world, the wealthiest country in the world, and the most powerful country in the world. That's not gonna happen on my watch.[39]

However, Western anxiety is not purely economic in reasoning. The possibility of a socialist democracy such as China becoming the world's foremost economy also signals the end of the unipolar global order led by the United States and the West.

A major goal for China, as President Xi Jinping explains, is the development of a community with a shared future for humankind. Included in this goal is a commitment to multipolarity, world peace, and win-win cooperation around issues of economic development and climate change.[40] China's foreign policy therefore aligns with its national commitment of improving living standards alongside robust participation of the people—a key component of socialist democracy. Socialist democracy thus runs counter to the West's record of championing procedural democracy to obscure the hegemony and exploitation inherent in its governance system.

The West' vision for democracy is monopolistic and incongruent with the current global situation. Development models possess a definite life course and the Western model liberal democracy is behaving as if it has reached the end of life. Instead of adjusting to the reality of a rising socialist democracy in China and the demand for a more egalitarian and multipolar world order, the West (led by the United States) is attempting to reassert its historic claim of holding monopoly over democracy and the trajectory of global politics. This article demonstrates that Western democracy is neither universally applicable across the world nor experienced the same way across social classes. An analysis of the class character of democracy is crucial for understanding the differences between its various forms and how these differences shape the aggressive posture of the US-led Western "democratic" order toward countries that chart an independent course of development.

## NOTES

1 Danny Haiphong and Carlos Martinez 2022, *The Universalization of "Liberal Democracy"*, International Critical Thought, 12:2, 213-224, DOI: 10.1080/21598282.2022.2074032

2 Mao Zedong 1940, *On New Democracy*, Marxist Internet Archive, accessed 28 February 2023, <https://www.marxists.org/reference/archive/mao/selected-works/volume-2/mswv2_26.htm>.

3 Mao Zedong 1937, *On Contradiction*, Marxist Internet Archive, accessed 28 February 2023, <https://www.marxists.org/reference/archive/mao/selected-works/volume-1/mswv1_17.htm>.

4 Karl Marx. *Capital: A Critique of Political Economy. V. 1* (1867): Penguin Classics. London ; New York, N.Y: Penguin Books in association with New Left Review, 1981, p799

5 Vladimir Lenin 1917, *The State and Revolution*, Marxist Internet Archive, accessed 28 February 2023, <https://www.marxists.org/archive/lenin/works/1917/staterev/>.

6 *ibid*

7 Abraham Lincoln 1863, *The Gettysburg Address*, Abraham Lincoln Online, accessed 28 February 2023, <https://www.abrahamlincolnonline.org/lincoln/speeches/gettysburg.htm>.

8 Joseph Stiglitz 2011, *Of 1%, by the 1%, for 1%*, Vanity Fair, accessed 28 February 2023, <https://www.vanityfair.com/news/2011/05/top-one-percent-201105>.

9 Vladimir Lenin 1918, *Democracy and Dictatorship*, Marxist Internet Archive, accessed 28 February 2023, <https://www.marxists.org/archive/lenin/works/1918/dec/23.htm>.

10 Ernesto Guevara 1963, *Guerrilla warfare: A method*, Marxist Internet Archive, accessed 28 February 2023, <https://www.marxists.org/archive/guevara/1963/09/guerrilla-warfare.htm>.

11 Mao Zedong 1949, *On the People's Democratic Dictatorship*, Marxist Internet Archive, accessed 28 February 2023, <https://www.marxists.org/reference/archive/mao/selected-works/volume-4/mswv4_65.htm>.

12 *ibid*

13 Michael Parenti. *Blackshirts & Reds: Rational Fascism & the Overthrow of Communism*. San Francisco, Calif: City Lights Books, 1997, p52

14 Fidel Castro 1961, *Fidel Castro's speech to intellectuals on 30 June 1961*, Latin American Network Information Centre, accessed 28 February 2023, <http://lanic.utexas.edu/project/castro/db/1961/19610630.html>.

15 Deng Xiaoping 1979, *Uphold the Four Cardinal Principles*, Marxist Internet Archive, accessed 28 February 2023, <https://www.

marxists.org/reference/archive/deng-xiaoping/1979/115.htm>.

16 Xi Jinping 2021, *Highlights of Xi Jinping's latest remarks on democracy*, China Daily, accessed 28 February 2023, <https://www.chinadaily.com.cn/a/202110/15/WS61692284a310cdd39bc6f3af.html>.

17 Cited in Lenin 1917, *op cit*

18 Roland Boer 2021, *We need to talk more about China's socialist democracy*, Friends of Socialist China, accessed 28 February 2023, <https://socialistchina.org/2021/09/26/roland-boer-we-need-to-talk-more-about-chinas-socialist-democracy/>.

19 Zhang Weiwei. *The China Wave: Rise of a Civilizational State.* Hackensack, N.J: World Century, 2012, p158

20 Gerald Horne. *The Counter-Revolution Of 1776: Slave Resistance and the Origins of the United States of America.* New York: New York University Press, 2014.

21 Reed Akil Amar 2016, *The Troubling Reason the Electoral College Exists*, Time, accessed 28 February 2023, <https://time.com/4558510/electoral-college-history-slavery/>.

22 Lenin, *The State and Revolution, op cit*

23 Ashik Siddique 2021, *COVID Shrank the Global Economy, but U.S. Military Spending is Still More Than the Next 11 Countries Combined*, Institute for Policy Studies, accessed 28 February 2023, <https://ips-dc.org/covid-shrank-the-global-economy-but-u-s-military-spending-is-still-more-than-next-11-countries-combined/>.

24 Roberto Sirvent and Danny Haiphong. *American Exceptionalism and American Innocence: A Peoples History of Fake News-From the Revolutionary War to the War on Terror.* New York: Skyhorse Publishing, 2019.

25 Áine Cain 2018, *The 30 Fortune 500 Companies That Have Thrown the Most Money at Republicans and Democrats in the Last Decade*, Business Insider, accessed 28 February 2023, <https://www.businessinsider.com/fortune-500-companies-republican-democrat-political-donations-2018-2>.

26 Brian Schwartz 2020, *Wall Street Spent Over $74 million to back Joe Biden's Run for President, Topping Trump's Haul*, CNBC, accessed 28 February 2023, <https://www.cnbc.com/2020/10/28/wall-street-spends-74-million-to-support-joe-biden.html>.

27 Leslie Josephs and Christina Wilkie 2020, *Boeing CEO Confident in Defense Spending, No Matter Who Wins 2020 Election*, CNBC, accessed 28 February 2023, <https://www.cnbc.com/2020/07/29/boeing-ceo-confident-in-defense-spending-no-matter-who-wins-the-2020-election.html>.

28 Carla Johnson at al 2021, *As US Death Toll Nears 600,000, Racial Gaps Persist*, Associated Press, accessed 28 February

2023, <https: / / www.usnews.com / news / health-news / articles / 2021-06-14 / as-us-covid-19-death-toll-nears-600-000-racial-gaps-persist>.

29 Albert Szymanski. *Is the Red Flag Flying? The Political Economy of the Soviet Union.* Imperialism Series, no. 5. London: Zed Press, 1979.

30 Ursula Wolfe-Rocca 2021, *The Attack on Activism Students Don't Learn from Their Textbooks,* The Zinn Education Project, accessed 28 February 2023, <https: / / www.zinnedproject.org / if-we-knew-our-history / more-than-mccarthyism>.

31 Mark Landler 2021, *20 Years on, The War on Terror Grinds on, with No End in Sight,* New York Times, accessed 28 February 2023, <https: / / www.nytimes.com / 2021 / 09 / 10 / world / europe / war-on-terror-bush-biden-qaeda.html>.

32 Mary Ellen Cagnassola 2021, *Defense Contractors Benefited from Nearly Half of $14 Trillion Spent on Afghan War: Study,* Newsweek, accessed 28 February 2023, <https: / / www.newsweek.com / defense-contractors-benefited-nearly-half-14-trillion-spent-afghan-war-study-1628485>.

33 JoAnne Allen 2007, *Greenspan Clarifies Iraq War and Oil Link,* Reuters, accessed 28 February 2023, <https: / / www.reuters.com / article / uk-greenspan / greenspan-clarifies-iraq-war-and-oil-link-idUKN1728646120070917>.

34 Neta Crawford 2019, *Pentagon Fuel Use, Climate Change, and the Costs of War,* Watson Institute for International and Public Affairs, accessed 28 February 2023, <https: / / watson.brown.edu / costsofwar / papers / ClimateChangeandCostofWar>.

35 Cornell Overfield 2021, *Biden's 'Strategic Competition' Is a Step Back,* Foreign Policy, accessed 28 February 2023, <https: / / foreignpolicy.com / 2021 / 10 / 13 / biden-strategic-competition-national-defense-strategy / >.

36 Chen Weihua 2021, *US Should Correct Wrongs by Ending Propaganda War Against China,* China Daily, accessed 28 February 2023, <http: / / www.chinadaily.com.cn / a / 202110 / 15 / WS6168b867a310cdd39bc6f0b4.html>.

37 Mike Patton 2016, *US Role in Global Economy Declines by 50%,* Forbes, accessed 28 February 2023, <https: / / www.forbes.com / sites / mikepatton / 2016 / 02 / 29 / u-s-role-in-global-economy-declines-nearly-50 / ?sh=3c80b5885e9e>.

38 Naomi Xu Elegant 2021, *China's 2020 GDP Means That It Will Overtake U.S. as World's No. 1 Economy Sooner Than Expected,* Fortune, accessed 28 February 2023, <https: / / fortune.com / 2021 / 01 / 18 / chinas-2020-gdp-world-no-1-economy-us / >.

39 John Haltiwanger 2021, *Biden Says China Wants to Become the*

*Most Wealthy, Powerful Country But It's 'Not Gonna Happen on My Watch*, Business Insider, accessed 28 February 2023, <https://www.businessinsider.com/biden-says-wont-let-china-become-most-wealthy-powerful-country-2021-3?r=US&IR=T>.

40 Xi Jinping 2017, *Work Together to Build a Community of Shared Future for Mankind*, Xinhua, accessed 28 February 2023, <http://www.xinhuanet.com/english/2017-01/19/c_135994707.htm>.

# Recommended reading

For those wanting to deepen their understanding of Chinese socialism, it's obviously important to read the classics of the genre, starting with Mao Zedong – the pre-eminent leader of the Chinese Revolution. *On Contradiction, On Practice, On New Democracy, On Protracted War, Combat Liberalism, The Chinese Revolution and the Chinese Communist Party, On the People's Democratic Dictatorship* and *On the Correct Handling of Contradictions Among the People* constitute a reasonable selection of pamphlets and speeches to get going with.

The selected works of Deng Xiaoping are crucial for understanding the evolution of Chinese socialism from the late 1970s. The selected works of Zhou Enlai and Liu Shaoqi also offer valuable insight, as do those of Chen Yun, Jiang Zemin and Hu Jintao. The four volumes of Xi Jinping's *The Governance of China* are in my view indispensable.

There are numerous brilliant accounts of the early decades of the Chinese Revolution written by foreign friends of China. Among the most noteworthy are Edgar Snow's epic *Red Star Over China*, Israel Epstein's *From Opium War To Liberation*, William Hinton's *Fanshen: A Documentary of Revolution in a Chinese Village*, Agnes Smedley's *The Great Road: The Life and Times of Chu Teh*, Ted Allen and Sydney Gordon's *The Scalpel, the Sword: The Story of Doctor Norman Bethune*, and Isabel and David Crook's *Ten Mile Inn*.

In terms of a general overview of modern China, Roland Boer's *Socialism with Chinese Characteristics: A Guide for Foreigners* is extremely useful. Martin Jacques' best-selling *When China Rules the World*, although more than a decade old, contains a great deal of valuable insight, and the same is true of

Zhang Weiwei's books *China Wave* and *China Horizon*.

On China's modern economy, *Delving into the Issues of the Chinese Economy and the World by Marxist Economists* by Cheng Enfu, *Demystifying the Chinese Economy* by Justin Yifu Lin, and *China's Great Road: Lessons for Marxist Theory and Socialist Practices* by John Ross are all very helpful. Peter Nolan has written a number of important books on China's development, including his groundbreaking 1995 study, *China's Rise, Russia's Fall*. Although it's not written from a Marxist perspective, Arthur Kroeber's *China's Economy: What Everyone Needs to Know* is packed with valuable information. Isabella Weber's *How China Escaped Shock Therapy: The Market Reform Debate* is also interesting and relevant.

On foreign policy and the New Cold War, *China's Global Strategy: Towards a Multipolar World* by Jenny Clegg is essential, as is *The US Vs China: Asia's New Cold War?* by Jude Woodward. Kishore Mahbubani's *Has China Won?: The Chinese Challenge to American Primacy* is a thought-provoking challenge to the Cold War mania that pervades Washington. *The Dragon's Gift* by Deborah Brautigan and *The China Triangle: Latin America's China Boom and the Fate of the Washington Consensus* by Kevin Gallagher are essential for understanding the nature of China's engagement with Africa and Latin America respectively.

Han Suyin's *Eldest Son: Zhou Enlai and the Making of Modern China* provides an abundance of historical information. And although basically unsympathetic to their subjects, Alexander Pantsov and Steven Levine's biographies of Mao and Deng (*Mao: The Real Story* and *Deng Xiaoping: A Revolutionary Life*) are very much worth reading, as is Graham Hutchings' *China 1949: Year of Revolution*.

On China's approach to ecological issues, Barbara Finamore's *Will China Save the Planet?* is unsurpassed.

For up-to-date English-language news related to China, visit the Friends of Socialist China website (socialistchina.org) and Chinese media such as Xinhua, China Daily, CGTN and Global Times.

# Index


## A

Afghanistan 52, 77, 79, 80, 86, 124, 133, 169, 196
African National Congress 39
African Union 40, 58
Afwerki, Isaias 39
Agriculture 105
Algeria 51, 110, 168, 190
Amin, Samir 23, 29, 36, 53, 56, 63, 96, 104, 171, 179, 181, 185
Andropov, Yuri 82
Angola 40, 42, 52, 59, 77, 79, 168, 169

## B

Belarus 83
Belt and Road Initiative 32, 45, 47, 61, 62, 124, 149
Biden, Joe 68, 81, 84, 116, 117, 129, 146, 148, 163, 164, 171, 172, 173, 174, 175, 176, 177, 182, 183, 184, 194, 197, 200, 201
Black Panther Party 189
Bolivia 45, 46, 47, 60
Brautigam, Deborah 40, 41, 42, 49, 57, 58, 62
BRICS 53
Britain iii, ix, xvi, xvii, xxiii, 2, 3, 8, 21, 32, 33, 37, 38, 42, 44, 50, 51, 63, 80, 115, 128, 147, 150, 175, 189, 214
Brunei 49, 178

## C

Cambodia 169, 178
Capitalism xxiii, xxiv, 31, 35, 48, 56, 84, 85, 104, 163, 165
Carbon dioxide emissions 139
Chávez, Hugo 45, 46, 61
Chen Yun 12, 67, 70, 93, 203
Chiang Kai-shek 3, 4, 6, 8
Chile 168, 169
Climate change 156
Colonialism 58, 110, 127
Comintern 34
Common prosperity 104
Confucius Institutes 177
Congo Brazzaville 39
Corbyn, Jeremy 189

Covid-19 x, 113, 118, 126, 167, 188, 194
Cuba xx, xxi, 45, 46, 60, 77, 81, 83, 86, 87, 123, 133, 150, 164, 168, 187, 190, 195
Cultural Revolution 2, 10, 12, 13, 14, 15, 16, 17, 23, 26, 69, 76, 94

## D

Debt 41, 58, 62
Democracy 6, 7, 8, 9, 20, 25, 28, 56, 76, 113, 115, 120, 129, 131, 193, 197, 199, 203
Democratic People's Republic of Korea 81, 187
Deng Xiaoping xi, xvi, xviii, xix, xxii, xxiii, xxiv, 12, 14, 15, 17, 19, 22, 26, 27, 28, 29, 52, 66, 73, 75, 76, 77, 81, 84, 85, 86, 87, 92, 97, 100, 102, 103, 105, 106, 107, 174, 182, 192, 199, 203, 204
Development x, xxii, 60, 62, 68, 84, 85, 95, 104, 106, 121, 136, 149, 155, 161, 162, 185, 197

## E

Education 98, 184, 201
Engels xv, xxiii, 63, 98, 105, 188, 189
Epstein 2, 25, 103, 203
Eric X Li xii
Ethiopia 40, 57, 58, 77, 150

## F

Famine 17, 26
Feudalism 1, 36
Fidel Castro xx, xxi, xxiv, 15, 46, 74, 77, 83, 85, 87, 191, 199
Five Eyes 175
Foreign investment xiv
Forum on China-Africa Cooperation 43, 53
Four Cardinal Principles xxiii, 15, 16, 75, 86, 192, 199
Four Modernisations 12, 23
France 33, 42, 44, 50, 51, 80, 131, 142

## G

Gang of Four 14
Gross Domestic Product (GDP) 11, 37, 68, 72, 73, 80, 85, 87, 95, 99, 133, 137, 138, 143, 145, 146, 160, 163, 178, 197, 201
Genocide 115, 116, 122, 129, 130, 131, 132
Germany 2, 3, 33, 37, 38, 44, 80, 142, 148, 163, 171
Great Leap Forward 8, 10, 11, 14, 76
Grenada 168
Griswold, Deirdrie xvii, xxiii, 153, 165
Guinea 40
Guinea Bissau 77, 168
Guomindang 3, 5, 191

## H

Han Suyin 3, 4, 13, 14, 15, 25, 204
Hinton, William 4, 25, 91, 103, 203
Ho Chi Minh 77, 87
Hollywood 110
Hong Kong 1, 19, 22, 37, 62, 67, 93, 103, 109, 112, 113, 118, 127, 128, 130, 197
Hua Guofeng 19
Huawei 167, 172, 174, 183
Hu Jintao 100, 106, 203
Human Development Index 68
Hungary 19
Hutchings, Graham 6, 8, 25, 29, 204
Hydropower 150

## I

Imperialism xxii, 34, 35, 40, 48, 56, 59, 110, 127, 201
India xvi, xxiii, 11, 21, 23, 24, 47, 53, 68, 92, 95, 124, 172, 187
Indonesia 21, 49, 67, 110, 169, 178

Infant mortality 95
Infrastructure 45, 80, 159
International Monetary Fund 53
Iran 187
Ireland 37, 145, 147, 162

**J**

Jacobin 32, 55, 115, 129
Japan xiii, 2, 3, 6, 8, 9, 19, 22, 37, 38, 49, 52, 53, 62, 67, 93, 147, 150, 167, 171, 172, 173, 176, 178, 180, 184, 187
Jiang Qing 14
Jiangxi Soviet 4, 5
Jiang Zemin 100, 106, 203
Ji Chaozhu 10, 11, 26

**K**

Kazakhstan 117, 124
Khrushchev, Nikita 10, 13, 76
Kim Il Sung 77
Kissinger, Henry 22, 29, 49, 62, 77, 94
Korea xiii, 9, 19, 52, 63, 67, 77, 80, 81, 83, 93, 167, 168, 169, 171, 178, 187, 190, 195
Korean War 9, 14, 80
Kyrgyzstan 124

**L**

Land reform 7, 8, 90
Laos 81, 83, 169, 178, 187
Lenin 1, 15, 20, 25, 28, 33, 34, 35, 36, 38, 48, 56, 75, 77, 94, 104, 188, 189, 199, 200
Liberia 44
Libya 110, 169
Literacy 31
Liu Shaoqi 2, 12, 13, 14, 203
Living standards 54
Losurdo, Domenico 69, 84, 85, 96, 104

**M**

Macao 1, 19
Malaysia 49, 50, 52, 67, 178
Malcolm X 109, 125, 134
Mali 39
Malnutrition 11
Manchukuo 5, 6
Mandela, Nelson 39, 57
Mao Zedong xxii, 2, 4, 10, 11, 14, 15, 16, 25, 26, 27, 28, 37, 57, 67, 75, 77, 84, 113, 135, 154, 166, 187, 190, 199, 203
Marx, Karl xv, xviii, xxiii, 1, 20, 28, 36, 44, 56, 59, 63, 69, 98, 128, 192, 193, 199
Marxism vii, xv, xviii, xix, xxiv, 2, 15, 16, 17, 18, 24, 31, 65, 75, 76, 82, 83, 86
May 4 Movement 3
McCarthyism 170, 176, 177, 184
Media 55, 111, 112, 127
Mnangagwa, Emmerson 39
Mongolia 124
Monroe Doctrine 44
Morales, Evo 46, 60
Mozambique xx, 37, 51, 77, 79, 168, 169
Multipolarity 51, 53, 179

**N**

Namibia 77, 168
NATO 111, 119, 148, 169, 172, 173, 175, 181, 183
New Cold War ii, v, ix, xiv, 28, 34, 35, 48, 54, 61, 62, 63, 81, 84, 85, 110, 114, 115, 124, 125, 133, 170, 172, 175, 178, 179, 180, 181, 196, 197, 204
New Democracy 6, 7, 8, 9, 20, 25, 28, 199, 203
New Economic Policy 9, 20
Nicaragua 45, 60, 77, 79, 168
Nigeria 40
Nixon 94
Nkrumah, Kwame 110, 127
Non-Proliferation Treaty 175
Nuclear power 142, 143

Nyerere, Julius xix

**O**
Obama, Barack 81, 167, 171, 172, 181
October Revolution 3, 85
Opium 5, 25, 103, 203

**P**
Pakistan 21, 49, 117, 124, 131, 150, 164
Palestine 190
Parenti, Michael 113, 114, 128, 191, 199
Paris Climate Agreement 172
Paris Commune xx
Peaceful coexistence 77
Peng Dehuai 5, 14, 91
Perestroika 73
Philippines 49, 50, 52, 175, 178, 183
Pilger, John xii, xxii
Pivot to Asia 81, 167, 169
Planning xxii, xxiii, 85, 169
Pollution 157
Poverty 97, 103, 104, 105, 126, 155
Propaganda 110, 127, 201

**R**
Reform and Opening Up ix, 15, 16, 70, 91, 92, 93, 95, 97, 192
Regional Comprehensive Economic Partnership 178
Rodney, Walter 59
Russia xxii, 3, 49, 53, 58, 72, 73, 85, 87, 124, 126, 143, 148, 163, 173, 176, 187, 196, 204

**S**
Sachs, Jeffrey 18, 27, 52, 63, 116, 122, 130, 132
Sanctions 60, 164, 173
Science 139, 160, 165, 173, 184
Second International 33, 34
Shanghai ix, xii, xxiv, 4, 6, 84, 96, 150
Singapore xxii, 27, 67, 127, 162, 178
Sino-Soviet Split ix, 26
Sisulu, Walter 39
Slavery 193
Smedley, Agnes 2, 25, 203
Snow, Edgar 5, 7, 25, 90, 103, 203
South Africa 37, 39, 53, 77, 168, 181
South China Sea 39, 49, 50, 51, 62, 63, 109, 167, 175, 196
South Korea 19, 67, 80, 93, 167, 171, 178, 187
Soviet Union v, xv, xix, xx, xxii, 3, 6, 7, 9, 13, 15, 23, 32, 34, 52, 54, 55, 65, 66, 69, 70, 71, 73, 74, 75, 77, 78, 79, 80, 82, 83, 85, 86, 125, 168, 169, 177, 178, 179, 195, 196, 201
Sri Lanka 49
Stalin, Joseph 10, 74, 76, 77, 85
Sun Yat-sen 3, 7
Sweden 37

**T**
Taiwan 1, 3, 8, 9, 19, 37, 50, 67, 80, 93, 109, 167, 174, 175, 176, 183, 184, 197
Tajikistan 124
Tazara Railway 36, 39
Technology xiv, 27, 63
Terminal High Altitude Area Defence (THAAD) 167
Terrorism 133
Thailand 21, 52, 67, 178
Trade xiv, 57, 102, 106, 181, 185
Trans-Pacific Partnership 167
Tricontinental Institute 97, 104
Truman, Harry S 9, 94, 168
Trump, Donald 55, 81, 115, 117, 149, 167, 171, 172, 173, 175, 177, 181, 182, 194, 200

**U**
uMkhonto we Sizwe 39
United Front 6

United Nations 22, 50, 52, 103, 123, 128, 129, 133, 143
United States ii, xii, xiv, xv, 9, 19, 22, 28, 29, 44, 46, 50, 63, 78, 85, 93, 95, 112, 116, 119, 121, 124, 132, 161, 165, 177, 193, 194, 195, 196, 197, 200
Uyghur people 115, 124

**V**

Venezuela xx, 45, 46, 61, 187
Vietnam xii, xx, xxii, xxiv, 49, 50, 51, 77, 80, 81, 83, 110, 168, 169, 178, 187, 190

**W**

Washington Consensus 46, 48, 60, 204
Wolfowitz, Paul 169
World Bank 43, 48, 67, 85, 87, 89, 91, 95, 130, 155, 157, 160, 162, 163
World Trade Organisation xiv

**X**

Xi Jinping xi, xvi, xvii, xviii, xix, xxii, xxiii, xxiv, 6, 20, 24, 28, 29, 39, 57, 68, 75, 86, 87, 91, 94, 97, 99, 100, 101, 103, 104, 105, 106, 113, 125, 134, 135, 137, 138, 139, 144, 145, 150, 154, 155, 156, 162, 166, 180, 182, 185, 192, 197, 200, 202, 203
Xinjiang 109, 110, 111, 114, 115, 116, 117, 118, 119, 120, 121, 122, 124, 125, 128, 129, 130, 131, 132, 133, 142, 149, 173

**Y**

Yan'an 5, 6, 14, 25
Yemen 79
Yugoslavia 19, 169

**Z**

Zambia 36, 39, 150, 164
Zenz, Adrian 120, 121, 122, 131, 132
Zhou Enlai 12, 14, 22, 23, 25, 29, 39, 203, 204
Zimbabwe 39, 40, 51, 58

# About the author

Carlos Martinez is an author and political activist from London, Britain. His first book, *The End of the Beginning: Lessons of the Soviet Collapse*, was published in 2019 by LeftWord Books. He is a co-editor of Friends of Socialist China, a co-founder of No Cold War, and a coordinating committee member of the International Manifesto Group. He writes regularly in the *Morning Star*, *Global Times*, *China Daily* and CGTN.

# RELATED READING

China, after its revolution, has achieved the greatest improvement in life of the largest proportion of humanity of any country in history. *China's Great Road* explains how China achieved this step forward. The unequivocal conclusion is that socialism is responsible for this advance. *China's Great Road* analyses Chinese reality and argues socialists worldwide can learn from China.

https://redletterspp.com/products/chinas-great-road

Milton Keynes UK
Ingram Content Group UK Ltd.
UKHW021215050524
442175UK00013B/490

9 781899 155163